The Big Book of
ORIGAMI

ARCTURUS

ARCTURUS

This edition published in 2021 by Arcturus Publishing Limited
26/27 Bickels Yard, 151–153 Bermondsey Street,
London SE1 3HA

Origami models: Belinda Webster and Rita Storey
Photography: Michael Wiles and Rita Storey
Authors: Joe Fullman and Rita Storey
Editors: Frances Evans and Becca Clunes
Designers: Trudi Webb, Emma Randall, Tokiko Morishima,
    Rita Storey, and Amy McSimpson
Art director: Jessica Holliland
Editorial manager: Joe Harris

ISBN: 978-1-3988-0906-2
CH008648NT
Supplier 29, Date 0821, Print run 11638

Printed in China

Contents

INTRODUCTION

Valley Fold......................5
Mountain Fold..................5
Step Fold......................6
Kite Base......................6
Fish Base......................7
Waterbomb Base.................7
Square Base....................8
Bird Base......................9
Inside Reverse Fold...........10
Outside Reverse Fold..........10

CHAPTER 1: ANIMALS

Gorilla........................12
Seahorse.......................16
Fox............................20
Monkey.........................22
Squid..........................27
Polar Bear.....................30
Lion...........................34
Squirrel.......................36
Vulture........................40
Narwhal........................45
Parrot.........................48

CHAPTER 2: DINOSAURS

Velociraptor...................52
Megalosaurus...................54
Triceratops....................58
Ichthyosaurus..................66
Utahraptor.....................68
Pteranodon.....................73
Parasaurolophus................76
Quetzalcoatlus.................82
Spinosaurus....................84
Dinosaur Egg...................90
Argentinosaurus................94
Apatosaurus....................98

CHAPTER 3: ACTION MODELS

Dice...................................102
Magician's Rabbit...............106
Kissing Frog.......................111
Magic Cup..........................116
Flapping Bird......................118
Dominoes...........................120
Lotus Flower.......................122
Gulping Fish........................126
Barking Dog........................128
Helicopter..........................132
Motorboat..........................135
Duckling.............................138
Jumping Horse....................142
Jet Plane............................146
Egg-laying Hen....................148

CHAPTER 4: CHRISTMAS

Santa.................................154
Holly Leaves.......................158
Letter to Santa...................160
Reindeer............................162
Christmas Tree....................166
Wreath..............................168
Reindeer Face.....................171
Elf....................................176
Stocking.............................179
Snowflake..........................182
Candy Cane........................184
Candle...............................186
Sleigh................................190
Present..............................193
Snowman............................196
Star Chain..........................200

CHAPTER 5: MONSTERS

Dracula..............................202
Vampire Fangs....................204
Alien..................................208
Giant Snake........................212
Snapping Nessie..................214
Witch and Broomstick.....216
Witch's Cat.........................220
Werewolf............................222
Wizard...............................227
Spider................................232
The Mummy........................238
Dragon...............................240
The Grim Reaper..................244
Octopod.............................249
Ghost.................................254

Index.................................256

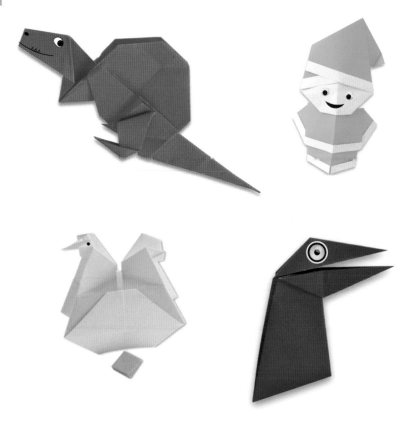

INTRODUCTION

Origami has been popular in Japan for hundreds of years and is now loved all around the world. The paper used in origami is thin but strong, so that it can be folded many times. It is usually white on one side. Where measurements appear in this book, it is assumed that you are using standard origami paper which is 15 x 15 cm/6 x 6 inches.

A lot of origami models begin using the same folds or "bases." The bases you'll need for the models in this book are explained in this introduction. It's a good idea to master these folds before you get started.

VALLEY FOLD

To make a valley fold, fold the paper so that the crease is pointing away from you, like a valley.

MOUNTAIN FOLD

To make a mountain fold, fold the paper so that the crease is pointing up at you, like a mountain.

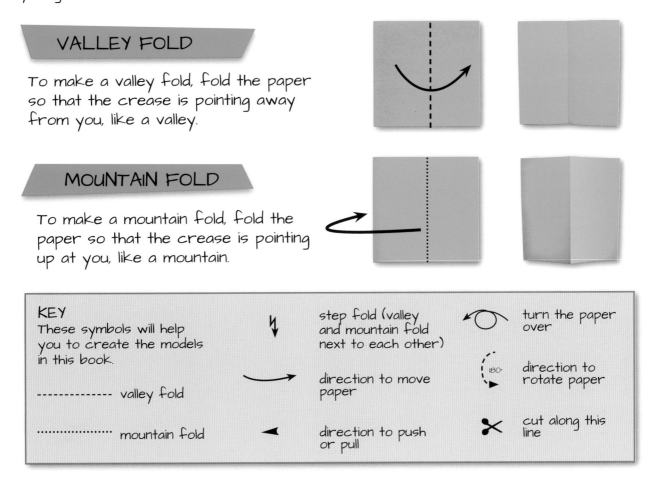

KEY
These symbols will help you to create the models in this book.

-------------- valley fold

·················· mountain fold

step fold (valley and mountain fold next to each other)

direction to move paper

direction to push or pull

turn the paper over

180° direction to rotate paper

cut along this line

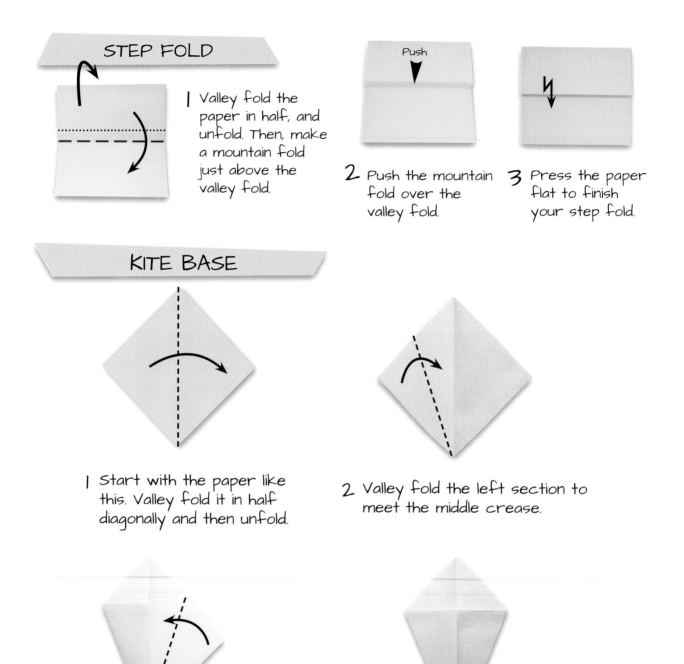

STEP FOLD

1 Valley fold the paper in half, and unfold. Then, make a mountain fold just above the valley fold.

Push

2 Push the mountain fold over the valley fold.

3 Press the paper flat to finish your step fold.

KITE BASE

1 Start with the paper like this. Valley fold it in half diagonally and then unfold.

2 Valley fold the left section to meet the middle crease.

3 Then, do the same on the right.

4 You now have a kite base.

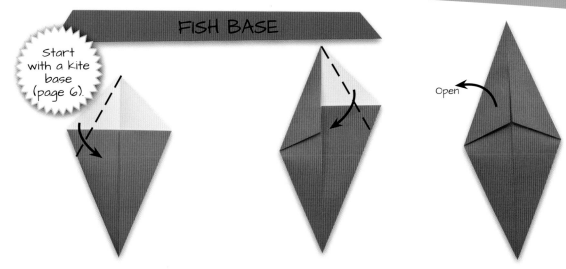

FISH BASE

Start with a kite base (page 6).

1 Valley fold the left-hand corner to the middle crease.

2 Valley fold the right-hand corner to the middle crease.

3 Your paper should look like this. Open out the left-hand pocket.

4 Pull the corner down to meet the middle crease.

5 Flatten the paper. Repeat steps 3-4 on the right-hand side.

6 You now have a fish base.

WATERBOMB BASE

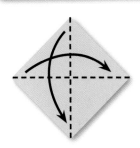

1 Start with your paper like this. Make two diagonal valley folds.

2 Your paper should now look like this. Turn it over.

3 Make two valley folds along the horizontal and vertical lines.

4 Push the left and right sides in, so the middle point pops up.

5 Keep pushing in the sides, until the back and front sections meet.

6 Flatten the paper. You now have a waterbomb base.

SQUARE BASE

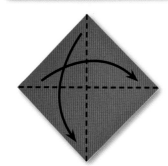

1 Place your paper like this. Make two diagonal valley folds.

2 The paper should now look like this. Turn it over.

3 Valley fold along the horizontal and vertical lines, then unfold.

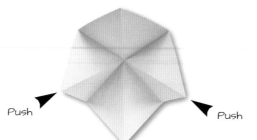

4 Your paper should now look like this.

5 Hold the paper by opposite diagonal corners. Push the corners to collapse the shape.

6 Flatten the paper. You now have a square base.

Start with a square base (page 8).

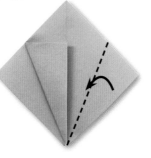

1 Place your square base so the open end is facing you. Fold the left-hand point of the top layer to the central crease.

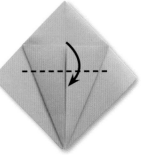

2 Do the same on the other side.

3 Valley fold the top point down.

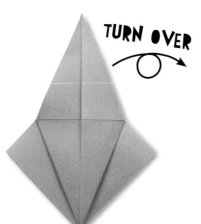

4 Unfold the top and sides and you have the shape shown here.

5 Take the bottom corner and lift it up to the top.

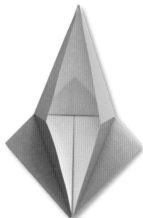

6 The paper should open like a bird's beak. Open out the flap as far as it will go.

TURN OVER

7 Flatten the paper down so that you now have this shape. Turn the paper over.

8 The paper should now look like this. Repeat steps 1 to 7 on this side as well.

9 You now have a bird base. The two flaps at the bottom should be separated by an open slit.

INSIDE REVERSE FOLD

This is useful if you want to flatten the shape of part of your model.

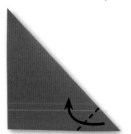

1 Fold a piece of paper diagonally in half. Make a valley fold on one point and crease.

2 Make sure that the paper is creased well. Run your finger over the fold several times.

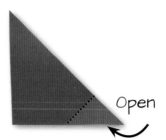

3 Unfold and open up the corner slightly. Refold the crease into a mountain fold.

4 Open up the paper a little more and then tuck the tip of the point inside. Close the paper. This is the view from the underside of the paper.

5 Flatten the paper. You now have an inside reverse fold.

OUTSIDE REVERSE FOLD

This is useful if you want to make part of your model stick out.

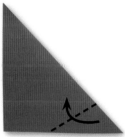

1 Fold a piece of paper diagonally in half. Make a valley fold on one point so the tip is overlapping the edge. Crease.

2 Run your finger over the fold two or three times, to make sure the paper is creased really well.

3 Unfold and open up the corner slightly. Refold the crease into a mountain fold.

4 Open up the paper and turn the corner inside out. Close the paper and crease it well. You now have an outside reverse fold.

CHAPTER 1

ANIMALS

Will you visit the Arctic or a jungle today? Create your own wild world with this bunch of exciting origami animals, from a cute little squirrel to a magnificent lion!

GORILLA

Gorillas are the world's largest apes. Follow these steps to fold your own gentle giant.

1 Place your paper white side down with a corner facing you. Valley fold it in half from top to bottom, and unfold. Then valley fold it in half from left to right, and unfold.

2 Fold the top tip down to the middle of the paper where the creases cross.

3 Make a small valley fold, as shown.

4 Turn the paper over from left to right.

5 Fold the top left edge in so it is about 5 mm (¼ in) from the central crease, as shown.

6 Repeat step 5 on the right-hand side.

12

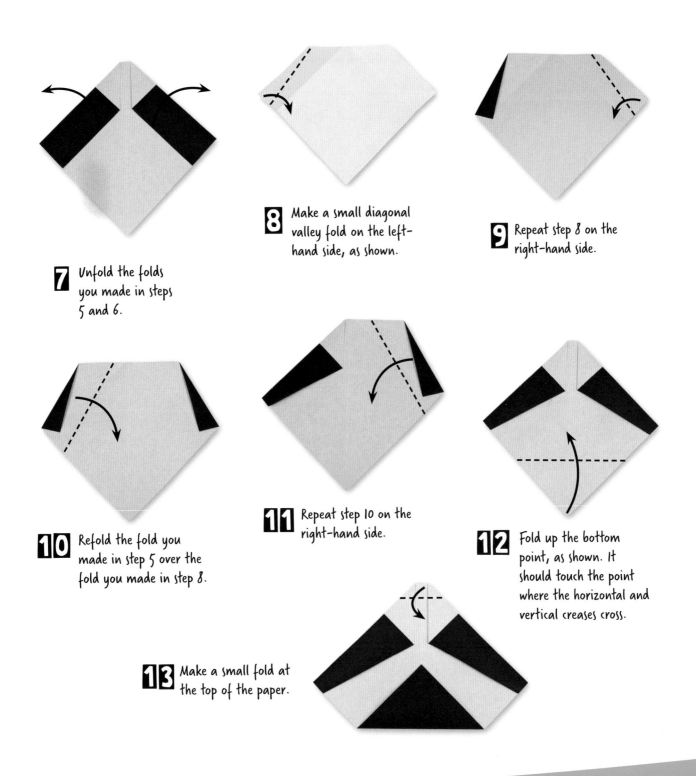

7 Unfold the folds you made in steps 5 and 6.

8 Make a small diagonal valley fold on the left-hand side, as shown.

9 Repeat step 8 on the right-hand side.

10 Refold the fold you made in step 5 over the fold you made in step 8.

11 Repeat step 10 on the right-hand side.

12 Fold up the bottom point, as shown. It should touch the point where the horizontal and vertical creases cross.

13 Make a small fold at the top of the paper.

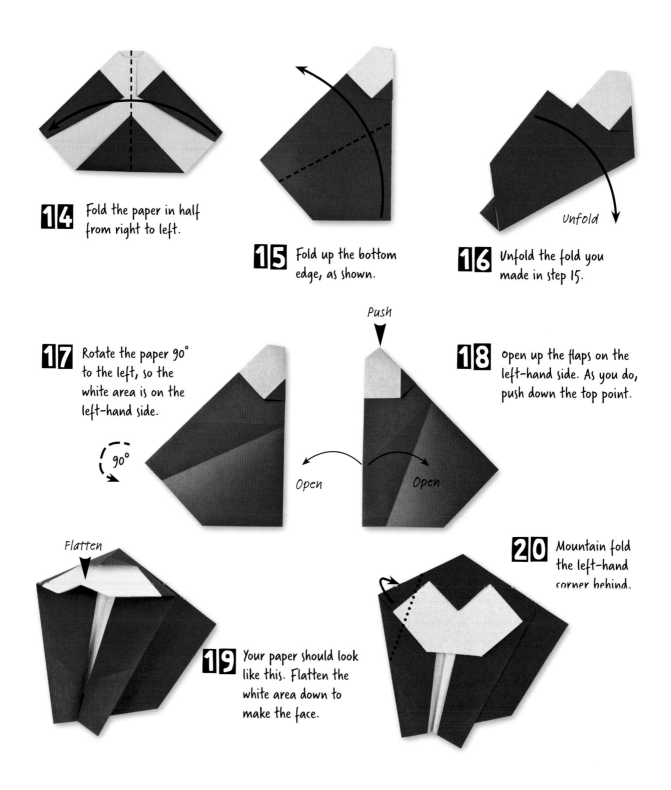

14 Fold the paper in half from right to left.

15 Fold up the bottom edge, as shown.

16 Unfold the fold you made in step 15.

Unfold

17 Rotate the paper 90° to the left, so the white area is on the left-hand side.

90°

Push

18 Open up the flaps on the left-hand side. As you do, push down the top point.

Open

Open

Flatten

19 Your paper should look like this. Flatten the white area down to make the face.

20 Mountain fold the left-hand corner behind.

21 Fold it the other way, so it's also a valley fold.

Tuck

22 Tuck the fold inside to make an inside reverse fold (see page 10).

23 Your paper should look like this. Repeat steps 20 to 22 on the other side of the face.

Unfold

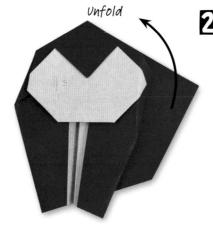

24 Unfold the body and your gorilla should stand up.

25

Use your pens to draw your gorilla's face. Will you make it fierce or friendly?

SEAHORSE

A seahorse swims through the water using tiny fins on its back, so make sure you fold them well!

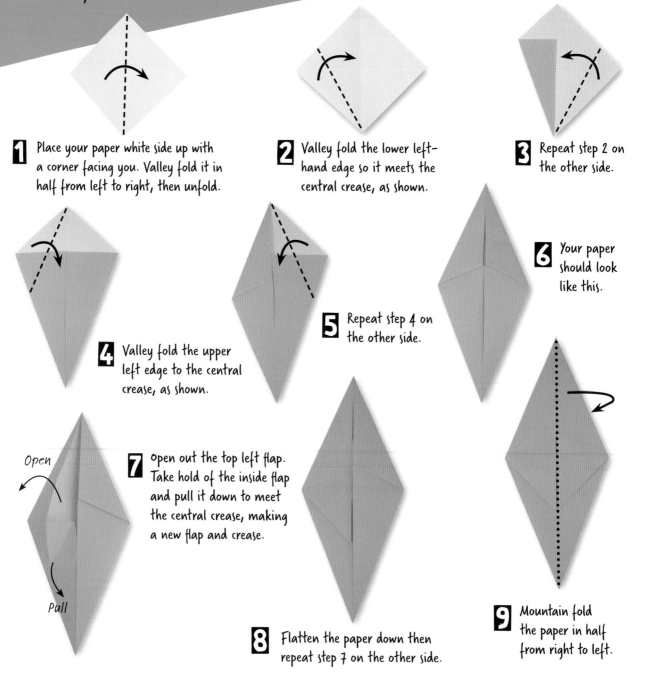

1 Place your paper white side up with a corner facing you. Valley fold it in half from left to right, then unfold.

2 Valley fold the lower left-hand edge so it meets the central crease, as shown.

3 Repeat step 2 on the other side.

4 Valley fold the upper left edge to the central crease, as shown.

5 Repeat step 4 on the other side.

6 Your paper should look like this.

Open

Pull

7 Open out the top left flap. Take hold of the inside flap and pull it down to meet the central crease, making a new flap and crease.

8 Flatten the paper down then repeat step 7 on the other side.

9 Mountain fold the paper in half from right to left.

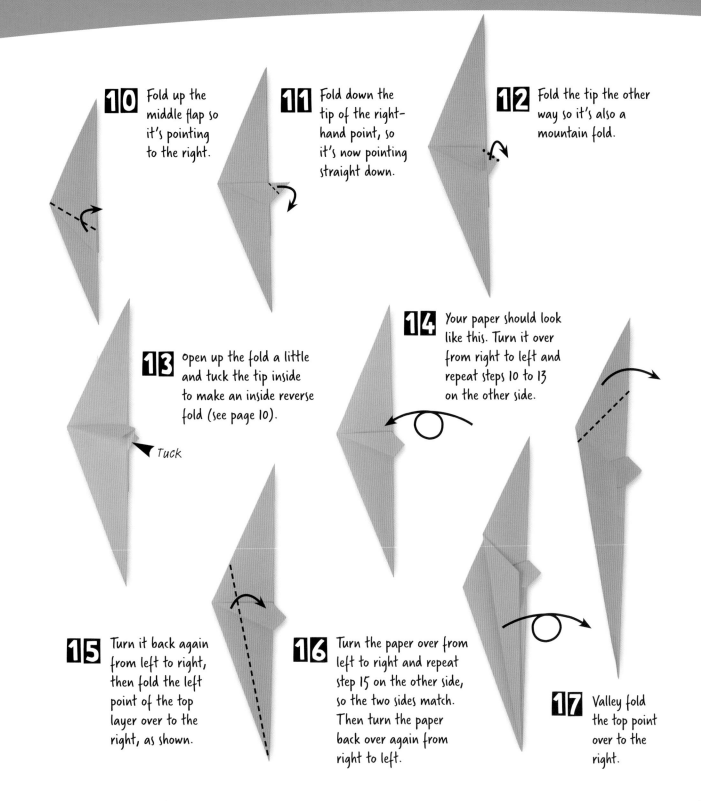

10 Fold up the middle flap so it's pointing to the right.

11 Fold down the tip of the right-hand point, so it's now pointing straight down.

12 Fold the tip the other way so it's also a mountain fold.

13 Open up the fold a little and tuck the tip inside to make an inside reverse fold (see page 10).

Tuck

14 Your paper should look like this. Turn it over from right to left and repeat steps 10 to 13 on the other side.

15 Turn it back again from left to right, then fold the left point of the top layer over to the right, as shown.

16 Turn the paper over from left to right and repeat step 15 on the other side, so the two sides match. Then turn the paper back over again from right to left.

17 Valley fold the top point over to the right.

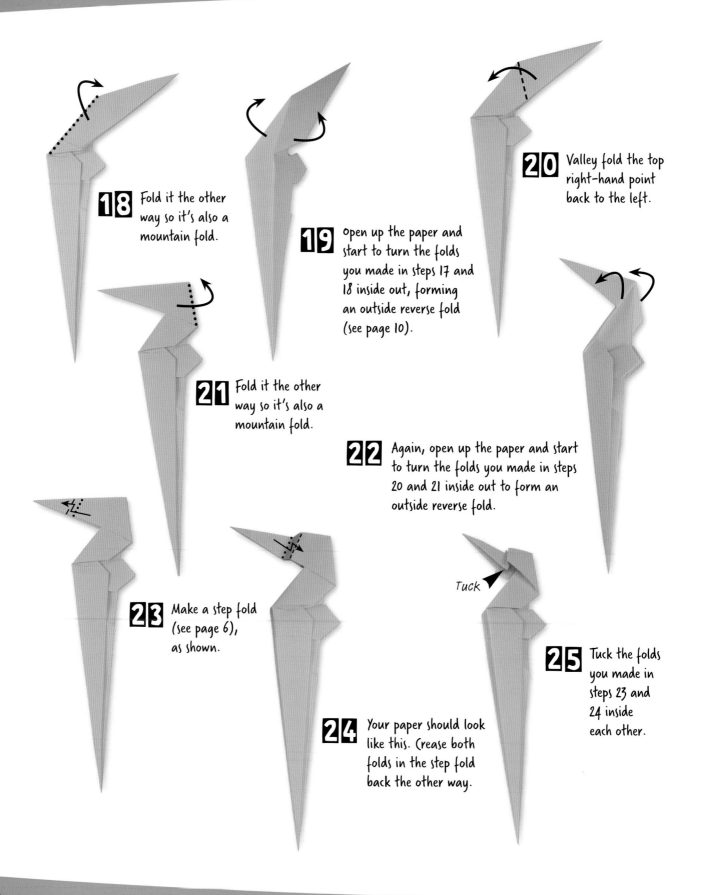

18 Fold it the other way so it's also a mountain fold.

19 Open up the paper and start to turn the folds you made in steps 17 and 18 inside out, forming an outside reverse fold (see page 10).

20 Valley fold the top right-hand point back to the left.

21 Fold it the other way so it's also a mountain fold.

22 Again, open up the paper and start to turn the folds you made in steps 20 and 21 inside out to form an outside reverse fold.

23 Make a step fold (see page 6), as shown.

24 Your paper should look like this. Crease both folds in the step fold back the other way.

Tuck

25 Tuck the folds you made in steps 23 and 24 inside each other.

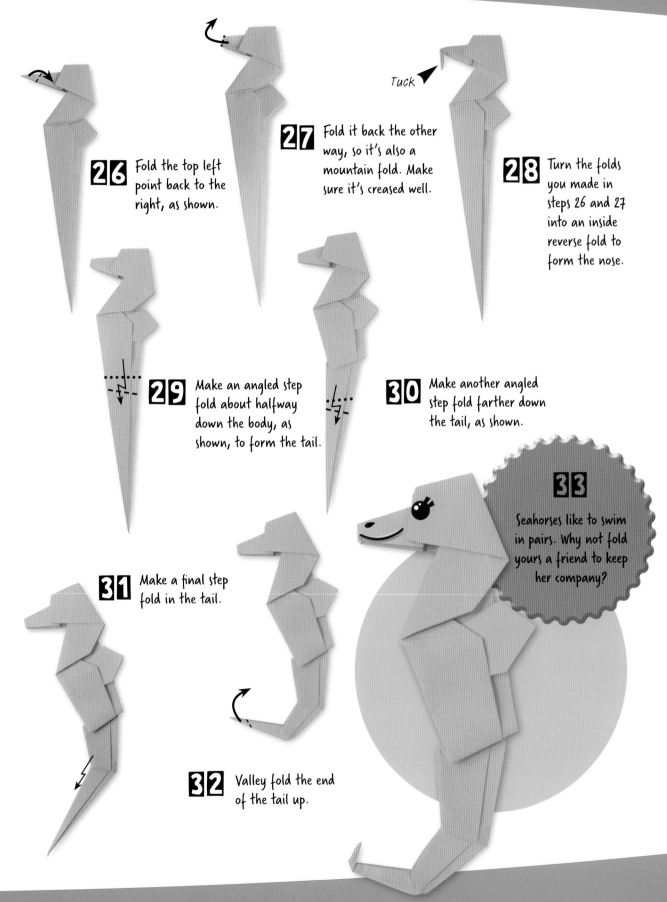

26 Fold the top left point back to the right, as shown.

27 Fold it back the other way, so it's also a mountain fold. Make sure it's creased well.

Tuck

28 Turn the folds you made in steps 26 and 27 into an inside reverse fold to form the nose.

29 Make an angled step fold about halfway down the body, as shown, to form the tail.

30 Make another angled step fold farther down the tail, as shown.

33 Seahorses like to swim in pairs. Why not fold yours a friend to keep her company?

31 Make a final step fold in the tail.

32 Valley fold the end of the tail up.

Fox

Use red or orange paper to make your own origami fox.

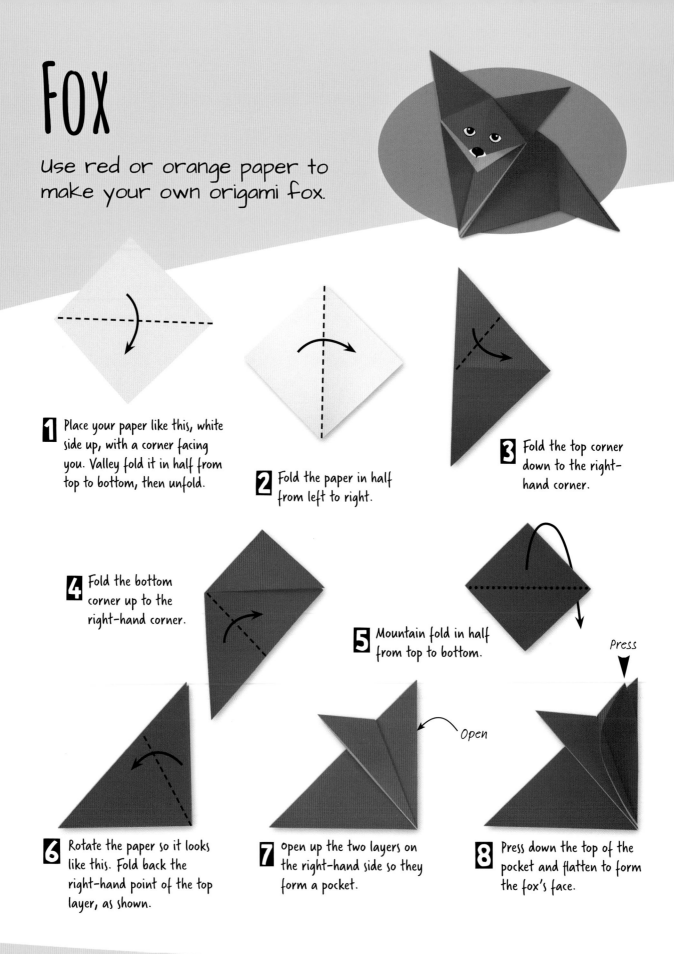

1 Place your paper like this, white side up, with a corner facing you. Valley fold it in half from top to bottom, then unfold.

2 Fold the paper in half from left to right.

3 Fold the top corner down to the right-hand corner.

4 Fold the bottom corner up to the right-hand corner.

5 Mountain fold in half from top to bottom.

Press

Open

6 Rotate the paper so it looks like this. Fold back the right-hand point of the top layer, as shown.

7 Open up the two layers on the right-hand side so they form a pocket.

8 Press down the top of the pocket and flatten to form the fox's face.

9 Fold the left-hand point to the right to form the tail.

10 Open up the flaps at the bottom of the face to form the mouth.

Open

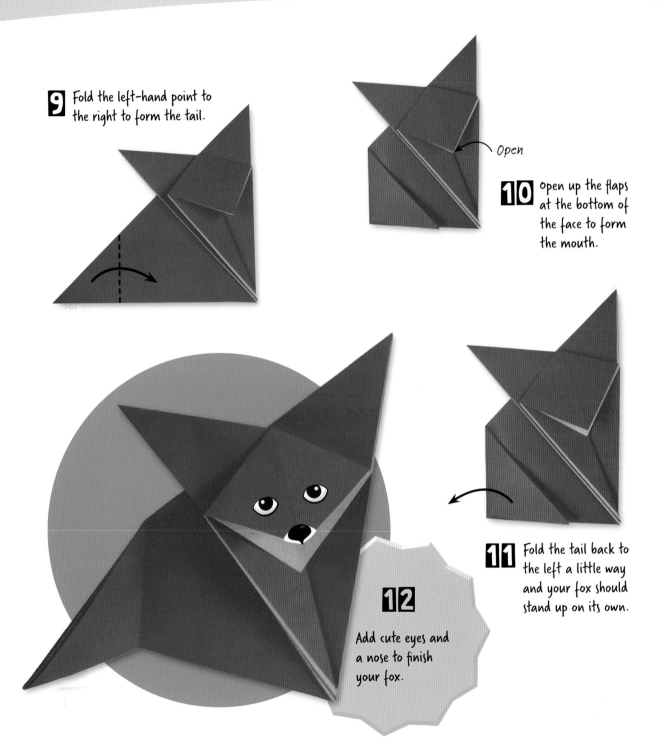

11 Fold the tail back to the left a little way and your fox should stand up on its own.

12 Add cute eyes and a nose to finish your fox.

MONKEY

Follow these steps to fold a funny paper monkey. You can hang him up wherever you like!

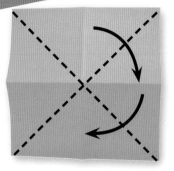

Push   Push

1 Place your paper white side up with a straight edge facing you. Valley fold it in half from top to bottom, and unfold. Then valley fold it in half from left to right, and unfold.

2 Turn the paper over, so that the orange side is facing up. Diagonally valley fold it one way, and unfold. Then diagonally valley fold it the other way, and unfold.

3 Turn the paper over again, so the white side is facing up, and rotate it so a corner is facing you. Then start pushing the two outer corners in to meet each other.

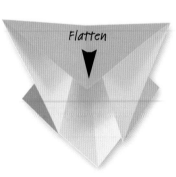

Flatten

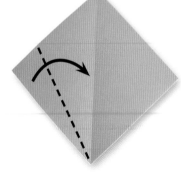

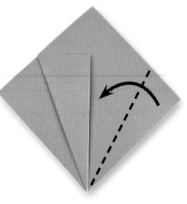

4 As you push, the paper should start folding up into a small square like this. Flatten it down.

5 Your paper should look like this. Valley fold the left bottom edge of the top layer over to the central line.

6 Valley fold the right bottom edge of the top layer over to the central line.

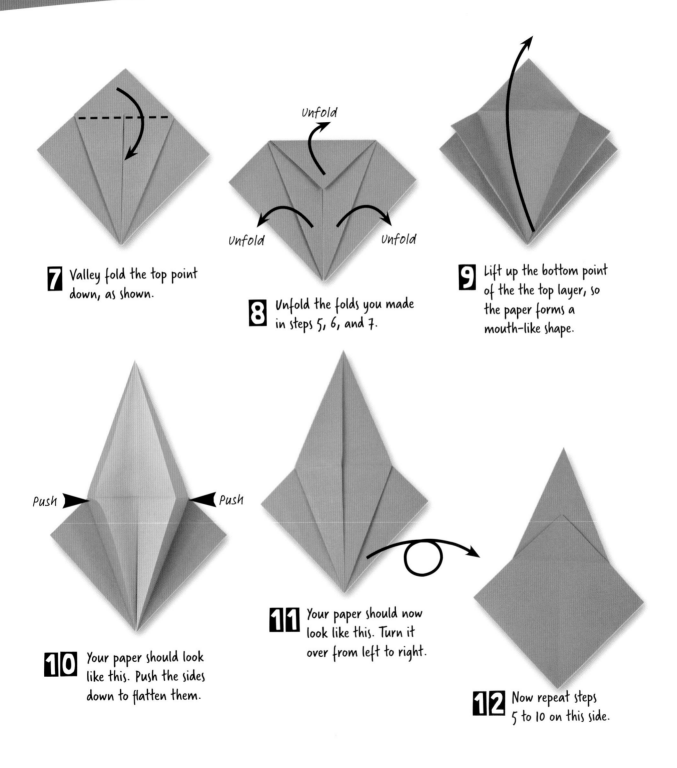

7 Valley fold the top point down, as shown.

Unfold

Unfold   Unfold

8 Unfold the folds you made in steps 5, 6, and 7.

9 Lift up the bottom point of the the top layer, so the paper forms a mouth-like shape.

Push ◄   ► Push

10 Your paper should look like this. Push the sides down to flatten them.

11 Your paper should now look like this. Turn it over from left to right.

12 Now repeat steps 5 to 10 on this side.

23

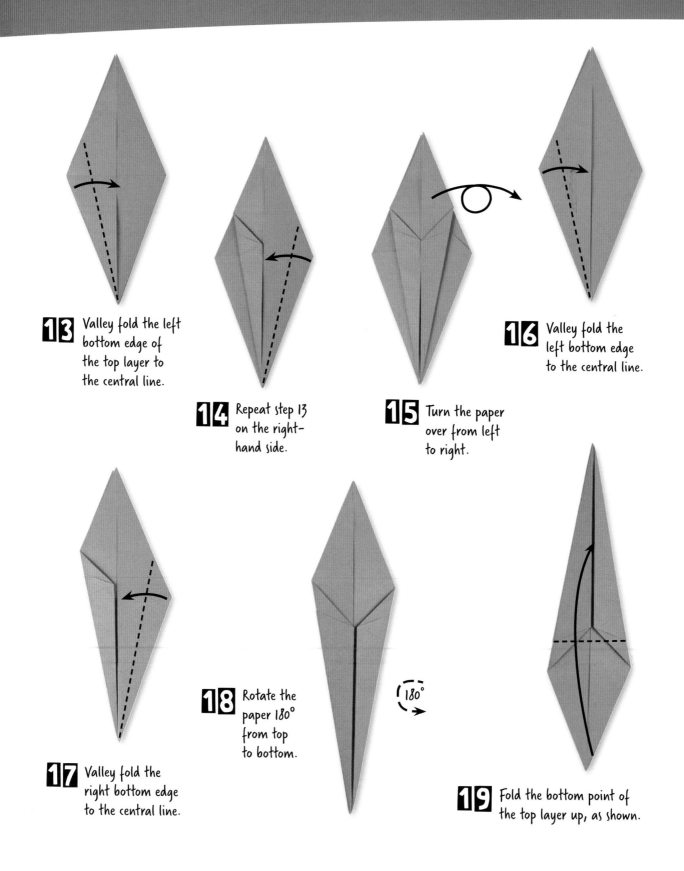

13 Valley fold the left bottom edge of the top layer to the central line.

14 Repeat step 13 on the right-hand side.

15 Turn the paper over from left to right.

16 Valley fold the left bottom edge to the central line.

17 Valley fold the right bottom edge to the central line.

18 Rotate the paper 180° from top to bottom.

180°

19 Fold the bottom point of the top layer up, as shown.

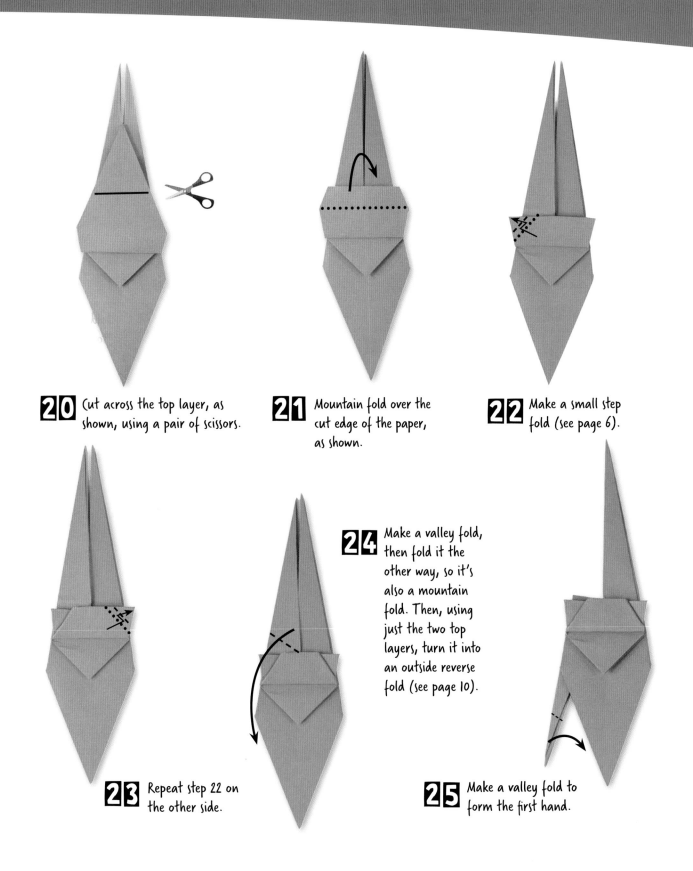

20 Cut across the top layer, as shown, using a pair of scissors.

21 Mountain fold over the cut edge of the paper, as shown.

22 Make a small step fold (see page 6).

23 Repeat step 22 on the other side.

24 Make a valley fold, then fold it the other way, so it's also a mountain fold. Then, using just the two top layers, turn it into an outside reverse fold (see page 10).

25 Make a valley fold to form the first hand.

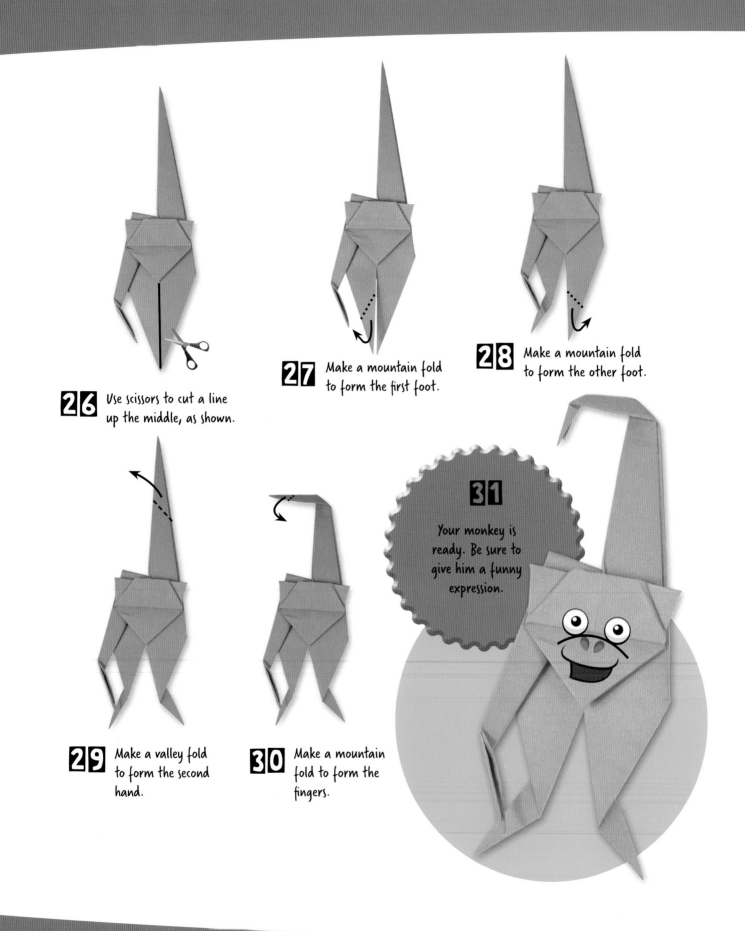

26 Use scissors to cut a line up the middle, as shown.

27 Make a mountain fold to form the first foot.

28 Make a mountain fold to form the other foot.

29 Make a valley fold to form the second hand.

30 Make a mountain fold to form the fingers.

31 Your monkey is ready. Be sure to give him a funny expression.

SQUID

Giant squid can be as long as a school bus! Here's how to fold a paper version.

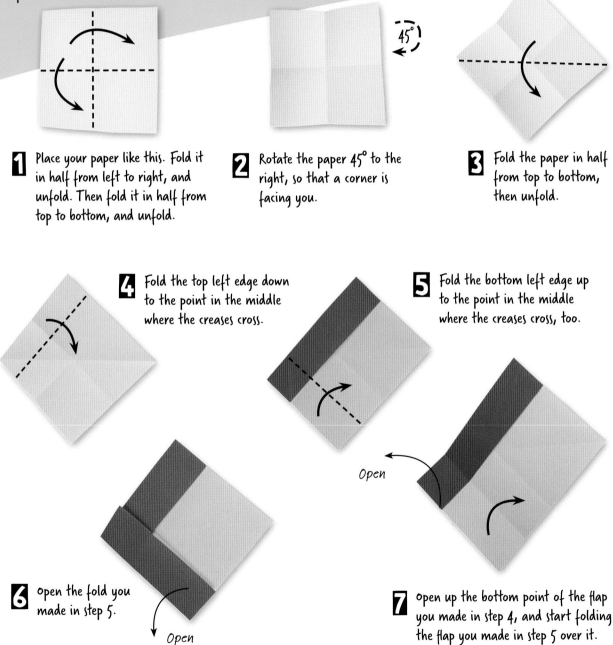

1 Place your paper like this. Fold it in half from left to right, and unfold. Then fold it in half from top to bottom, and unfold.

2 Rotate the paper 45° to the right, so that a corner is facing you.

3 Fold the paper in half from top to bottom, then unfold.

4 Fold the top left edge down to the point in the middle where the creases cross.

5 Fold the bottom left edge up to the point in the middle where the creases cross, too.

Open

6 Open the fold you made in step 5.

Open

7 Open up the bottom point of the flap you made in step 4, and start folding the flap you made in step 5 over it.

27

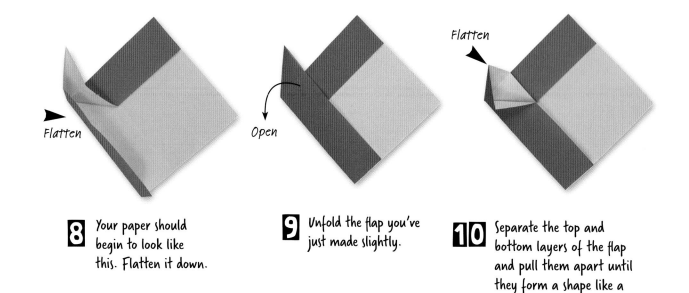

Flatten

8 Your paper should begin to look like this. Flatten it down.

Open

9 Unfold the flap you've just made slightly.

Flatten

10 Separate the top and bottom layers of the flap and pull them apart until they form a shape like a bird's mouth, like this, then flatten the shape down.

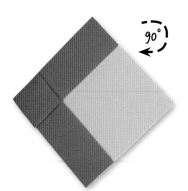

90°

11 Your paper should look this. Rotate it 90° to the right, so the shape you made in step 10 is at the top and a corner is facing you.

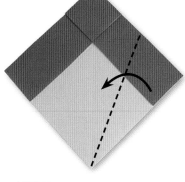

12 Fold the lower right edge over to the central line, as shown.

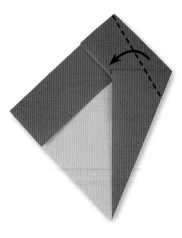

13 Fold the upper right edge over to the central line, tucking it under the shape you made in step 10.

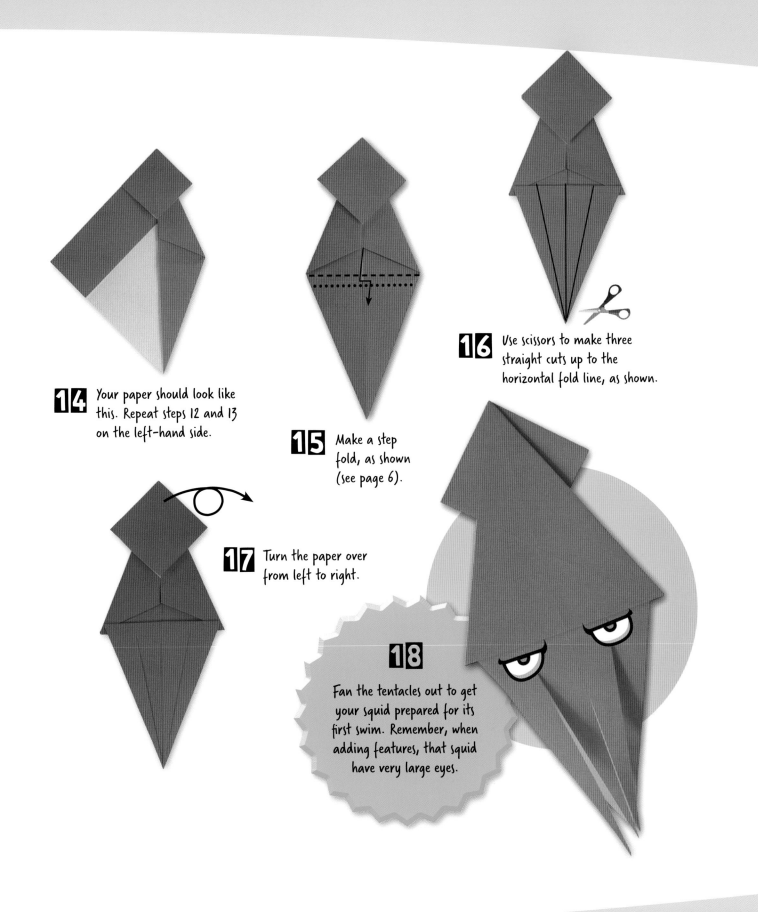

14 Your paper should look like this. Repeat steps 12 and 13 on the left-hand side.

15 Make a step fold, as shown (see page 6).

16 Use scissors to make three straight cuts up to the horizontal fold line, as shown.

17 Turn the paper over from left to right.

18 Fan the tentacles out to get your squid prepared for its first swim. Remember, when adding features, that squid have very large eyes.

POLAR BEAR

These enormous bears are the world's largest land predators. And they can swim well, too!

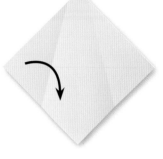

1 Place your paper white side up with a corner facing you. Valley fold it in half from right to left, then unfold.

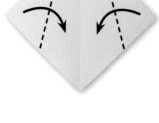

2 Make two valley folds on either side, as shown, then unfold.

3 Fold the left side back in.

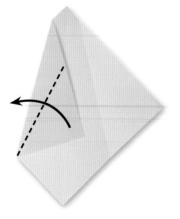

4 Make a small valley fold on the left-hand side, as shown.

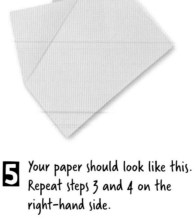

5 Your paper should look like this. Repeat steps 3 and 4 on the right-hand side.

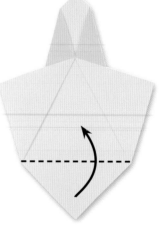

6 Fold the bottom point up.

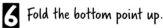

30

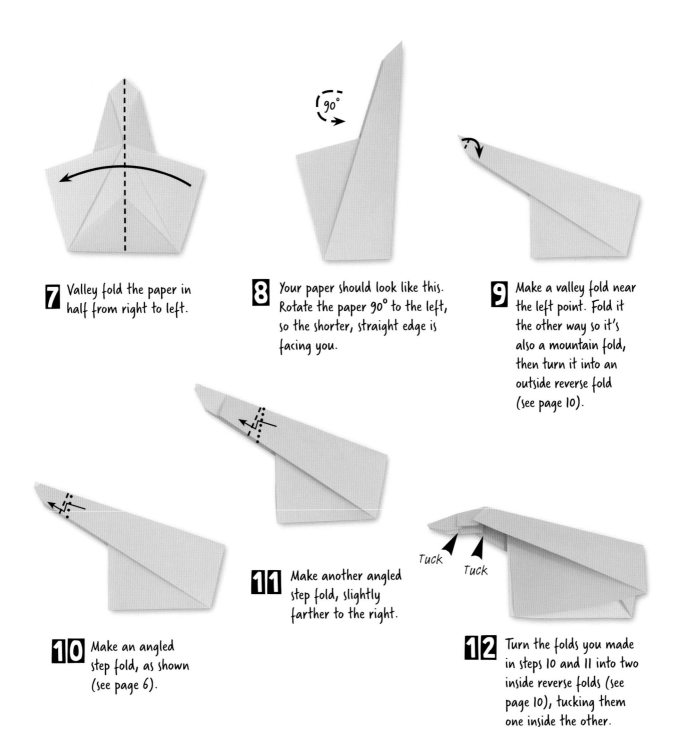

7 Valley fold the paper in half from right to left.

8 Your paper should look like this. Rotate the paper 90° to the left, so the shorter, straight edge is facing you.

9 Make a valley fold near the left point. Fold it the other way so it's also a mountain fold, then turn it into an outside reverse fold (see page 10).

10 Make an angled step fold, as shown (see page 6).

11 Make another angled step fold, slightly farther to the right.

Tuck   Tuck

12 Turn the folds you made in steps 10 and 11 into two inside reverse folds (see page 10), tucking them one inside the other.

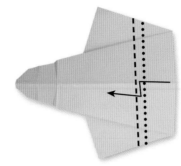

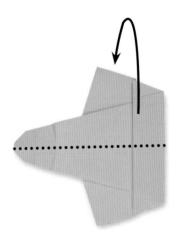

 Your paper should look like this. Open up the fold you made in step 7, so the paper is lying flat.

14 Make a step fold on the right-hand side.

15 Refold the paper in half from top to bottom.

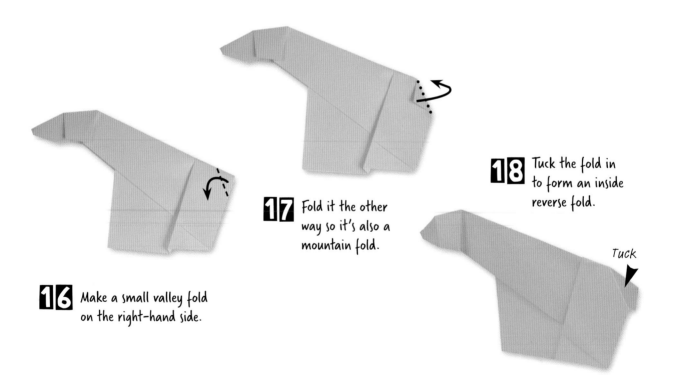

17 Fold it the other way so it's also a mountain fold.

16 Make a small valley fold on the right-hand side.

18 Tuck the fold in to form an inside reverse fold.

Tuck

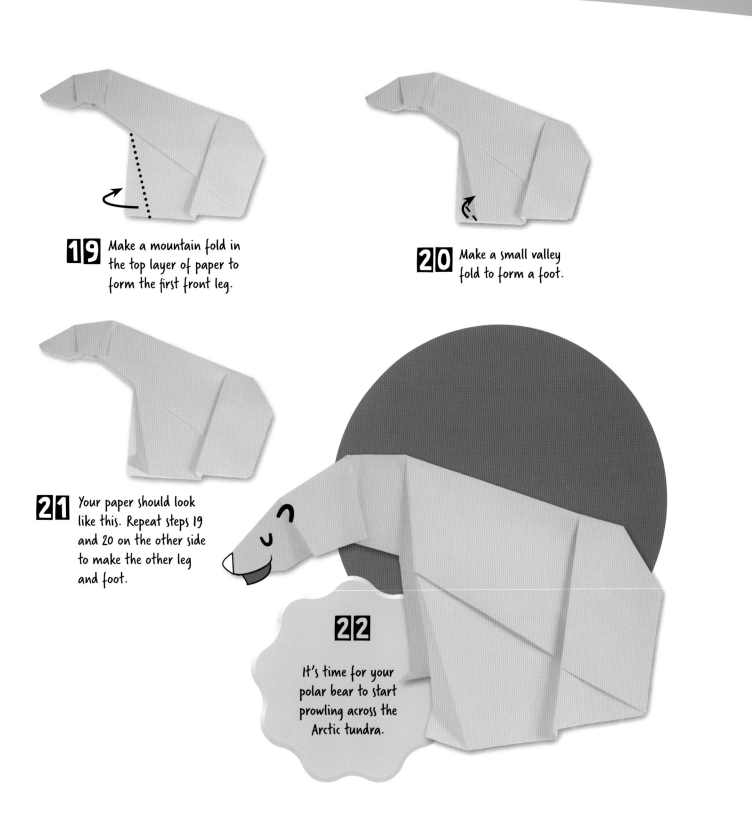

19 Make a mountain fold in the top layer of paper to form the first front leg.

20 Make a small valley fold to form a foot.

21 Your paper should look like this. Repeat steps 19 and 20 on the other side to make the other leg and foot.

22

It's time for your polar bear to start prowling across the Arctic tundra.

LION

Follow these steps to create your own king of the beasts with a magnificent mane!

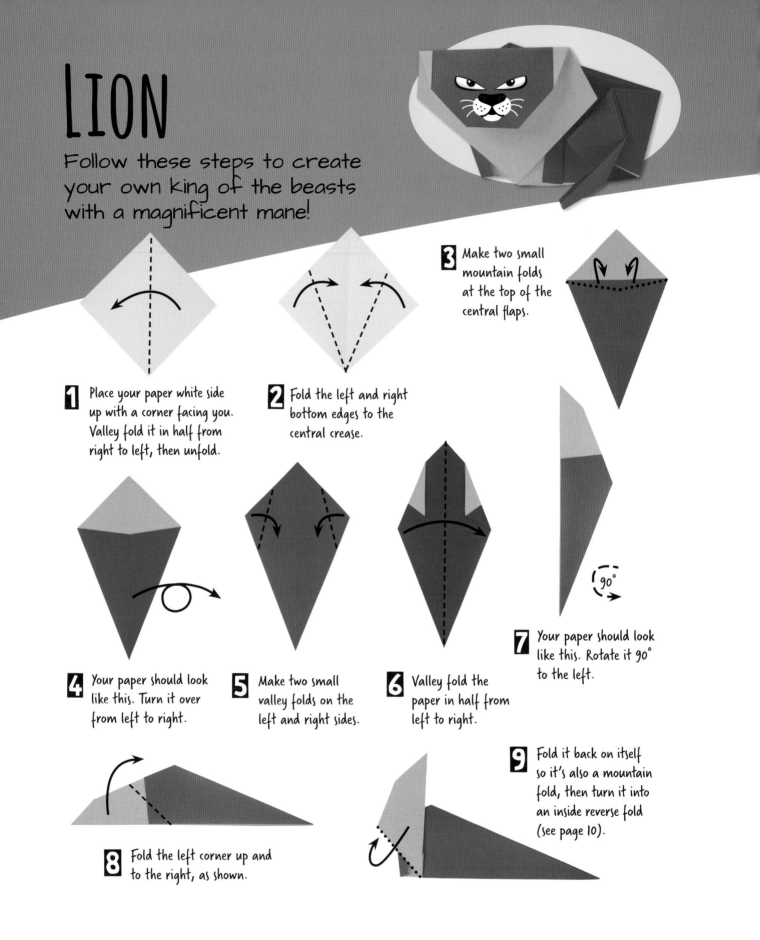

1 Place your paper white side up with a corner facing you. Valley fold it in half from right to left, then unfold.

2 Fold the left and right bottom edges to the central crease.

3 Make two small mountain folds at the top of the central flaps.

4 Your paper should look like this. Turn it over from left to right.

5 Make two small valley folds on the left and right sides.

6 Valley fold the paper in half from left to right.

7 Your paper should look like this. Rotate it 90° to the left.

8 Fold the left corner up and to the right, as shown.

9 Fold it back on itself so it's also a mountain fold, then turn it into an inside reverse fold (see page 10).

34

10 Fold the left-hand point of the top layer over to the right.

11 Your paper should look like this. Fold the top point down, as shown.

12 Make a small mountain fold, as shown, tucking the point behind.

13 Fold the right-hand point up and over to the left.

14 Now fold it down and to the right.

15 Make a third fold, taking it back over to the left.

16 Make a final fourth fold back to the right, then turn this into an inside reverse fold.

18 Add eyes, nose, whiskers, and a mouth, and your lion is ready to roar.

17 Your paper should look like this. Gently pull the tail out to help your lion stand.

Pull

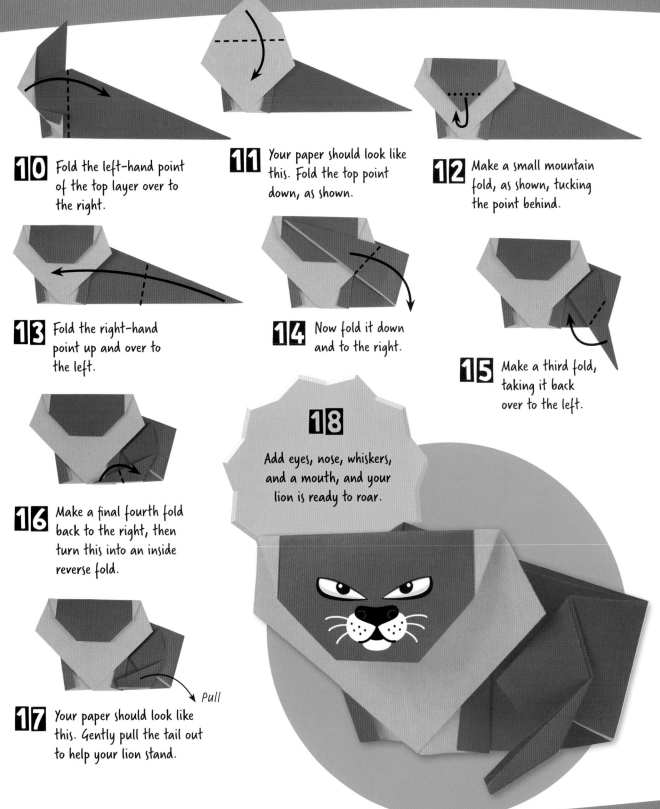

35

SQUIRREL

Look out for squirrels next time you are in a forest—or just make this cute origami version instead!

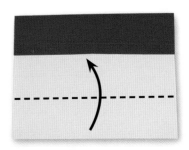

1 With your paper like this, valley fold it in half from top to bottom, and unfold. Then valley fold it in half from left to right, and unfold.

2 Now valley fold the top edge down to the central crease.

3 Valley fold the bottom edge up to the central crease, too.

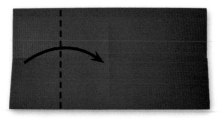

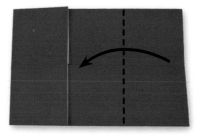

4 Valley fold the left edge to the central crease.

5 Valley fold the right edge to the central crease.

6 Unfold the folds you made in steps 4 and 5.

7 Fold the top-left corner down to the crease line.

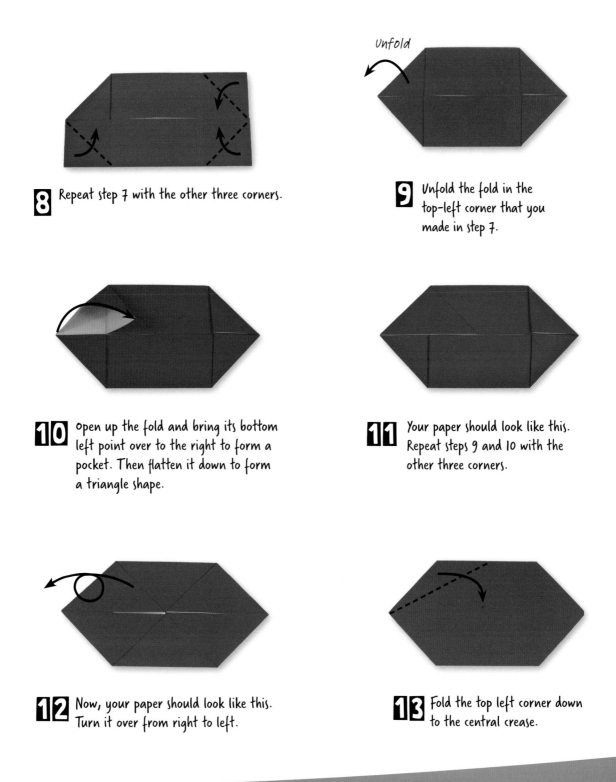

Unfold

8 Repeat step 7 with the other three corners.

9 Unfold the fold in the top-left corner that you made in step 7.

10 Open up the fold and bring its bottom left point over to the right to form a pocket. Then flatten it down to form a triangle shape.

11 Your paper should look like this. Repeat steps 9 and 10 with the other three corners.

12 Now, your paper should look like this. Turn it over from right to left.

13 Fold the top left corner down to the central crease.

14 Fold the bottom left corner up to the central crease.

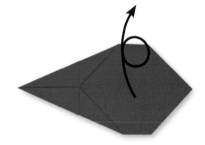

15 Your paper should look like this. Turn it over from bottom to top.

16 Fold this flap down to the left, as shown, to make the first foot.

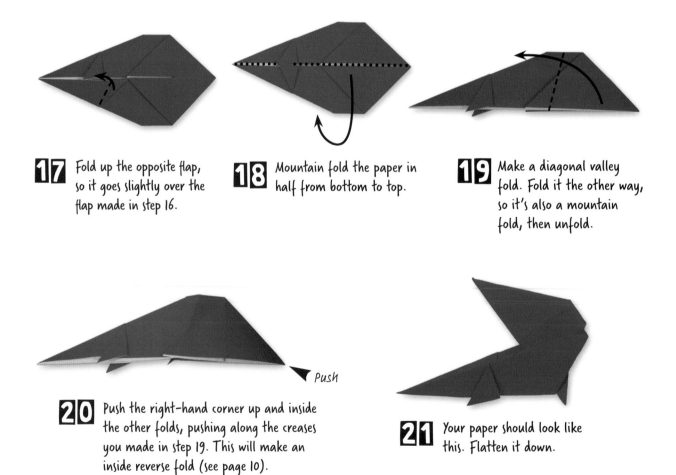

17 Fold up the opposite flap, so it goes slightly over the flap made in step 16.

18 Mountain fold the paper in half from bottom to top.

19 Make a diagonal valley fold. Fold it the other way, so it's also a mountain fold, then unfold.

Push

20 Push the right-hand corner up and inside the other folds, pushing along the creases you made in step 19. This will make an inside reverse fold (see page 10).

21 Your paper should look like this. Flatten it down.

22 Rotate your paper 90° to the right.

23 Fold the top point down and to the right, as shown.

24 Fold it the other way, so it's also a mountain fold, then turn it into an outside reverse fold (see page 10). This is the face.

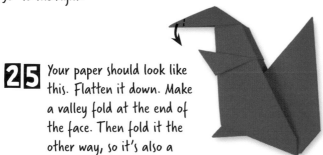

25 Your paper should look like this. Flatten it down. Make a valley fold at the end of the face. Then fold it the other way, so it's also a mountain fold.

26 Turn the fold you made in step 25 into an inside reverse fold (see page 10), tucking it into the face.

Tuck

27

Your squirrel is ready to collect her first nuts.

VULTURE

Vultures have excellent senses of sight and smell, which help them find food.

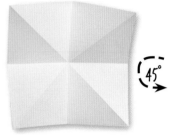

1 Place your paper white side up with a straight edge facing you. Valley fold it in half from top to bottom, and unfold. Then valley fold it in half from left to right, and unfold.

2 Turn the paper over, so that the white side is now facing down. Diagonally valley fold it one way and unfold. Then diagonally valley fold it the other way and unfold.

3 Turn the paper over again, so the white side is facing up. Rotate it 45° so a corner is facing you.

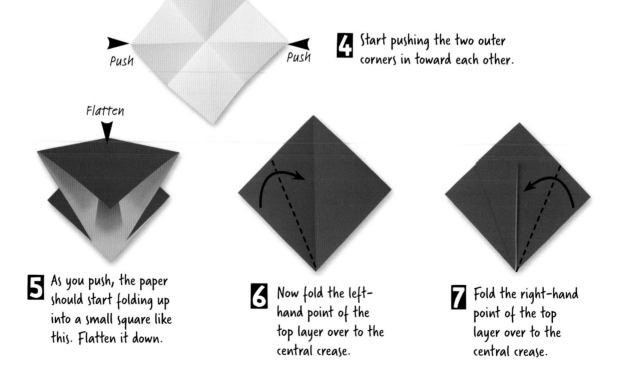

Push   Push

4 Start pushing the two outer corners in toward each other.

Flatten

5 As you push, the paper should start folding up into a small square like this. Flatten it down.

6 Now fold the left-hand point of the top layer over to the central crease.

7 Fold the right-hand point of the top layer over to the central crease.

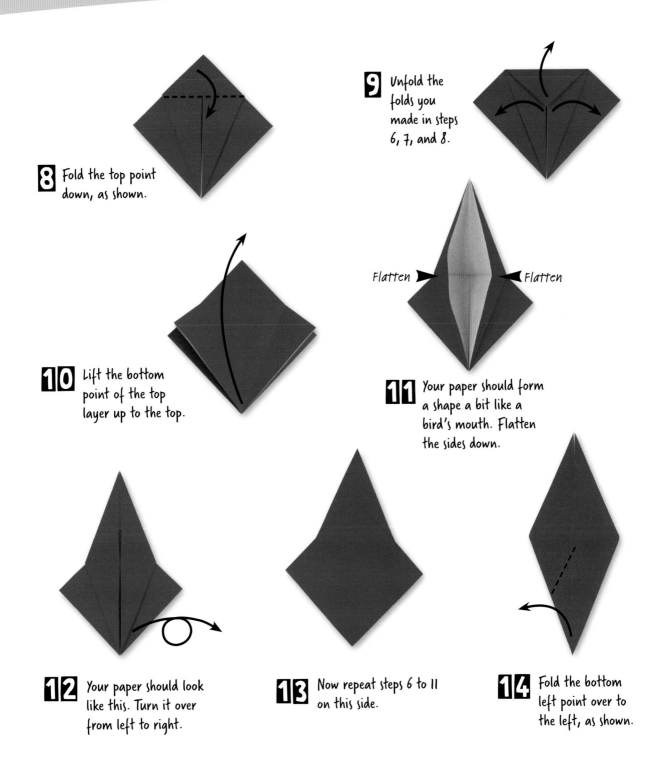

8 Fold the top point down, as shown.

9 Unfold the folds you made in steps 6, 7, and 8.

Flatten ◄   ► Flatten

10 Lift the bottom point of the top layer up to the top.

11 Your paper should form a shape a bit like a bird's mouth. Flatten the sides down.

12 Your paper should look like this. Turn it over from left to right.

13 Now repeat steps 6 to 11 on this side.

14 Fold the bottom left point over to the left, as shown.

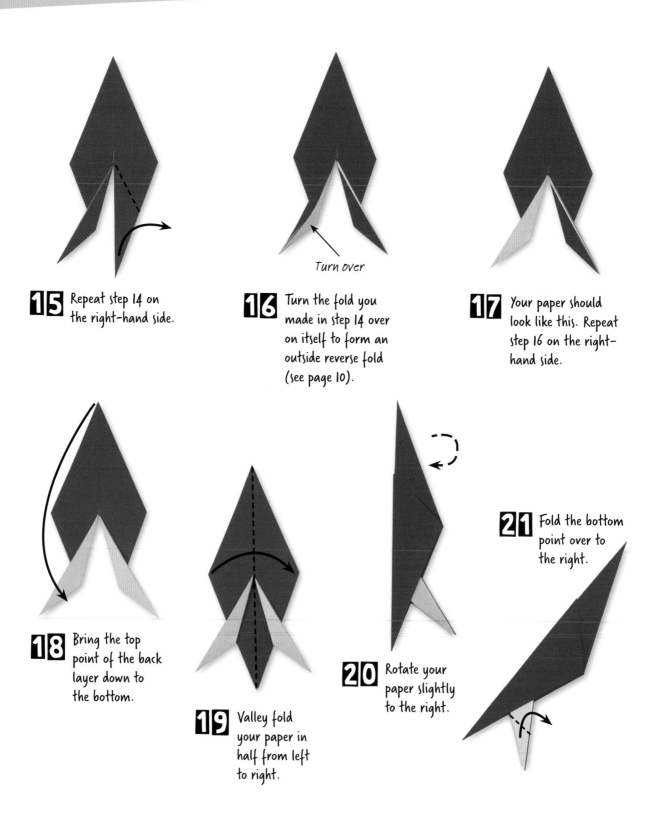

Turn over

15 Repeat step 14 on the right-hand side.

16 Turn the fold you made in step 14 over on itself to form an outside reverse fold (see page 10).

17 Your paper should look like this. Repeat step 16 on the right-hand side.

18 Bring the top point of the back layer down to the bottom.

19 Valley fold your paper in half from left to right.

20 Rotate your paper slightly to the right.

21 Fold the bottom point over to the right.

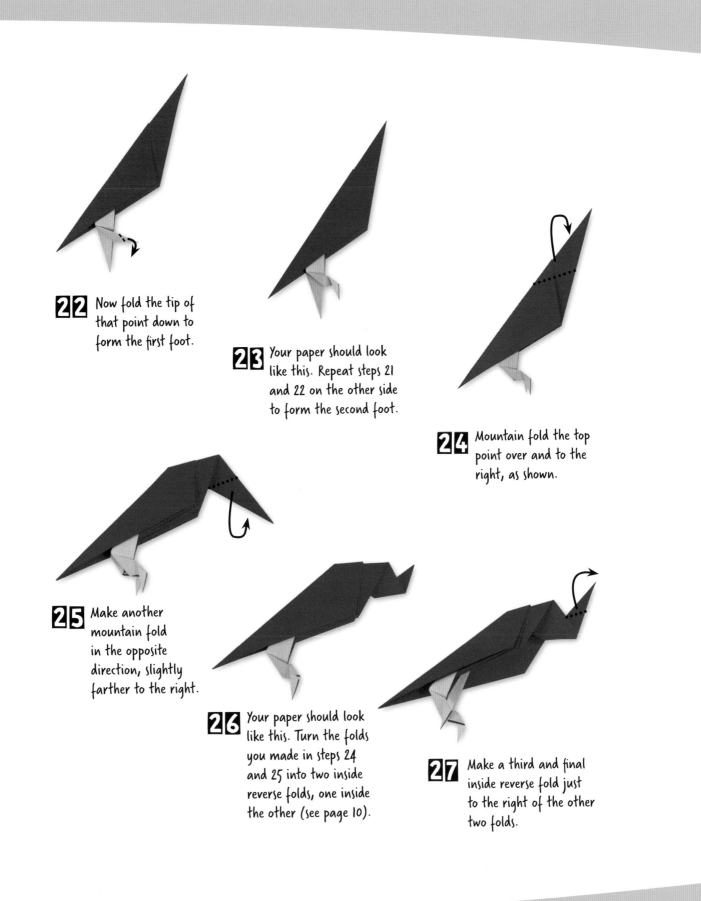

22 Now fold the tip of that point down to form the first foot.

23 Your paper should look like this. Repeat steps 21 and 22 on the other side to form the second foot.

24 Mountain fold the top point over and to the right, as shown.

25 Make another mountain fold in the opposite direction, slightly farther to the right.

26 Your paper should look like this. Turn the folds you made in steps 24 and 25 into two inside reverse folds, one inside the other (see page 10).

27 Make a third and final inside reverse fold just to the right of the other two folds.

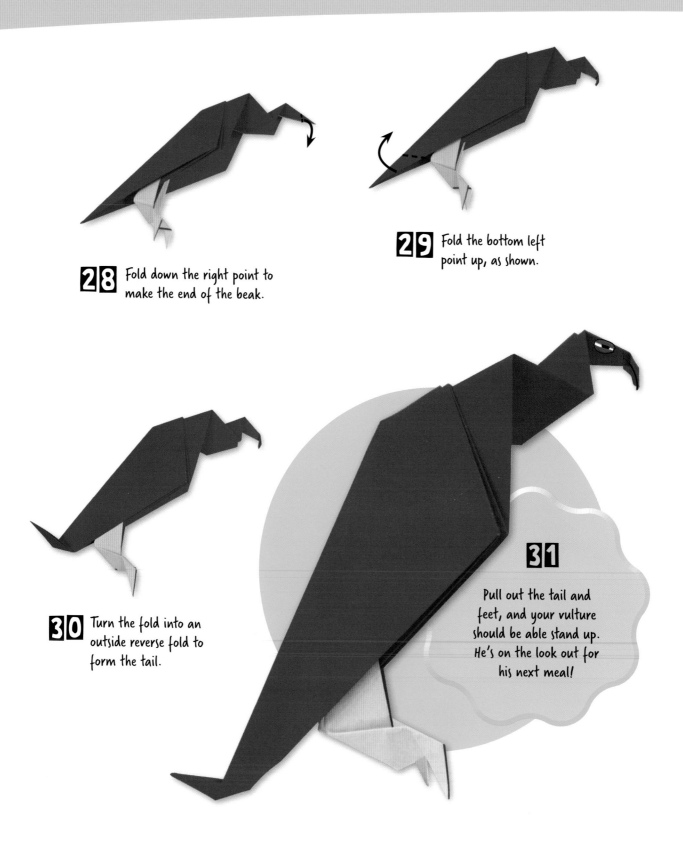

28 Fold down the right point to make the end of the beak.

29 Fold the bottom left point up, as shown.

30 Turn the fold into an outside reverse fold to form the tail.

31

Pull out the tail and feet, and your vulture should be able stand up. He's on the look out for his next meal!

NARWHAL

Sometimes called "sea unicorns," these whales have an enormous tusk on the front of their heads.

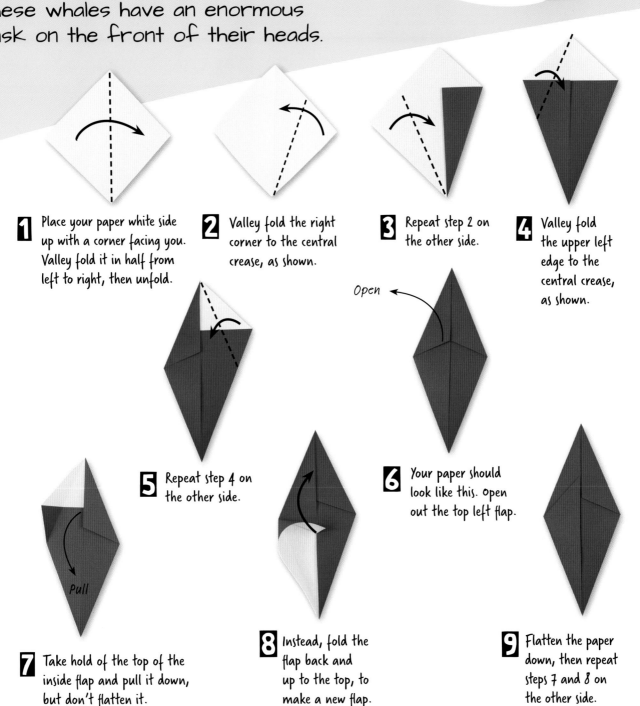

1 Place your paper white side up with a corner facing you. Valley fold it in half from left to right, then unfold.

2 Valley fold the right corner to the central crease, as shown.

3 Repeat step 2 on the other side.

4 Valley fold the upper left edge to the central crease, as shown.

Open

5 Repeat step 4 on the other side.

6 Your paper should look like this. Open out the top left flap.

Pull

7 Take hold of the top of the inside flap and pull it down, but don't flatten it.

8 Instead, fold the flap back and up to the top, to make a new flap.

9 Flatten the paper down, then repeat steps 7 and 8 on the other side.

45

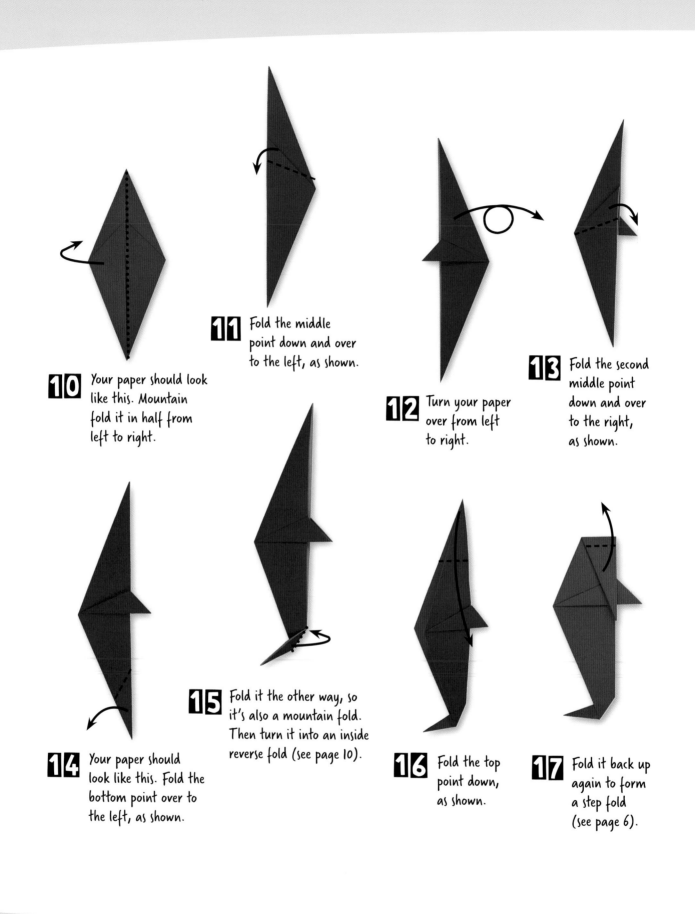

10 Your paper should look like this. Mountain fold it in half from left to right.

11 Fold the middle point down and over to the left, as shown.

12 Turn your paper over from left to right.

13 Fold the second middle point down and over to the right, as shown.

14 Your paper should look like this. Fold the bottom point over to the left, as shown.

15 Fold it the other way, so it's also a mountain fold. Then turn it into an inside reverse fold (see page 10).

16 Fold the top point down, as shown.

17 Fold it back up again to form a step fold (see page 6).

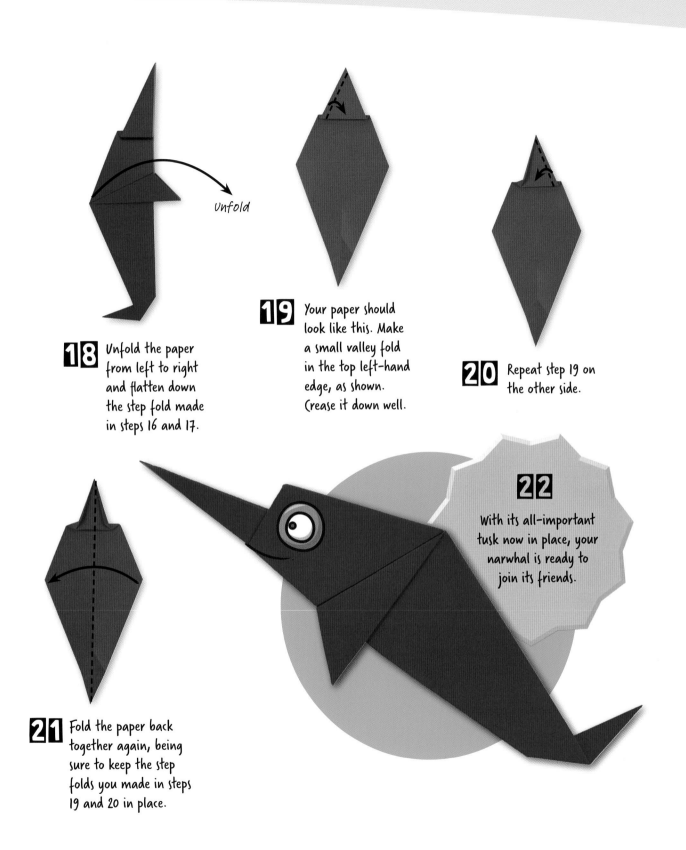

18 Unfold the paper from left to right and flatten down the step fold made in steps 16 and 17.

Unfold

19 Your paper should look like this. Make a small valley fold in the top left-hand edge, as shown. Crease it down well.

20 Repeat step 19 on the other side.

21 Fold the paper back together again, being sure to keep the step folds you made in steps 19 and 20 in place.

22 With its all-important tusk now in place, your narwhal is ready to join its friends.

PARROT

Parrots have beautiful, bright feathers. Choose a tropical shade of paper for yours!

1 Place your paper white side down with a corner facing you. Valley fold it in half from left to right, and unfold.

2 Fold the left corner in, so the tip meets the central crease, as shown.

3 Repeat step 2 on the right-hand side.

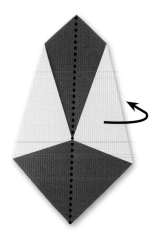

Tuck

4 Mountain fold the paper in half, so the vertical crease is on the right.

5 Your paper should look like this. Fold the top point over to the left.

6 Fold it back the other way so it's also a mountain fold.

7 Tuck the fold in on itself to form an inside reverse fold (see page 10).

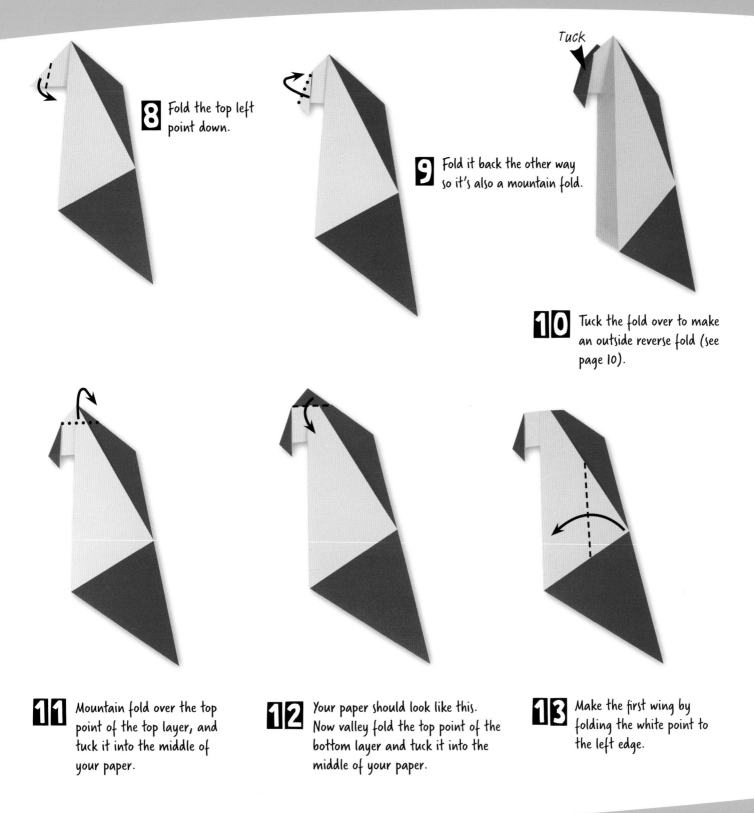

8 Fold the top left point down.

9 Fold it back the other way so it's also a mountain fold.

Tuck

10 Tuck the fold over to make an outside reverse fold (see page 10).

11 Mountain fold over the top point of the top layer, and tuck it into the middle of your paper.

12 Your paper should look like this. Now valley fold the top point of the bottom layer and tuck it into the middle of your paper.

13 Make the first wing by folding the white point to the left edge.

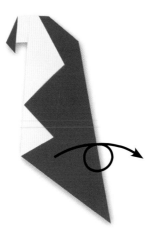

14 Your paper should look like this. Turn it over from left to right.

15 Repeat step 13 on this side, then turn the paper back from right to left.

16 Use a pair of scissors to make a cut in the bottom of the paper, as shown.

17 Valley fold the top layer over to the left to make the first foot.

18 Do the same on the bottom layer to make the other foot.

19

Spread the feet out and your parrot should be able to stand up.

50

CHAPTER 2

DINOSAURS

Create your own prehistoric world with these origami dinosaurs, from the terrible Triceratops to the giant Megalosaurus. There's even a dinosaur egg to make! Let's hope it doesn't hatch …

VELOCIRAPTOR

Say "veh-LOSS-ih-RAP-tor"

Though small and covered in feathers, Velociraptor was still a deadly predator. It probably hunted in packs, so why not make a whole group of them?

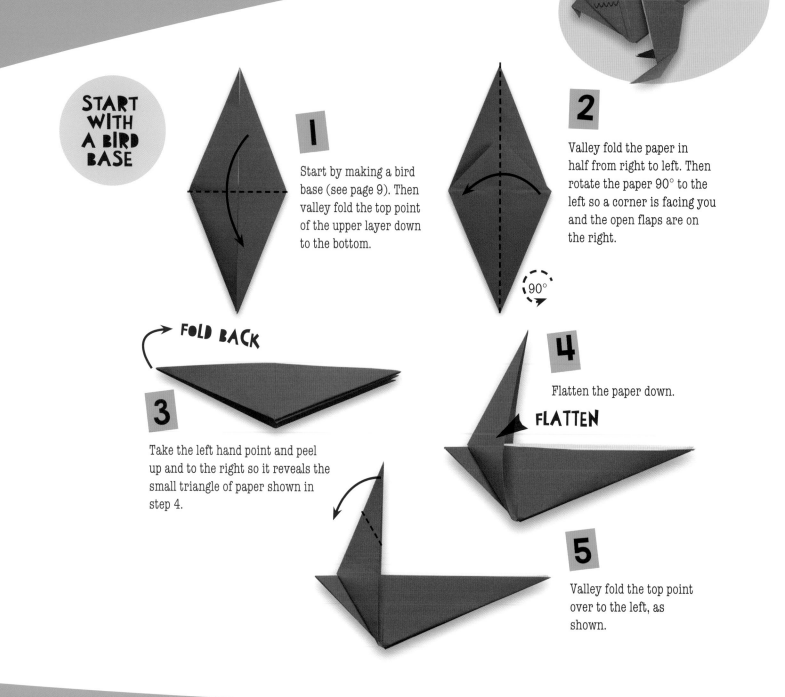

START WITH A BIRD BASE

1 Start by making a bird base (see page 9). Then valley fold the top point of the upper layer down to the bottom.

2 Valley fold the paper in half from right to left. Then rotate the paper 90° to the left so a corner is facing you and the open flaps are on the right.

90°

FOLD BACK

3 Take the left hand point and peel up and to the right so it reveals the small triangle of paper shown in step 4.

4 Flatten the paper down.

FLATTEN

5 Valley fold the top point over to the left, as shown.

6

Fold it the other way so it's also a mountain fold, then turn it into an outside reverse fold (see page 10). This is the head.

7

Tuck the tip of the nose inside the head by making an inside reverse fold (see page 10).

8

Valley fold the left-hand point down, as shown.

9

Fold it the other way so it's also a mountain fold, then turn it into an inside reverse fold to make the hands.

10

Fold the right-hand point of the upper layer down and to the left to form the first leg.

11

Valley fold the bottom point over to the left to form the first foot.

12

Your paper should look like this. Repeat steps 10 and 11 on the other side.

13

Finally, use your pens to give Velociraptor a feathery coat.

FINISHED!

MEGALOSAURUS

Say "MEG-ah-low-SAW-rus"

This dinosaur was a great two-legged hunter. When you finish the model, be sure to draw on some sharp teeth!

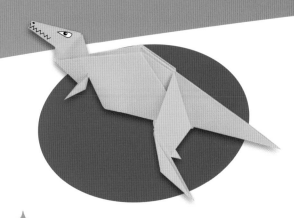

START WITH A BIRD BASE

1 Start by making a bird base (see page 9). Then, fold the left-hand point of the upper layer over to the right.

2 Your paper should look like this. Turn it over from left to right.

TURN OVER

3 Fold the left-hand point of the upper layer over to the right on this side too.

4 Your paper should now look like this with a clear gap between the top two points. Rotate it 90° to the right.

90°

54

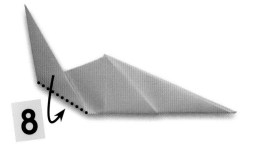

5 Valley fold the left-hand point of the upper layer all the way over to the right.

6 Valley fold the paper in half from bottom to top, as shown.

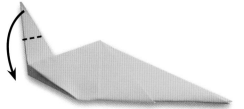

7 Valley fold the left-hand point up.

8 Fold it the other way so it's also a mountain fold, then turn it into an inside reverse fold (see page 10).

q Valley fold the left-hand point down, as shown.

10 Mountain fold it the other way, then unfold.

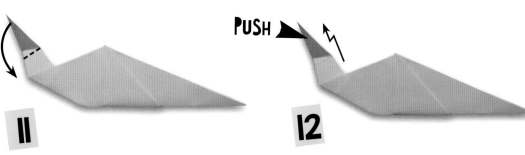

II Make another diagonal valley fold just below the fold you made in steps 9 and 10. Fold it the other way, so it's also a mountain fold, then unfold.

PUSH ►

12 Push the top left point down and to the right so that folds go out on either side of the paper, forming a step fold. Flatten the paper down. This is the head.

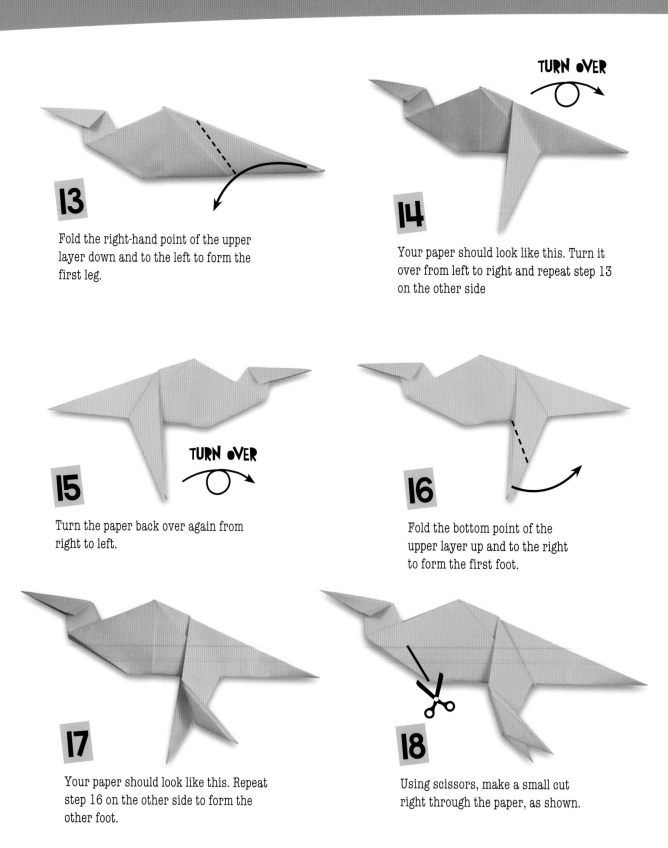

13

Fold the right-hand point of the upper layer down and to the left to form the first leg.

TURN OVER

14

Your paper should look like this. Turn it over from left to right and repeat step 13 on the other side

15

Turn the paper back over again from right to left.

TURN OVER

16

Fold the bottom point of the upper layer up and to the right to form the first foot.

17

Your paper should look like this. Repeat step 16 on the other side to form the other foot.

18

Using scissors, make a small cut right through the paper, as shown.

19

Valley fold the upper layer of paper to the left of your cut to make the first arm.

20

Your paper should look like this. Repeat step 19 on the other side.

21

Make a valley fold in the top left-hand point, then fold it the other way so it's also a mountain fold.

TUCK

22

Push the left-hand point down and to the right to form an inside reverse fold. Tuck it inside to form the snout.

23

Draw in your dinosaur's features—be sure to give it a fierce expression! Now your Megalosaurus is ready to go on its first hunt.

FINISHED!

TRICERATOPS

Say "Try-SER-ah-tops"

Triceratops is easy to recognize because of the three sharp horns on its head. You'll need two pieces of paper to make this beast!

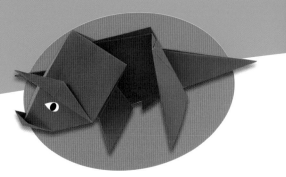

TAIL AND BACK LEGS

1

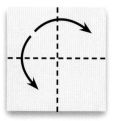

Place your paper like this, white side up with a straight edge facing you. Valley fold in half from top to bottom, and unfold. Then valley fold in half from left to right, and unfold.

2

Fold the bottom edge up to the central crease.

3

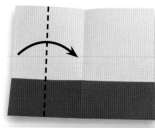

Fold the left edge over to the central crease.

4

Fold the right edge over to the central crease.

5

Fold the top left-hand corner over and down to the central crease.

6

Fold the top right-hand corner over to the central crease.

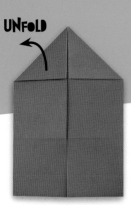

7 Open up the fold you made in step 5.

8 Bring the top central point of the fold down to form a pocket. Then flatten it down to form a triangle shape.

9 Your paper should look like this. Repeat steps 7 and 8 on the right-hand side.

10 Fold the top point down, as shown.

11 Unfold the fold you made in step 10.

12 Fold the top point over to the right so it meets the crease you made in step 10.

13 Unfold the fold you made in step 12.

14 Now fold the top point over to the left. Again, make sure it touches the crease you made in step 10.

15 Fold the left-hand central point up and to the left.

16 Repeat step 15 on the right-hand side.

17 Make a fold on the left-hand side, as shown.

18 Repeat step 17 on the right-hand side.

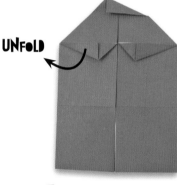

19 Unfold the fold you made in step 17.

20 Bring the left-hand point of the upper layer over to the right.

21 As you bring the point across, push the paper in as shown to make a new fold and then flatten the paper down.

22 Your paper should look like this. Repeat steps 19 to 21 on the right-hand side.

23 Open up the paper on the bottom left-hand side.

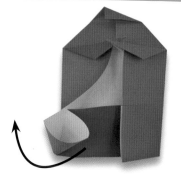

24

Lift the central point up and over to the left, so that the paper forms a triangle shape.

25

Flatten the paper down.

FLATTEN

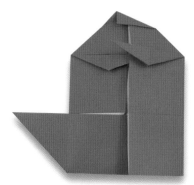

26

Your paper should look like this. Repeat steps 23 to 25 on the right-hand side.

Fold the left hand point down and to the right.

27

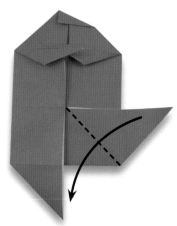

28

Fold the right-hand point down and to the left.

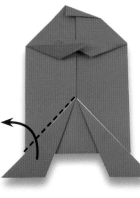

29

Fold the bottom left-hand point up and to the left, as shown.

30

Fold the bottom right-hand point up and to the right.

31

Fold the flap you made in step 29 over along its left edge.

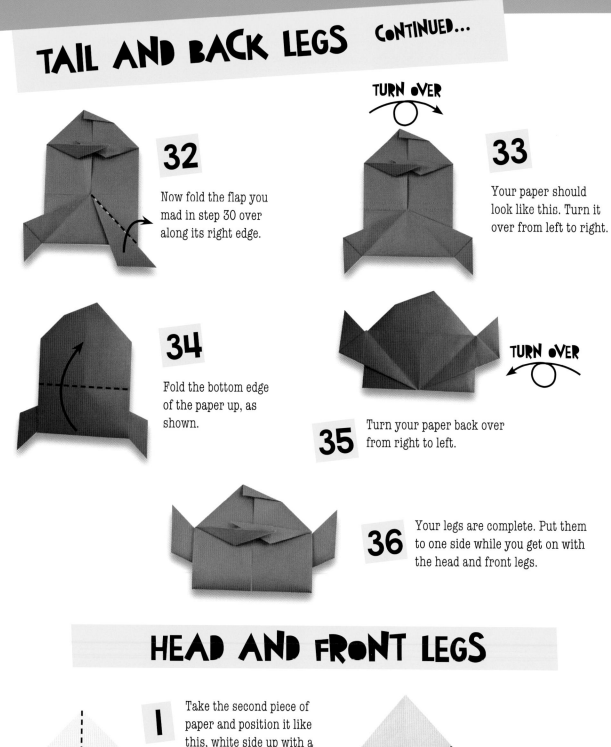

32 Now fold the flap you mad in step 30 over along its right edge.

33 Your paper should look like this. Turn it over from left to right.

TURN OVER

34 Fold the bottom edge of the paper up, as shown.

TURN OVER

35 Turn your paper back over from right to left.

36 Your legs are complete. Put them to one side while you get on with the head and front legs.

HEAD AND FRONT LEGS

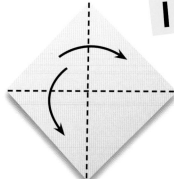

1 Take the second piece of paper and position it like this, white side up with a corner facing you. Fold it in half from top to bottom, and unfold. Then valley fold it in half from left to right, and unfold.

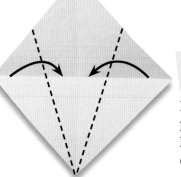

2 Fold the left-hand point and the right-hand point to the central line.

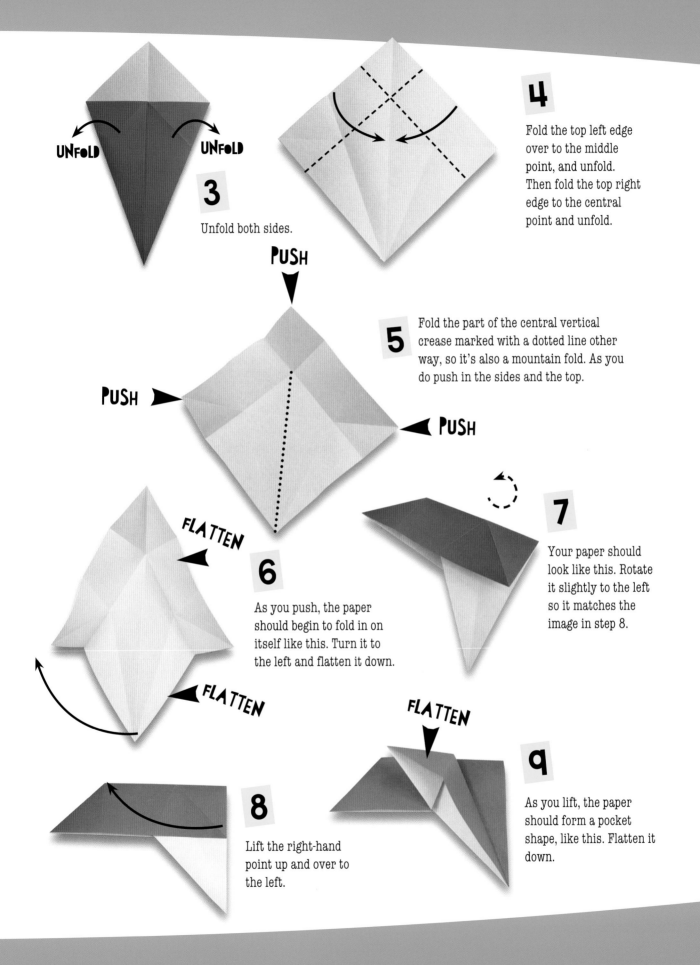

UNFOLD **UNFOLD**

3

Unfold both sides.

4

Fold the top left edge over to the middle point, and unfold. Then fold the top right edge to the central point and unfold.

PUSH

PUSH

PUSH

5

Fold the part of the central vertical crease marked with a dotted line other way, so it's also a mountain fold. As you do push in the sides and the top.

FLATTEN

6

As you push, the paper should begin to fold in on itself like this. Turn it to the left and flatten it down.

FLATTEN

7

Your paper should look like this. Rotate it slightly to the left so it matches the image in step 8.

FLATTEN

q

As you lift, the paper should form a pocket shape, like this. Flatten it down.

8

Lift the right-hand point up and over to the left.

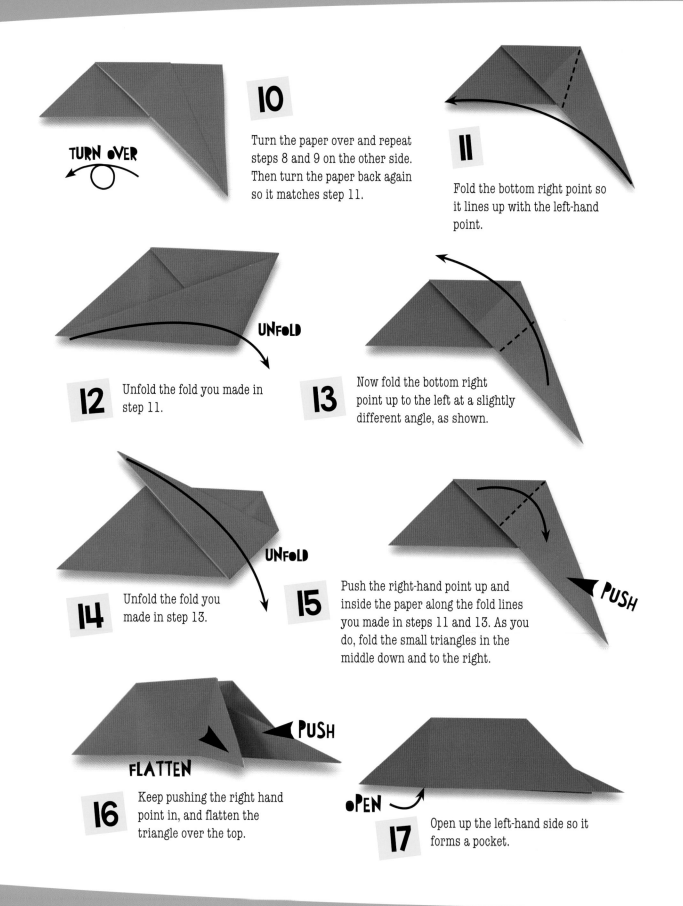

TURN OVER

10 Turn the paper over and repeat steps 8 and 9 on the other side. Then turn the paper back again so it matches step 11.

11 Fold the bottom right point so it lines up with the left-hand point.

UNFOLD

12 Unfold the fold you made in step 11.

13 Now fold the bottom right point up to the left at a slightly different angle, as shown.

UNFOLD

14 Unfold the fold you made in step 13.

15 Push the right-hand point up and inside the paper along the fold lines you made in steps 11 and 13. As you do, fold the small triangles in the middle down and to the right.

PUSH

PUSH

FLATTEN

16 Keep pushing the right hand point in, and flatten the triangle over the top.

OPEN

17 Open up the left-hand side so it forms a pocket.

FLATTEN ▶

18 Lift the middle point of the pocket up and to the right.

19 Flatten the paper down so it forms a square shape.

20 Make a fold on the right-hand side as shown.

21 Turn your paper over and repeat step 20 on the other side. Then turn your paper back again.

TURN OVER

22 Now take the first piece of paper. Fold it in half and then unfold.

23 Dab some glue in the areas shown. Start to fold your paper in half again.

24 Place the first piece of paper over the second piece of paper and hold in place.

25 Once the glue has dried, you've got one terrifying Triceratops. Charge!

FINISHED!

ICHTHYOSAURUS

Say "ICK-thee-oh-SAW-rus"

Ichthyosaurs looked quite a lot like modern dolphins. They swam fast through the oceans looking for fish to eat.

1

Place your paper like this, white side up with a corner facing you. Valley fold in half from top to bottom, and unfold. Then valley fold in half from left to right, and unfold.

2

Fold the top corner down to the central crease.

3

Fold the bottom corner up to the central crease.

4

Your paper should look like this. Turn it over from top to bottom.

TURN OVER

5

Fold the paper in half from left to right.

6

Open up the fold on the top left-hand side, and bring the point of this flap over to the left.

FLATTEN

7

The fold you opened in step 7 should begin to form a triangle shape, like this. Flatten it down.

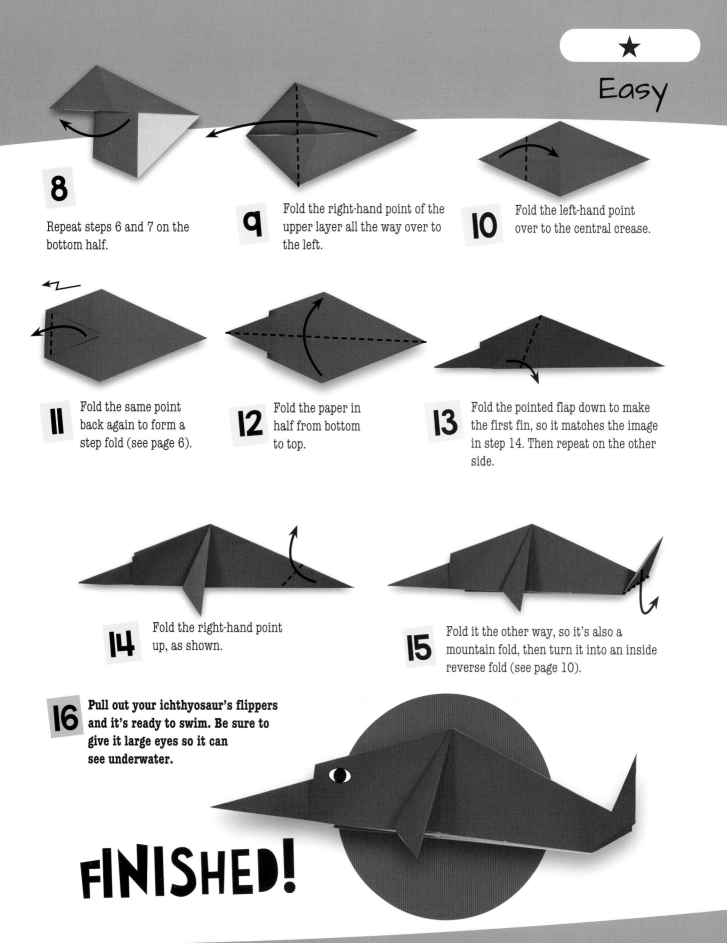

8 Repeat steps 6 and 7 on the bottom half.

9 Fold the right-hand point of the upper layer all the way over to the left.

10 Fold the left-hand point over to the central crease.

11 Fold the same point back again to form a step fold (see page 6).

12 Fold the paper in half from bottom to top.

13 Fold the pointed flap down to make the first fin, so it matches the image in step 14. Then repeat on the other side.

14 Fold the right-hand point up, as shown.

15 Fold it the other way, so it's also a mountain fold, then turn it into an inside reverse fold (see page 10).

16 Pull out your ichthyosaur's flippers and it's ready to swim. Be sure to give it large eyes so it can see underwater.

FINISHED!

UTAHRAPTOR

Say "YOO-tah-RAP-tor"

This dinosaur was a fast, agile predator that roamed the USA around 125 million years ago. It had one enormous claw on each of its hind legs.

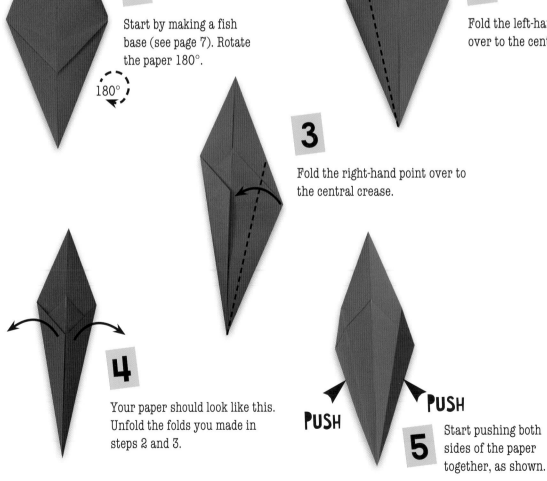

START WITH A FISH BASE

1 Start by making a fish base (see page 7). Rotate the paper 180°.

180°

2 Fold the left-hand point over to the central crease.

3 Fold the right-hand point over to the central crease.

4 Your paper should look like this. Unfold the folds you made in steps 2 and 3.

5 Start pushing both sides of the paper together, as shown.

PUSH PUSH

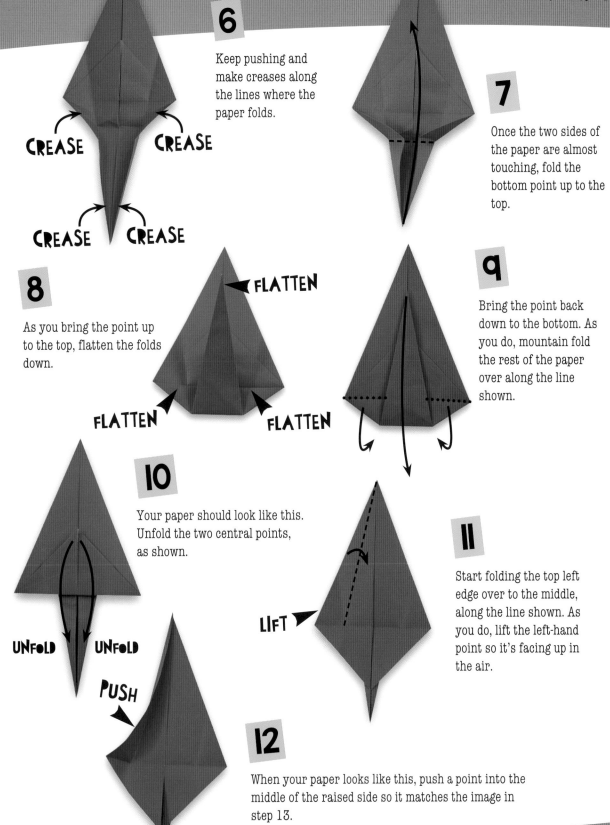

6

Keep pushing and make creases along the lines where the paper folds.

CREASE   CREASE

CREASE   CREASE

7

Once the two sides of the paper are almost touching, fold the bottom point up to the top.

8

As you bring the point up to the top, flatten the folds down.

◄ FLATTEN

FLATTEN   FLATTEN

9

Bring the point back down to the bottom. As you do, mountain fold the rest of the paper over along the line shown.

10

Your paper should look like this. Unfold the two central points, as shown.

UNFOLD   UNFOLD

PUSH

11

Start folding the top left edge over to the middle, along the line shown. As you do, lift the left-hand point so it's facing up in the air.

LIFT ►

12

When your paper looks like this, push a point into the middle of the raised side so it matches the image in step 13.

13

Fold the point you made in step 12 over to the middle. As you do, bring the left-hand point up and over to the middle and the bottom left-hand point over to the right-hand side. Flatten the paper down.

14

Valley fold the right-hand point of the upper layer back over to the left.

15

Repeat step 11 on the other side

16

Repeat steps 12 and 13 on the other side. Remember to bring the right-hand point over to the middle and the bottom right-hand point over to the left so it matches up with the left-hand point.

17

Valley fold the left-hand point of the upper layer back to the right.

18

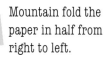

Mountain fold the paper in half from right to left.

19

90°

Your paper should look like this. Rotate it 90° to the left.

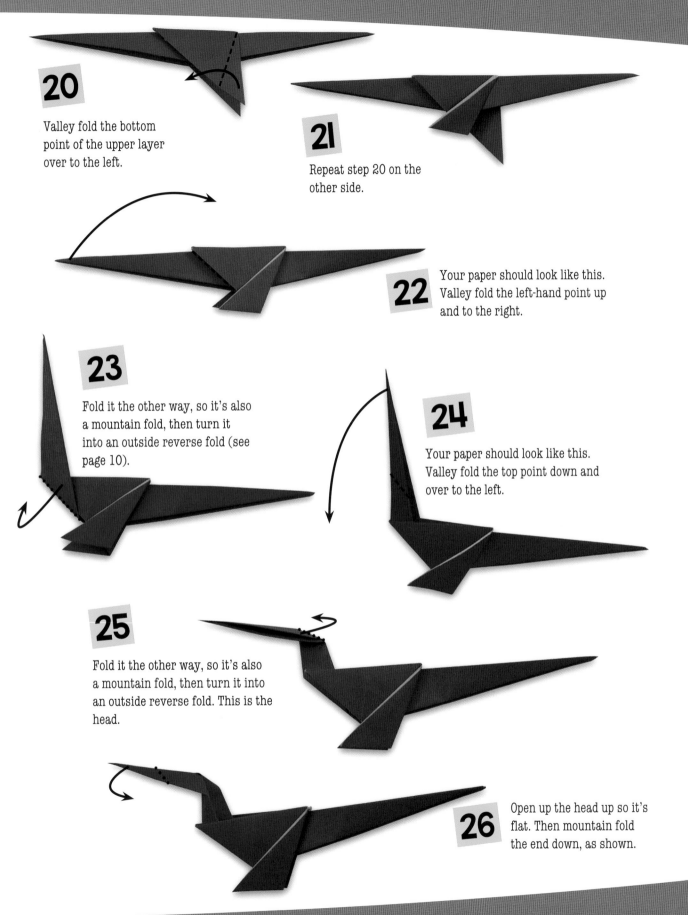

20

Valley fold the bottom point of the upper layer over to the left.

21

Repeat step 20 on the other side.

22

Your paper should look like this. Valley fold the left-hand point up and to the right.

23

Fold it the other way, so it's also a mountain fold, then turn it into an outside reverse fold (see page 10).

24

Your paper should look like this. Valley fold the top point down and over to the left.

25

Fold it the other way, so it's also a mountain fold, then turn it into an outside reverse fold. This is the head.

26

Open up the head up so it's flat. Then mountain fold the end down, as shown.

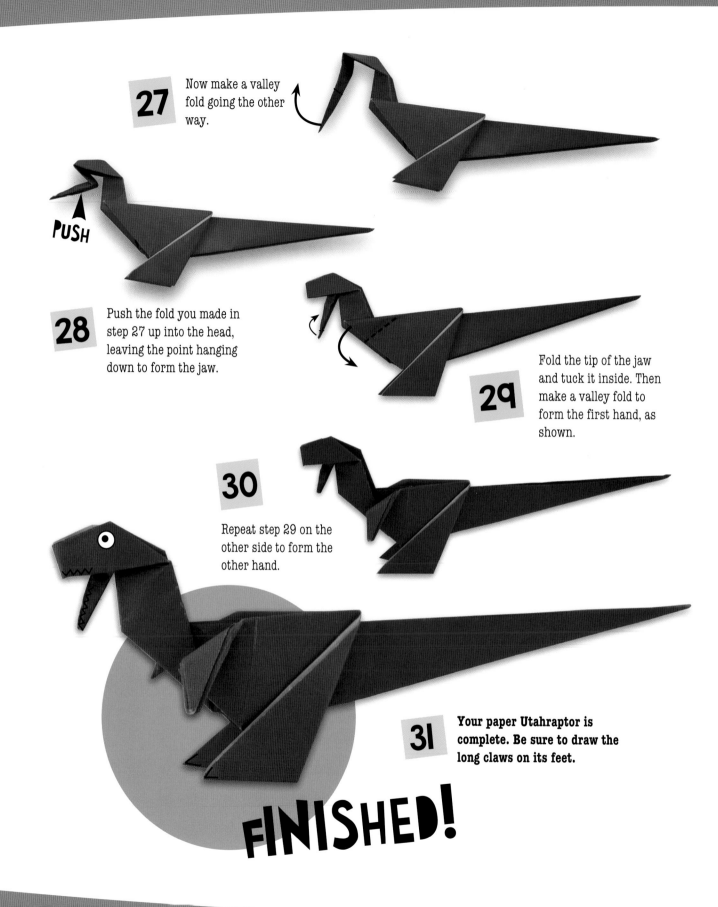

27 Now make a valley fold going the other way.

PUSH

28 Push the fold you made in step 27 up into the head, leaving the point hanging down to form the jaw.

29 Fold the tip of the jaw and tuck it inside. Then make a valley fold to form the first hand, as shown.

30 Repeat step 29 on the other side to form the other hand.

31 Your paper Utahraptor is complete. Be sure to draw the long claws on its feet.

FINISHED!

PTERANODON

Pteranodon had a distinctive crest on its head, and used its large leathery wings to soar through the prehistoric skies.

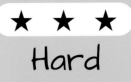

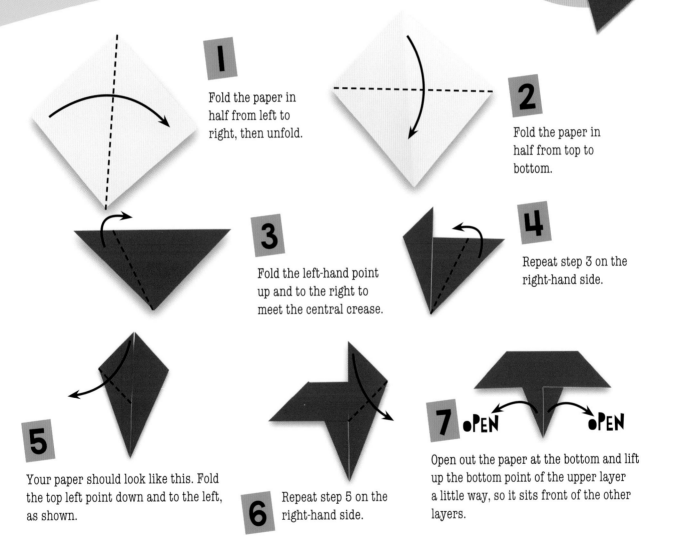

1 Fold the paper in half from left to right, then unfold.

2 Fold the paper in half from top to bottom.

3 Fold the left-hand point up and to the right to meet the central crease.

4 Repeat step 3 on the right-hand side.

5 Your paper should look like this. Fold the top left point down and to the left, as shown.

6 Repeat step 5 on the right-hand side.

7 OPEN   OPEN

Open out the paper at the bottom and lift up the bottom point of the upper layer a little way, so it sits front of the other layers.

TUCK BEHIND   TUCK BEHIND

8 As you lift, the white triangles at the top of the paper should tuck behind the central triangle. Flatten your paper down.

73

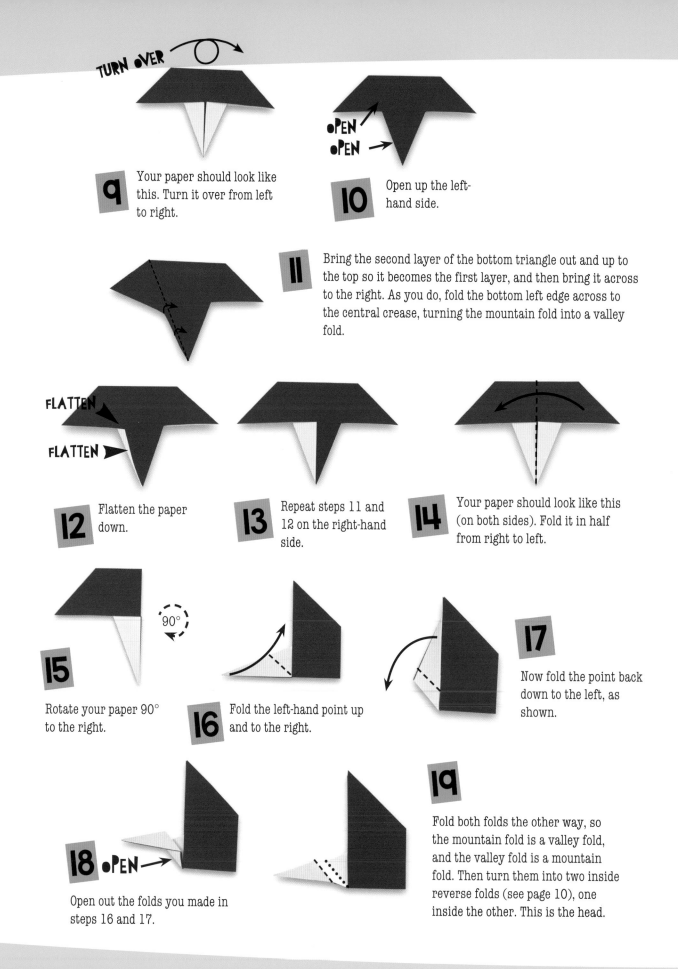

TURN OVER

9 Your paper should look like this. Turn it over from left to right.

OPEN
OPEN

10 Open up the left-hand side.

11 Bring the second layer of the bottom triangle out and up to the top so it becomes the first layer, and then bring it across to the right. As you do, fold the bottom left edge across to the central crease, turning the mountain fold into a valley fold.

FLATTEN

FLATTEN

12 Flatten the paper down.

13 Repeat steps 11 and 12 on the right-hand side.

14 Your paper should look like this (on both sides). Fold it in half from right to left.

15 Rotate your paper 90° to the right.

90°

16 Fold the left-hand point up and to the right.

17 Now fold the point back down to the left, as shown.

18 OPEN Open out the folds you made in steps 16 and 17.

19 Fold both folds the other way, so the mountain fold is a valley fold, and the valley fold is a mountain fold. Then turn them into two inside reverse folds (see page 10), one inside the other. This is the head.

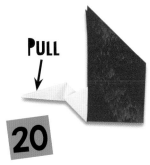

PULL

20

Pull back the top layer of the head.

21

Make a valley fold as shown.

22

Fold it the other way so it's also a mountain fold, then turn it into an outside reverse fold (see page 10). This is the crest.

FLATTEN

23

Flatten the paper down, and tuck the head between the wings.

24

Fold down the top wing, as shown.

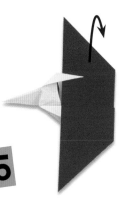

25

Now fold down the other wing, so it matches the first.

26

Your paper should look like this.

27

Spread your Pteranodon's wings out, and it's ready to take to the skies.

FINISHED!

PARASAUROLOPHUS

Say "PAR-uh-SAW-roh-LOW-fuss"

This dino had a crest on top of its head which it may have used to call to other dinosaurs— a bit like a trumpet. You'll need two pieces of paper for this model.

1

Let's start with the legs. Place your paper white side up with a straight edge facing you. Valley fold in half from top to bottom, and unfold. Then valley fold in half from left to right, and unfold.

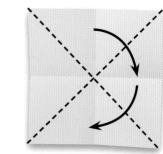

2

Diagonally fold the top-left corner to the bottom right, and unfold. Then diagonally fold the top right corner down to the bottom left, and unfold.

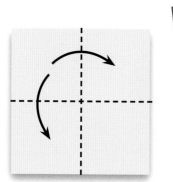

3

Fold the top left corner over to the central point.

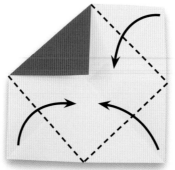

4

Repeat step 3 on the other three corners.

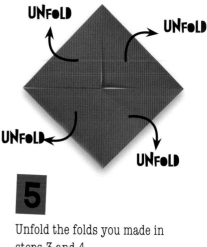

UNFOLD UNFOLD

UNFOLD UNFOLD

5

Unfold the folds you made in steps 3 and 4.

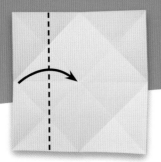

 Fold the left edge over to the middle.

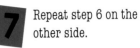 Repeat step 6 on the other side.

UNFOLD

 Fold the top edge down to the middle.

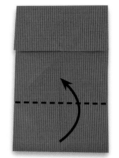

 Fold the bottom edge up to the middle.

 Unfold the fold you made in step 10 about half-way.

FLATTEN

11 Pull the central point of the second layer down and to the left so it forms a triangle shape, as in the image for step 12.

 Repeat step 11 on the right-hand side

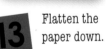 Flatten the paper down.

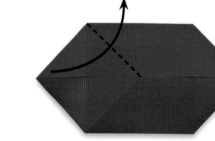

 Your paper should look like this. Repeat steps 10 to 13 on the bottom half.

 Fold the top left-hand point up and to the right, as shown.

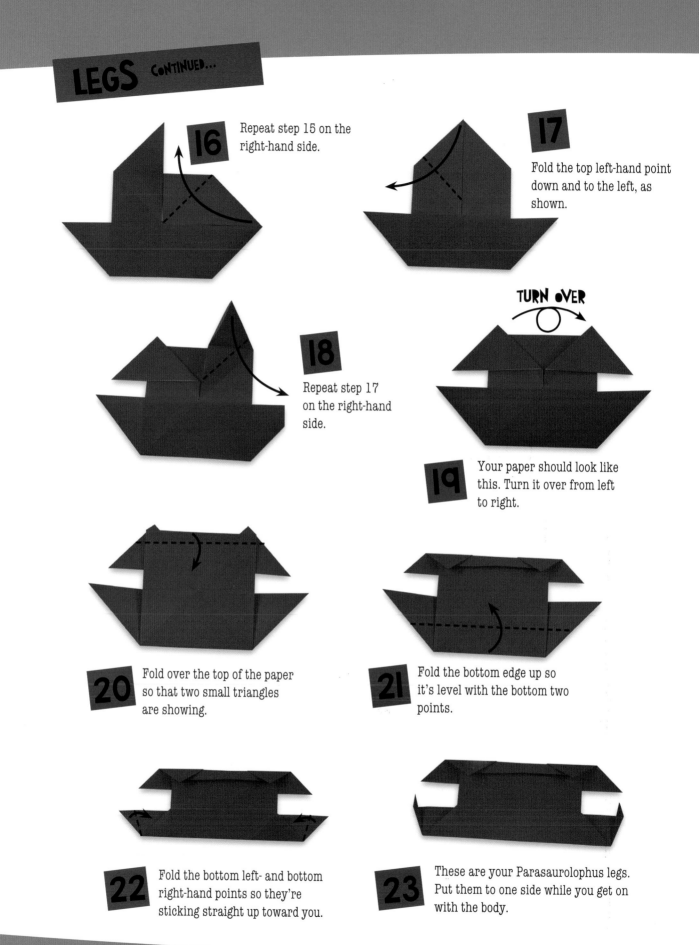

16 Repeat step 15 on the right-hand side.

17 Fold the top left-hand point down and to the left, as shown.

18 Repeat step 17 on the right-hand side.

TURN OVER

19 Your paper should look like this. Turn it over from left to right.

20 Fold over the top of the paper so that two small triangles are showing.

21 Fold the bottom edge up so it's level with the bottom two points.

22 Fold the bottom left- and bottom right-hand points so they're sticking straight up toward you.

23 These are your Parasaurolophus legs. Put them to one side while you get on with the body.

BODY

1 Take your other piece of paper and place it like this, white side up with a corner facing you. Valley fold it in half from right to left and unfold.

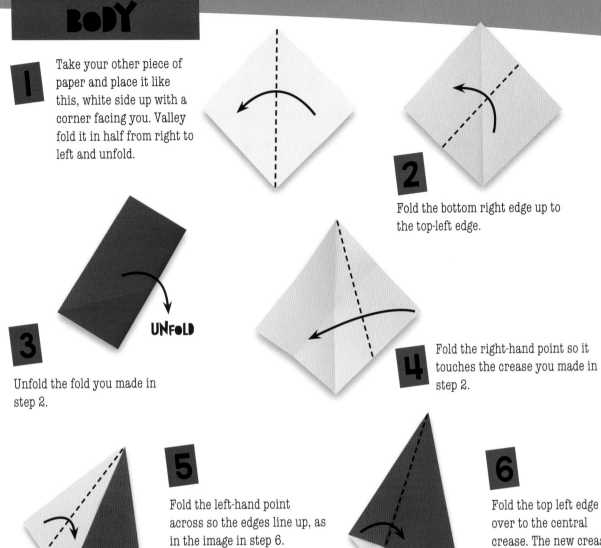

2 Fold the bottom right edge up to the top-left edge.

3 Unfold the fold you made in step 2.

UNFOLD

4 Fold the right-hand point so it touches the crease you made in step 2.

5 Fold the left-hand point across so the edges line up, as in the image in step 6.

6 Fold the top left edge over to the central crease. The new crease should go where the edges line up.

7 Fold the bottom left-hand point over to the central crease.

8 Repeat step 7 on the right-hand side.

q

Your paper should look like this. Fold it in half from left to right.

10

Now take your dinosaur's legs. Place the body over the legs. Make sure it lines up as in the image in step 11.

ll

Fold the top point of the body down and to the right, making sure it lines up with the legs.

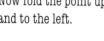

12

Now fold the point up and to the left.

13

Your two pieces of paper should look like this. Put the dinosaur's legs to one side again.

14

Your body should have two clear crease marks from steps 11 and 12: one mountain, one valley. Crease both so they also fold the other way.

PUSH

15

Turn the creases into two inside reverse folds (see page 10). Push the top fold down inside the bottom one.

16

Flatten down the paper, then fold the top point over to the right.

17

Fold it the other way so it's also a mountain fold, then turn it into an inside reverse fold.

18

Fold the top right-hand point back to the left to form the crest.

19

Fold it the other way, so it's also a mountain fold, then turn it into an outside reverse fold (see page 10).

20

Your paper should look like this. Fetch the other piece of paper.

21

Place your pieces of paper one on top of the other like this. Dab a bit of glue in the marked area. Turn the paper over and do the same on the other side.

22

Fold the dinosaur's legs down over the body.

23

Hold the paper in place for a minute. Once you let go, the paper should be stuck, which means your dino is ready to start calling out to its friends.

FINISHED!

QUETZALCOATLUS

Say "KWET-zal-koh-AT-luss"

This giant flying reptile is easier to make than it is to say. You'll need scissors to complete this project—cut carefully when you make its crest.

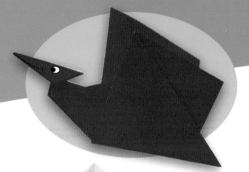

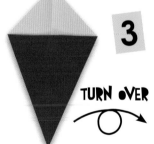

1

Place your paper like this, white side up with a corner facing you. Fold in half from left to right, and unfold. Then fold in half from top to bottom, and unfold.

2

Fold the left and right points to the central crease, as shown.

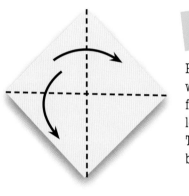

3

Your paper should look like this. Turn it over from left to right.

TURN OVER

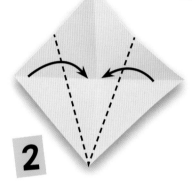

4

Make a large step fold, as shown (see page 6).

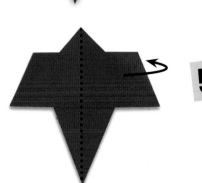

5

Your paper should look like this. Mountain fold it in half from right to left.

6

Now rotate your paper 90° to the right.

90°

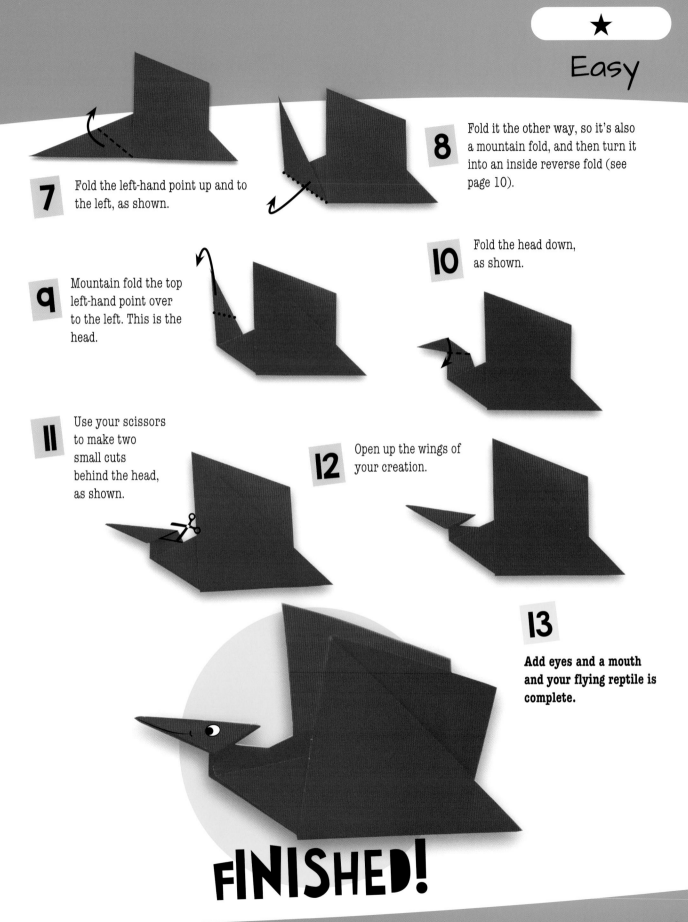

7 Fold the left-hand point up and to the left, as shown.

8 Fold it the other way, so it's also a mountain fold, and then turn it into an inside reverse fold (see page 10).

9 Mountain fold the top left-hand point over to the left. This is the head.

10 Fold the head down, as shown.

11 Use your scissors to make two small cuts behind the head, as shown.

12 Open up the wings of your creation.

13

Add eyes and a mouth and your flying reptile is complete.

FINISHED!

SPINOSAURUS

Say "SPY-noh-SAW-rus"

This fierce predator had a large sail on its back and probably spent most of its time in water, hunting for fish and other marine creatures.

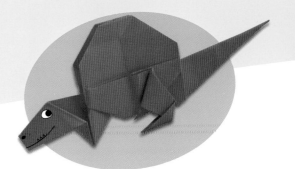

START WITH A BIRD BASE

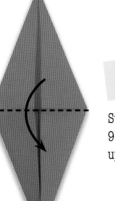

1

Start by making a bird base (see page 9). Then valley fold the top point of the upper layer down to the bottom.

2

Mountain fold the remaining top point down to the bottom.

3

Your paper should look like this. Fold the top point down to the horizontal crease, and then unfold.

4

Fold the top point down to the crease you made in step 3.

5

Your paper should look like this. Unfold the last fold.

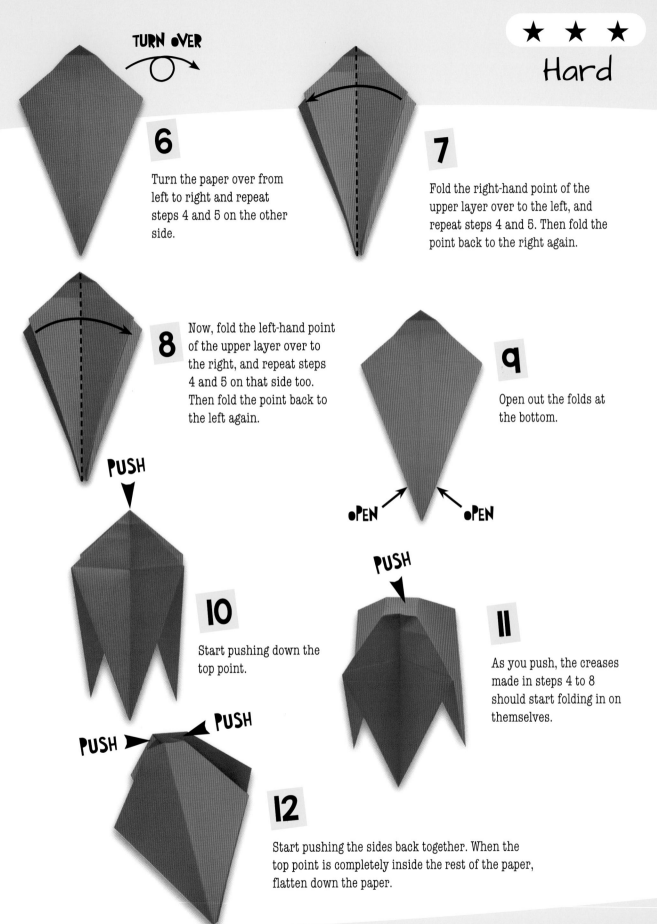

6

Turn the paper over from left to right and repeat steps 4 and 5 on the other side.

7

Fold the right-hand point of the upper layer over to the left, and repeat steps 4 and 5. Then fold the point back to the right again.

8

Now, fold the left-hand point of the upper layer over to the right, and repeat steps 4 and 5 on that side too. Then fold the point back to the left again.

9

Open out the folds at the bottom.

OPEN   OPEN

PUSH

10

Start pushing down the top point.

PUSH

11

As you push, the creases made in steps 4 to 8 should start folding in on themselves.

PUSH   PUSH

12

Start pushing the sides back together. When the top point is completely inside the rest of the paper, flatten down the paper.

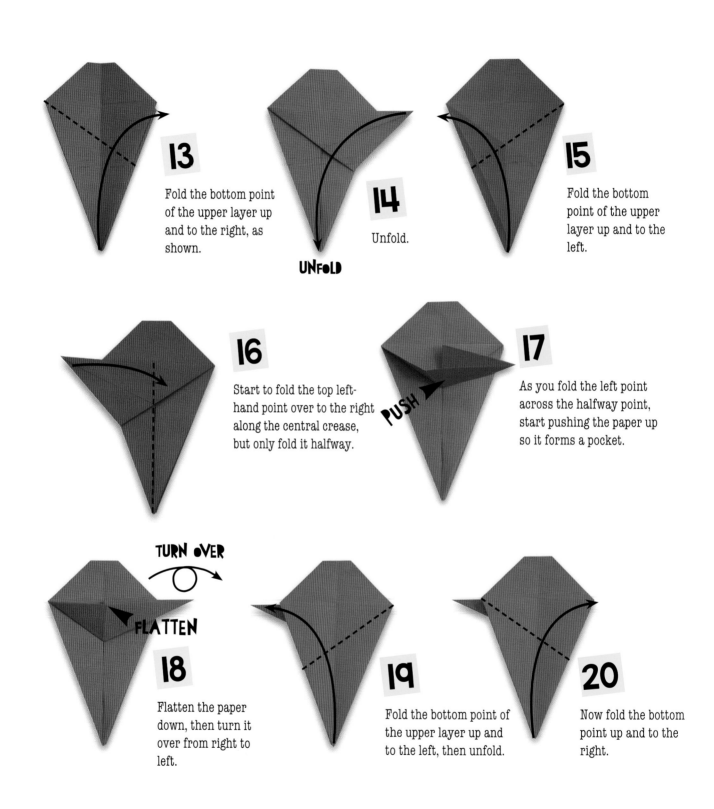

13

Fold the bottom point of the upper layer up and to the right, as shown.

14

UNFOLD

Unfold.

15

Fold the bottom point of the upper layer up and to the left.

16

Start to fold the top left-hand point over to the right along the central crease, but only fold it halfway.

PUSH

17

As you fold the left point across the halfway point, start pushing the paper up so it forms a pocket.

TURN OVER

FLATTEN

18

Flatten the paper down, then turn it over from right to left.

19

Fold the bottom point of the upper layer up and to the left, then unfold.

20

Now fold the bottom point up and to the right.

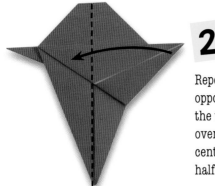

21

Repeat step 16 on the opposite side by folding the top right-hand point over to the left along the central crease. Only fold it halfway.

PUSH

22

As you fold the point across the halfway point, start pushing the paper up so it forms a pocket, then flatten it down.

TURN OVER

PULL

23

Your paper should look like this. Turn it over from left to right.

24

Take the bottom left-hand point and pull it out to the left and up, so it forms an inside reverse fold (see page 10).

PULL

25

Keep pulling the paper up until it's level with the fold you made in step 22, then flatten it down.

26

Your paper should look like this. Repeat steps 24 and 25 on the other side.

27

Make a valley fold, as shown, folding the point second from the right over to the left.

28

Tuck the bottom point behind by making a small mountain fold. Repeat on the other side.

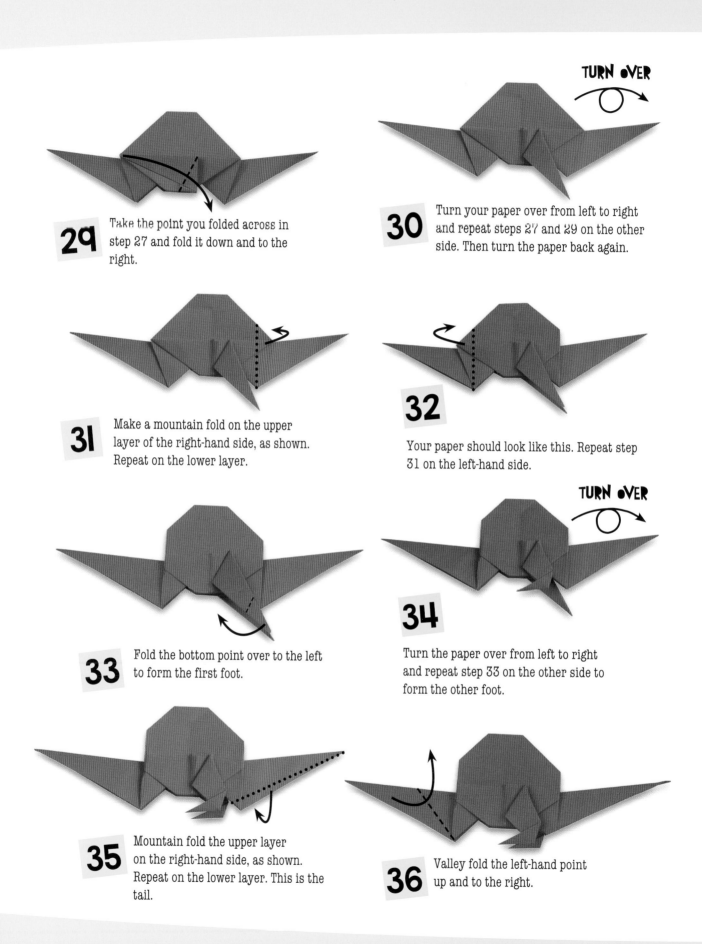

29 Take the point you folded across in step 27 and fold it down and to the right.

30 Turn your paper over from left to right and repeat steps 27 and 29 on the other side. Then turn the paper back again.

TURN OVER

31 Make a mountain fold on the upper layer of the right-hand side, as shown. Repeat on the lower layer.

32 Your paper should look like this. Repeat step 31 on the left-hand side.

33 Fold the bottom point over to the left to form the first foot.

34 Turn the paper over from left to right and repeat step 33 on the other side to form the other foot.

TURN OVER

35 Mountain fold the upper layer on the right-hand side, as shown. Repeat on the lower layer. This is the tail.

36 Valley fold the left-hand point up and to the right.

37

Now fold the point down and to the left.

38

Pull the point to the left, then push it back to the right so that folds go out on either side of the paper, forming a step fold. This is the head.

PUSH ▶

FOLDS GO EITHER SIDE OF PAPER

39

Push the tip of the left-hand point down and to the right.

PUSH ◀

40

Tuck the point inside the head to form the snout.

PUSH ◀

41

Your paper should look like this. All that's left now is to stand your Spinosaurus on its feet.

42

Give your dino big eyes to help it track down its prey.

FINISHED!

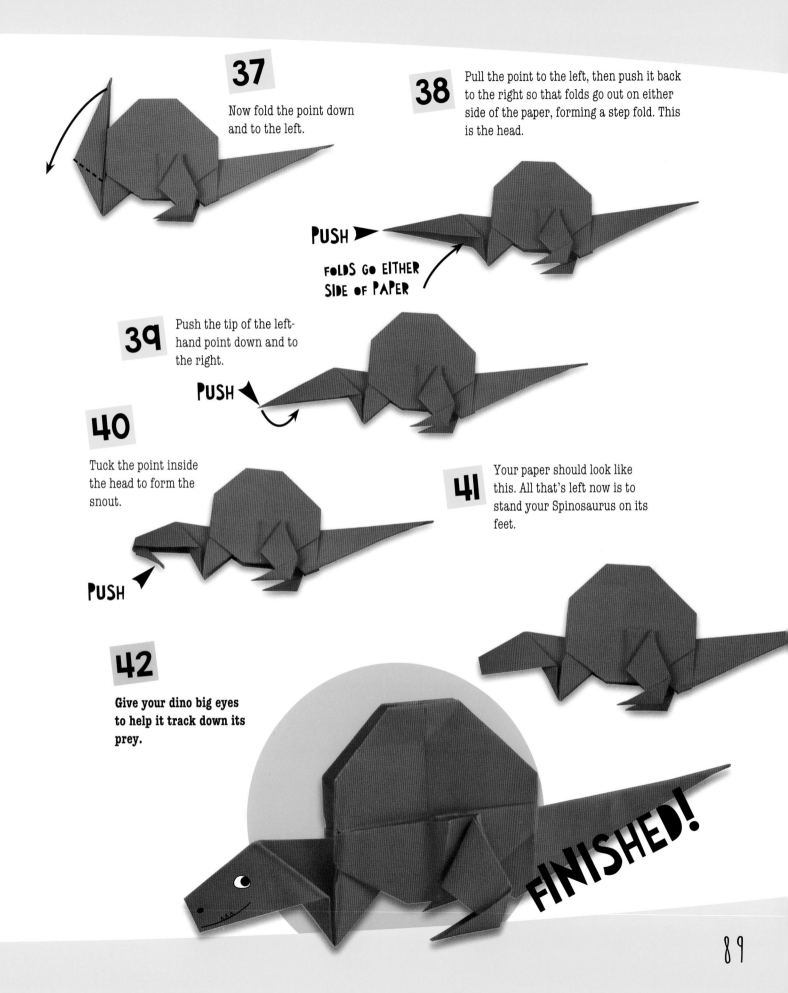

DINOSAUR EGG

All dinosaurs started life as an egg. Why not make several eggs so you can have your very own dinosaur nest?

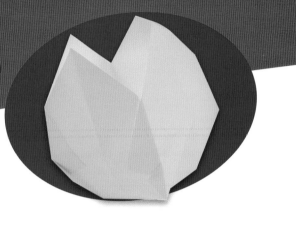

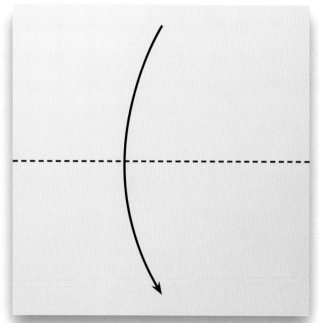

Place your paper like this, white side up, with a straight edge facing you. Fold in half from top to bottom.

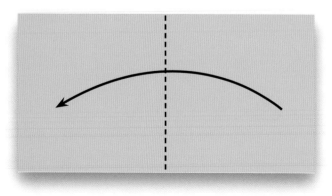

Fold the paper in half from right to left.

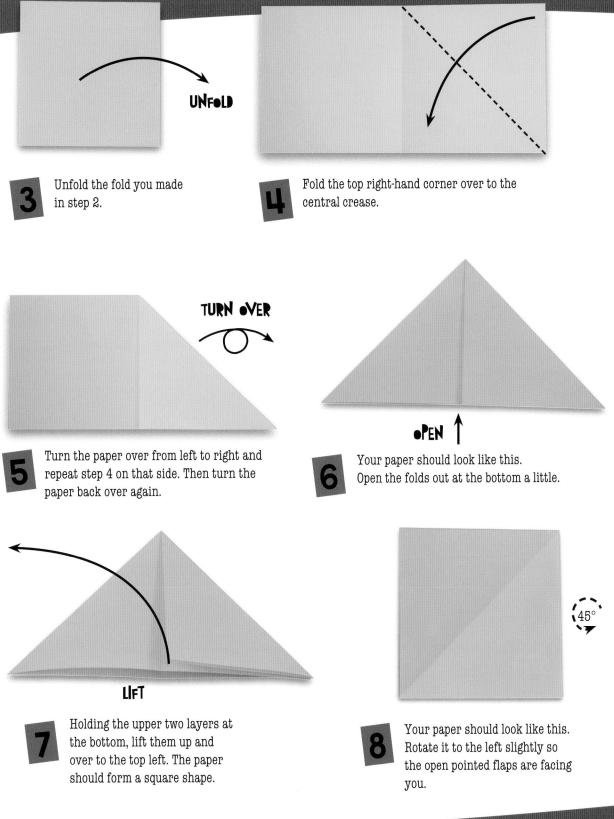

3 Unfold the fold you made in step 2.

UNFOLD

4 Fold the top right-hand corner over to the central crease.

TURN OVER

5 Turn the paper over from left to right and repeat step 4 on that side. Then turn the paper back over again.

OPEN ↑

6 Your paper should look like this. Open the folds out at the bottom a little.

LIFT

7 Holding the upper two layers at the bottom, lift them up and over to the top left. The paper should form a square shape.

45°

8 Your paper should look like this. Rotate it to the left slightly so the open pointed flaps are facing you.

91

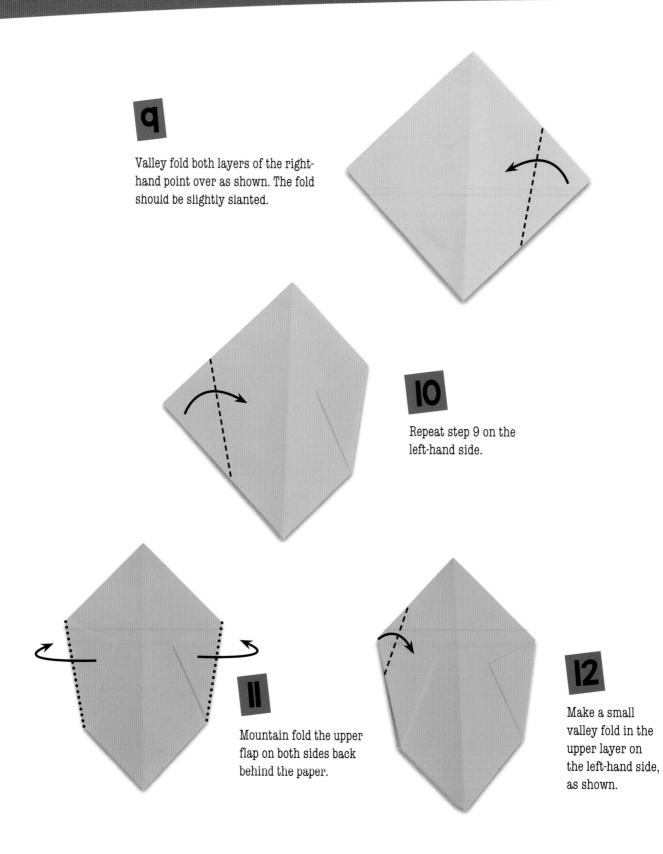

q

Valley fold both layers of the right-hand point over as shown. The fold should be slightly slanted.

10

Repeat step 9 on the left-hand side.

11

Mountain fold the upper flap on both sides back behind the paper.

12

Make a small valley fold in the upper layer on the left-hand side, as shown.

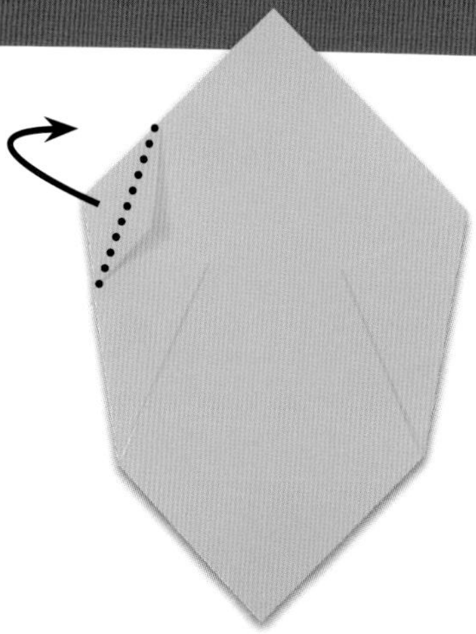

13

Mountain fold the lower layer behind so it matches the fold from step 12.

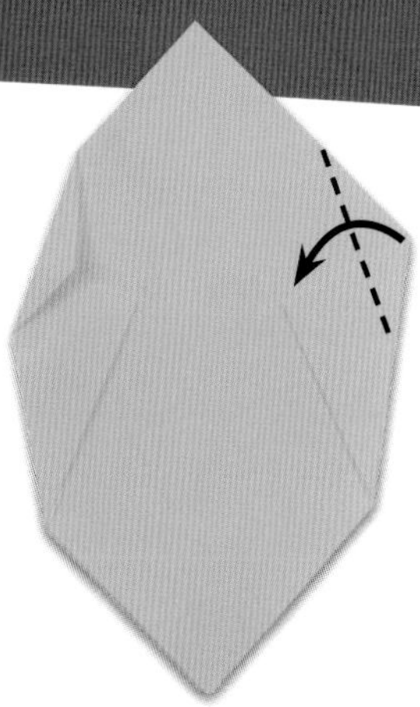

14

Repeat steps 12 and 13 on the right-hand side.

15

Your paper should look like this. Rotate it 180°.

180°

16

OPEN

Open out the paper at the top, and carefully push out all four sides.

17

And there's your egg, but where's the baby dino? It looks like it's already hatched and has scuttled away.

FINISHED!

ARGENTINOSAURUS

Say "ar-jen-TEE-noh-SAW-rus"

This enormous, long-necked dino was named after the country in which it was found—Argentina. You'll make the tail and back legs first.

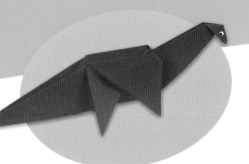

TAIL AND BACK LEGS

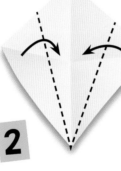

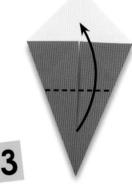

1 Start with your paper like this, white side up with a corner facing you. Valley fold it in half from top to bottom, and unfold. Then valley fold it in half from left to right, and unfold.

2 Fold the left- and right-hand points over to the central crease.

3 Fold the bottom point up to the top.

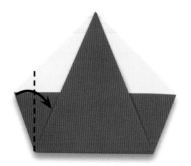

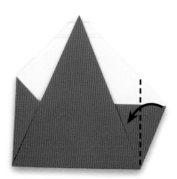

4 Fold the lower left edge across so it sits flush against the central triangle.

5 Repeat step 2 on the right-hand side.

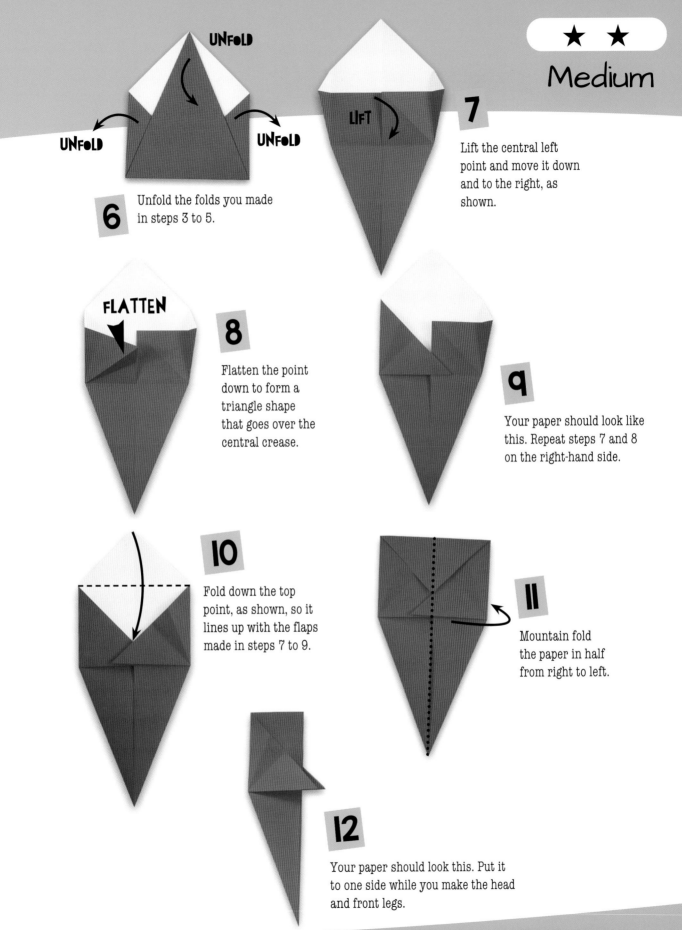

UNFOLD

UNFOLD

UNFOLD

6 Unfold the folds you made in steps 3 to 5.

LIFT

7 Lift the central left point and move it down and to the right, as shown.

FLATTEN

8 Flatten the point down to form a triangle shape that goes over the central crease.

9 Your paper should look like this. Repeat steps 7 and 8 on the right-hand side.

10 Fold down the top point, as shown, so it lines up with the flaps made in steps 7 to 9.

11 Mountain fold the paper in half from right to left.

12 Your paper should look this. Put it to one side while you make the head and front legs.

HEAD AND FRONT LEGS

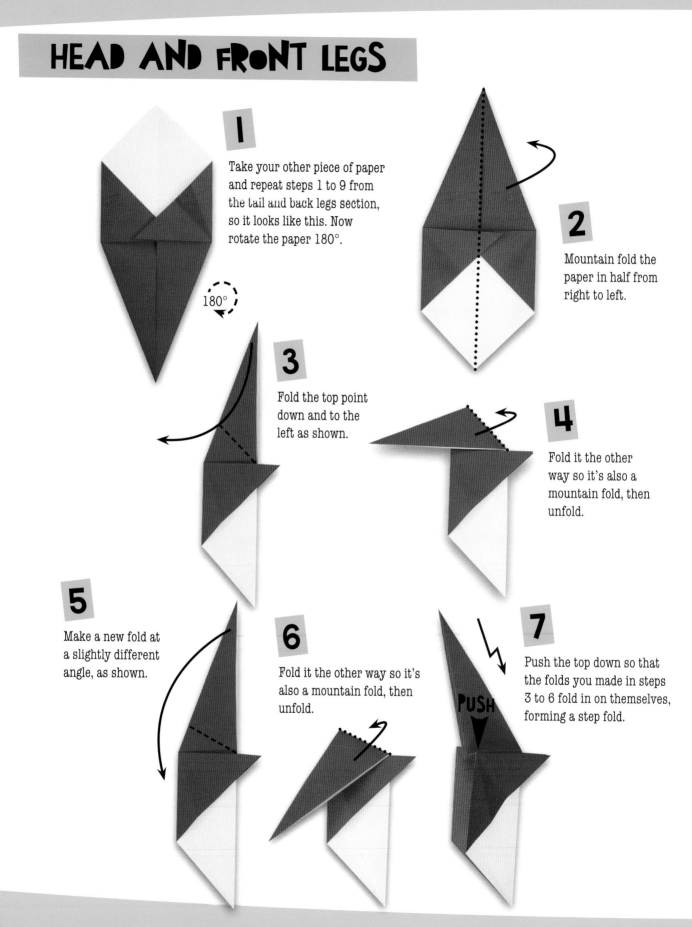

1

Take your other piece of paper and repeat steps 1 to 9 from the tail and back legs section, so it looks like this. Now rotate the paper 180°.

180°

2

Mountain fold the paper in half from right to left.

3

Fold the top point down and to the left as shown.

4

Fold it the other way so it's also a mountain fold, then unfold.

5

Make a new fold at a slightly different angle, as shown.

6

Fold it the other way so it's also a mountain fold, then unfold.

7

Push the top down so that the folds you made in steps 3 to 6 fold in on themselves, forming a step fold.

PUSH

8

Flatten the paper down.

FLATTEN

q

Fold the top point over to the right, as shown.

10

Fold it the other way so it's also a mountain fold, then turn it into an outside reverse fold (see page 10). This is the head.

11

Your paper should look like this. Rotate it 90° to the right.

90°

12

Now bring back the first piece of paper and place it below the second one, like this.

13

Carefully push the second piece of paper so that the white triangle goes inside the first piece of paper while the legs go on the outside.

PUSH

14

Keep pushing until the two pieces of paper fit neatly together.

15

Lift it up carefully and your giant dino should be able to stand upright.

FINISHED!

APATOSAURUS

Say "a-PAT-oh-SAW-rus"

From nose to tail, Apatosaurus was as long as a tennis court, making it one of the largest animals ever to walk the Earth. Your origami version will be a little smaller.

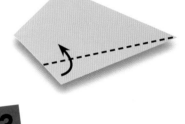

START WITH A KITE BASE

1 Make a kite base (see page 6), but start with the white side facing down, so your paper looks like this. Rotate it 90° to the left.

TURN OVER

2 Turn the paper over from top to bottom.

3 Fold the bottom point up to the central crease.

4 Fold the top point down to the central crease.

5 Unfold the lowest layer on both sides so that your paper matches the image in step 6.

6 Fold the bottom point up to the middle along the crease line, turning it from a mountain fold to a valley fold.

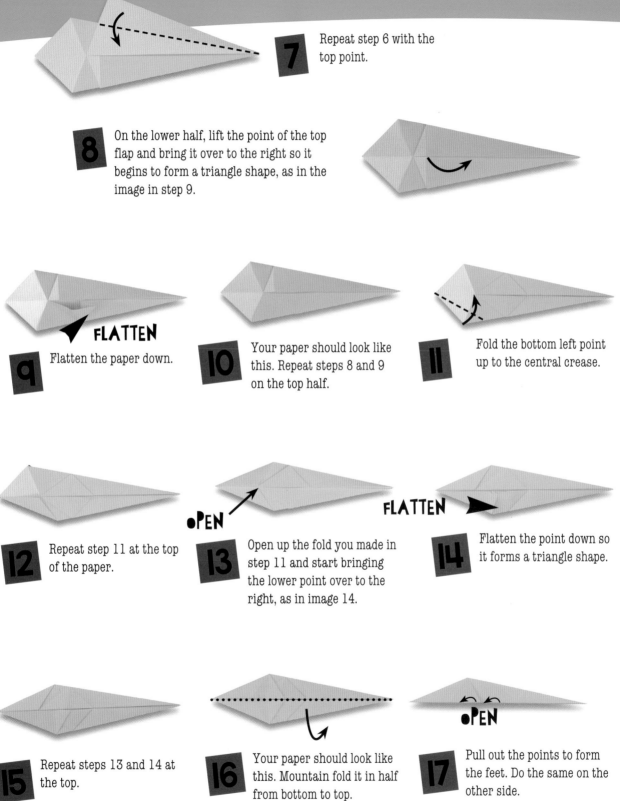

7 Repeat step 6 with the top point.

8 On the lower half, lift the point of the top flap and bring it over to the right so it begins to form a triangle shape, as in the image in step 9.

FLATTEN

9 Flatten the paper down.

10 Your paper should look like this. Repeat steps 8 and 9 on the top half.

11 Fold the bottom left point up to the central crease.

12 Repeat step 11 at the top of the paper.

OPEN

13 Open up the fold you made in step 11 and start bringing the lower point over to the right, as in image 14.

FLATTEN

14 Flatten the point down so it forms a triangle shape.

15 Repeat steps 13 and 14 at the top.

16 Your paper should look like this. Mountain fold it in half from bottom to top.

OPEN

17 Pull out the points to form the feet. Do the same on the other side.

18 Fold the right-hand point up, as shown.

19 Fold it the other way so it's also a mountain fold, then turn it into an inside reverse fold (see page 10).

20 Your paper should look like this. Fold the top right-hand point back to the left to start forming the head.

21 Fold it the other way so it's also a mountain fold. Then turn it into an inside reverse fold. This is the head.

22 Fold the upper layer of the head down, as shown to create a flat shape.

23 Mountain fold the right-hand point over, as shown, to form the snout.

24

Make sure the legs are standing straight out from the body and your Apatosaurus should be able to stand up. Doesn't it look fierce!

FINISHED!

CHAPTER 3

ACTION MODELS

These models are not only fun to make, you can play with them, too! From a jumping horse to a bird that can flap its wings, the models turn a simple piece of paper into a toy.

DICE

Dice are used in lots of different games. Follow these instructions to make some dice of your own, draw on the dots with a felt-tip pen, and get rolling!

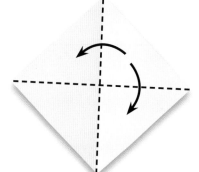

1 You'll need two pieces of paper for this project, which you'll need to fold in exactly the same way.

2 Place the first piece of paper like this. Valley fold in half from left to right, and unfold. Then valley fold in half from top to bottom, and unfold.

3 Take the left point and fold it over to meet the central line.

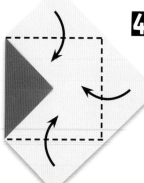

4 Repeat step 3 with the other three points.

5 Make a vertical valley fold a third of the way from the right side.

6 Fold the left edge all the way over to the right edge to form a tube shape.

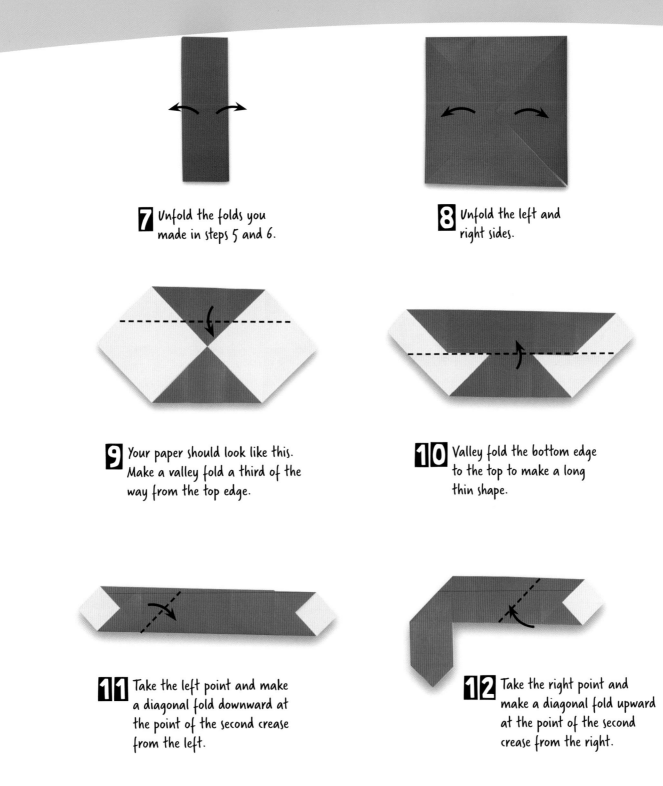

7 Unfold the folds you made in steps 5 and 6.

8 Unfold the left and right sides.

9 Your paper should look like this. Make a valley fold a third of the way from the top edge.

10 Valley fold the bottom edge to the top to make a long thin shape.

11 Take the left point and make a diagonal fold downward at the point of the second crease from the left.

12 Take the right point and make a diagonal fold upward at the point of the second crease from the right.

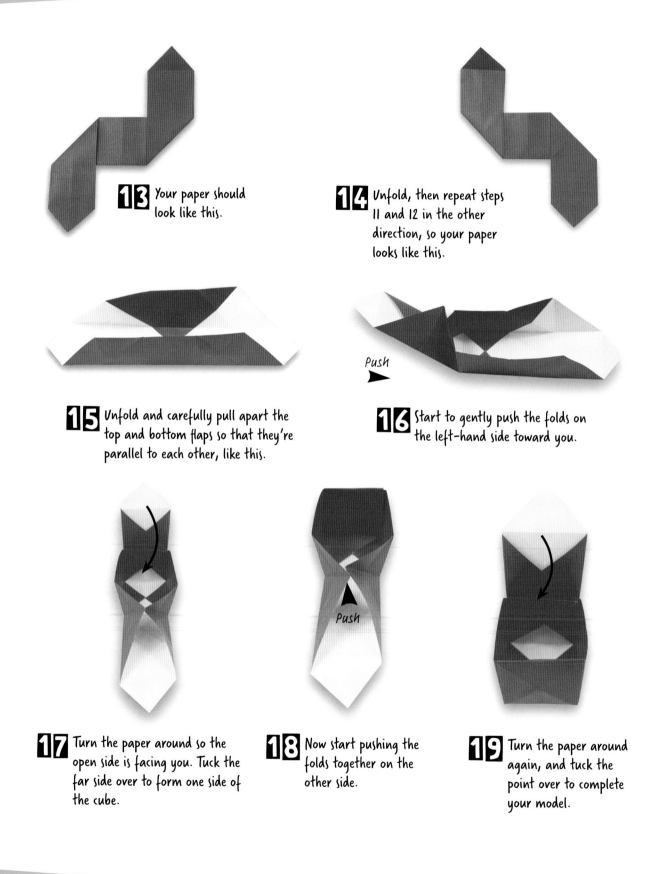

13 Your paper should look like this.

14 Unfold, then repeat steps 11 and 12 in the other direction, so your paper looks like this.

15 Unfold and carefully pull apart the top and bottom flaps so that they're parallel to each other, like this.

Push

16 Start to gently push the folds on the left-hand side toward you.

17 Turn the paper around so the open side is facing you. Tuck the far side over to form one side of the cube.

Push

18 Now start pushing the folds together on the other side.

19 Turn the paper around again, and tuck the point over to complete your model.

20 The first half of your dice is now complete.

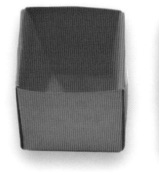

21 Use the other sheet of paper and repeat steps 1 to 19 to make the other half of the dice.

Push

22 Slightly squeeze the edges of one of the boxes, fit it carefully inside the other box, and push down.

23 Once the two boxes have slotted together, use a felt-tip pen to draw on some dots. Your dice is ready to roll!

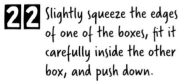

Magician's Rabbit

Making a rabbit disappear is one of the great magic tricks. But first you need to make your rabbit. Here's how!

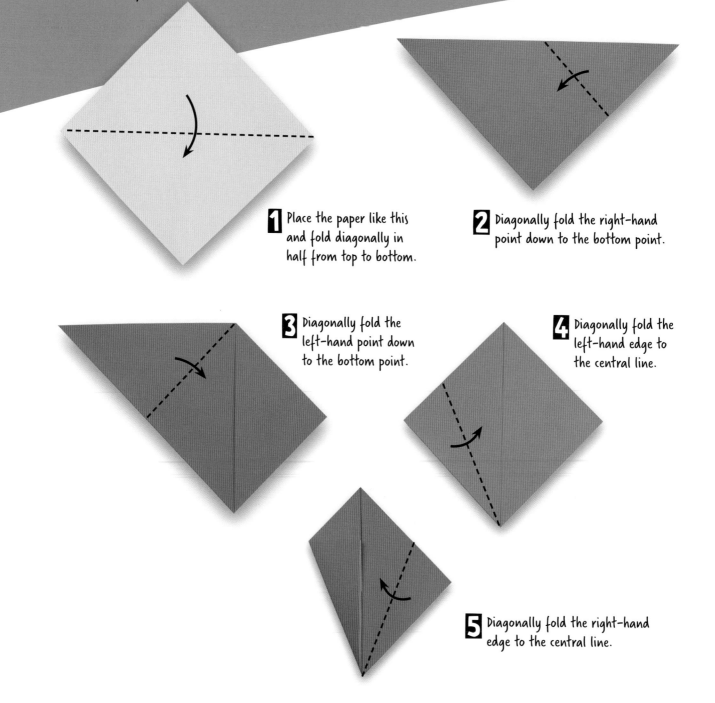

1 Place the paper like this and fold diagonally in half from top to bottom.

2 Diagonally fold the right-hand point down to the bottom point.

3 Diagonally fold the left-hand point down to the bottom point.

4 Diagonally fold the left-hand edge to the central line.

5 Diagonally fold the right-hand edge to the central line.

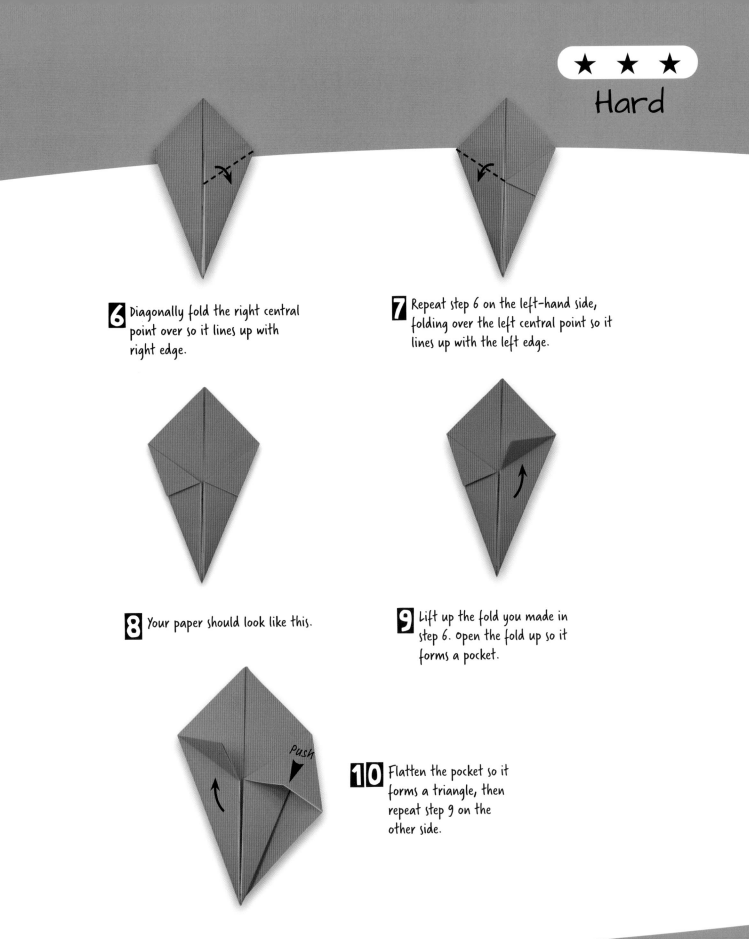

6 Diagonally fold the right central point over so it lines up with right edge.

7 Repeat step 6 on the left-hand side, folding over the left central point so it lines up with the left edge.

8 Your paper should look like this.

9 Lift up the fold you made in step 6. Open the fold up so it forms a pocket.

Push

10 Flatten the pocket so it forms a triangle, then repeat step 9 on the other side.

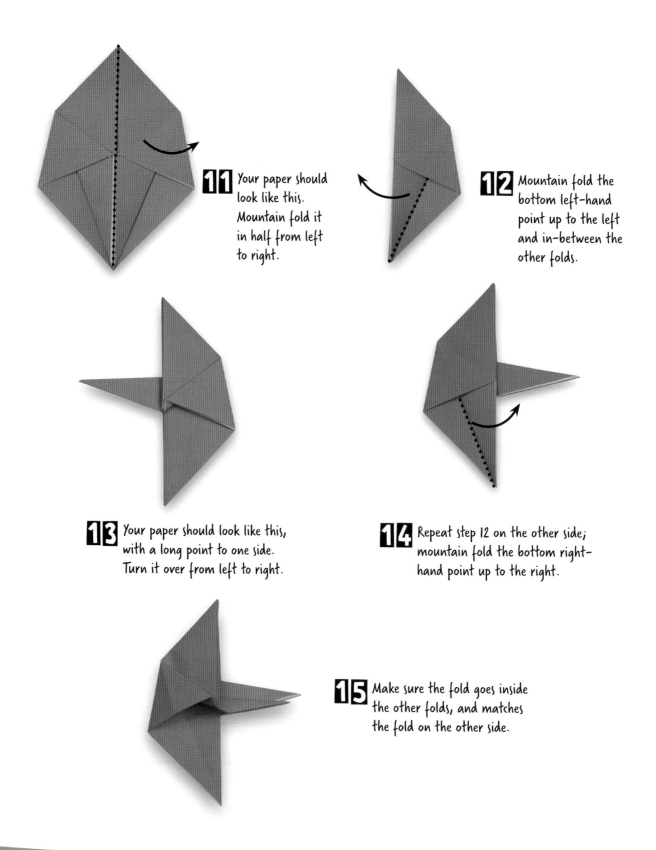

11 Your paper should look like this. Mountain fold it in half from left to right.

12 Mountain fold the bottom left-hand point up to the left and in-between the other folds.

13 Your paper should look like this, with a long point to one side. Turn it over from left to right.

14 Repeat step 12 on the other side; mountain fold the bottom right-hand point up to the right.

15 Make sure the fold goes inside the other folds, and matches the fold on the other side.

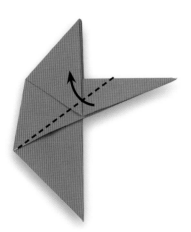

16 To make the first ear, valley fold the long point you made in step 14.

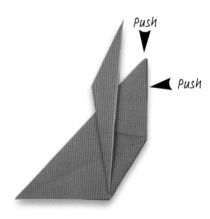

17 Your paper should look like this. Turn it over from left to right.

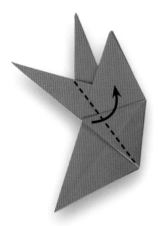

18 To make the second ear, valley fold the long point you made in step 12 to match the other one.

Push

Push

19 Holding the ears at the base, start to make the face by pushing open the top right point and folding it around the ears.

Push

Push

20 Your paper should look like this. Push down the folds to make the face.

21 Make a small inside reverse fold for the nose (see page 10). Open out the ears so that the white is showing on the inside.

22 To make the tail, make a vertical valley fold like this. Then fold it the other way, so it's also a mountain fold.

23 Make another smaller valley fold near the first fold. Again, fold it the other way, so it's also a mountain fold.

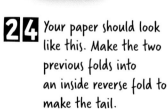

24 Your paper should look like this. Make the two previous folds into an inside reverse fold to make the tail.

25 Draw on eyes and whiskers. Your magic rabbit is ready to perform his first trick!

KISSING FROG

In most fairy tales, the combination of a frog and a kiss usually results in a handsome prince appearing. Here, it'll just provide plenty of origami fun.

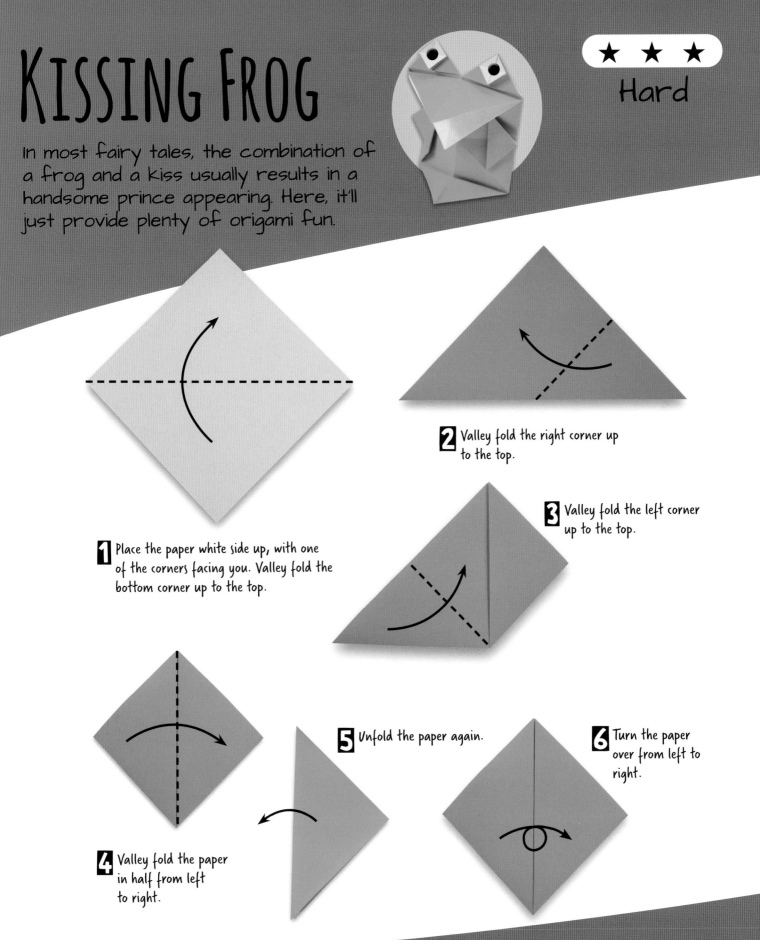

1 Place the paper white side up, with one of the corners facing you. Valley fold the bottom corner up to the top.

2 Valley fold the right corner up to the top.

3 Valley fold the left corner up to the top.

4 Valley fold the paper in half from left to right.

5 Unfold the paper again.

6 Turn the paper over from left to right.

111

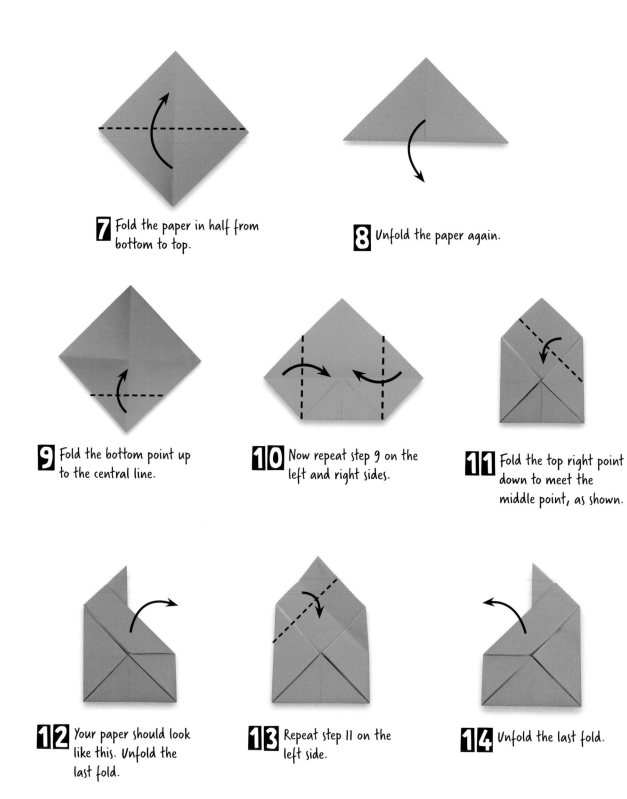

7 Fold the paper in half from bottom to top.

8 Unfold the paper again.

9 Fold the bottom point up to the central line.

10 Now repeat step 9 on the left and right sides.

11 Fold the top right point down to meet the middle point, as shown.

12 Your paper should look like this. Unfold the last fold.

13 Repeat step 11 on the left side.

14 Unfold the last fold.

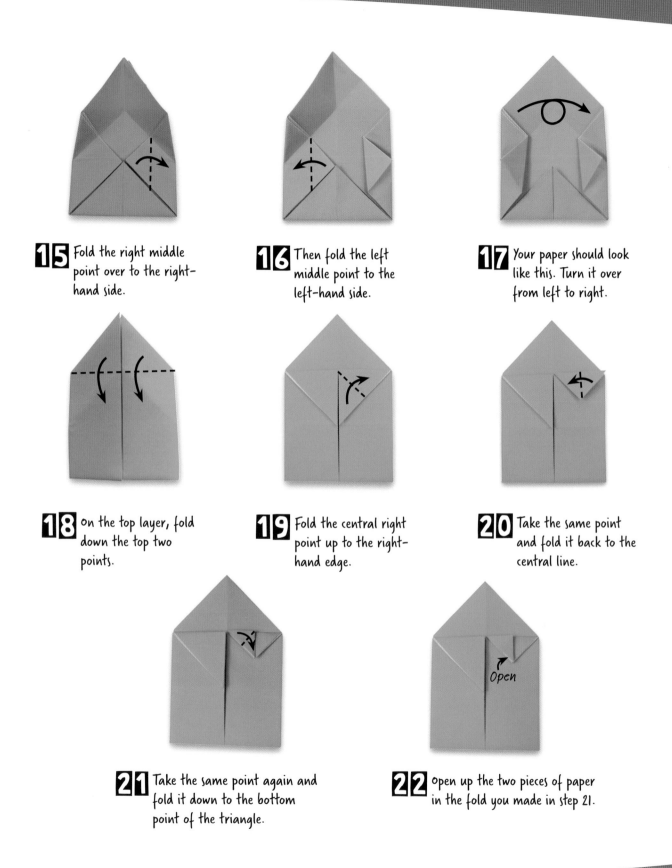

15 Fold the right middle point over to the right-hand side.

16 Then fold the left middle point to the left-hand side.

17 Your paper should look like this. Turn it over from left to right.

18 On the top layer, fold down the top two points.

19 Fold the central right point up to the right-hand edge.

20 Take the same point and fold it back to the central line.

21 Take the same point again and fold it down to the bottom point of the triangle.

22 Open up the two pieces of paper in the fold you made in step 21.

Open

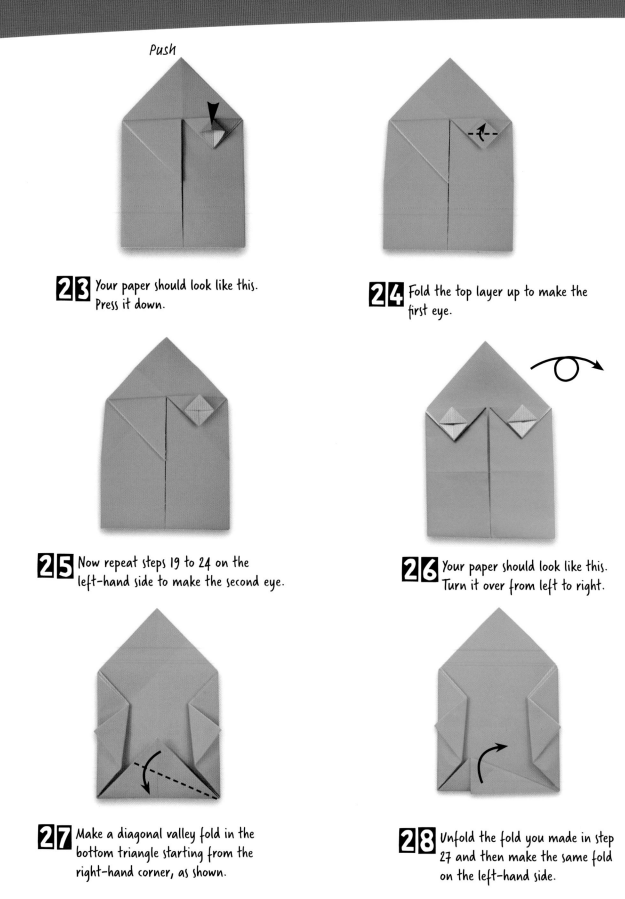

Push

23 Your paper should look like this. Press it down.

24 Fold the top layer up to make the first eye.

25 Now repeat steps 19 to 24 on the left-hand side to make the second eye.

26 Your paper should look like this. Turn it over from left to right.

27 Make a diagonal valley fold in the bottom triangle starting from the right-hand corner, as shown.

28 Unfold the fold you made in step 27 and then make the same fold on the left-hand side.

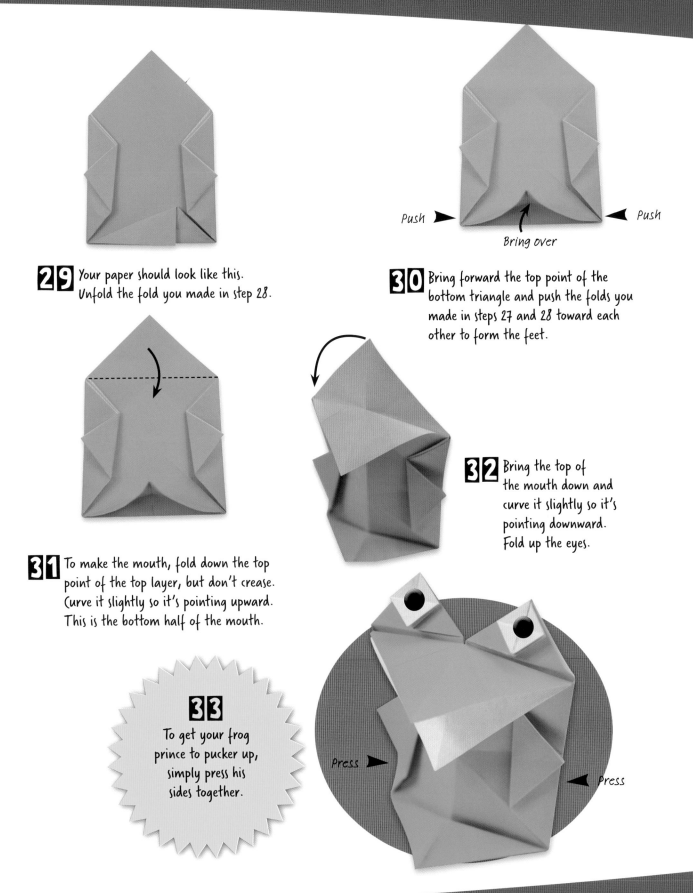

29 Your paper should look like this. Unfold the fold you made in step 28.

Push ► ◄ Push

Bring over

30 Bring forward the top point of the bottom triangle and push the folds you made in steps 27 and 28 toward each other to form the feet.

31 To make the mouth, fold down the top point of the top layer, but don't crease. Curve it slightly so it's pointing upward. This is the bottom half of the mouth.

32 Bring the top of the mouth down and curve it slightly so it's pointing downward. Fold up the eyes.

33 To get your frog prince to pucker up, simply press his sides together.

Press ► ◄ Press

MAGIC CUP

You can use this simple origami cup to perform lots of tricks. Held one way, it's just a normal cup, but turn it around and you've got a special magic cup without a base.

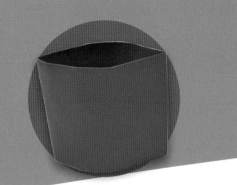

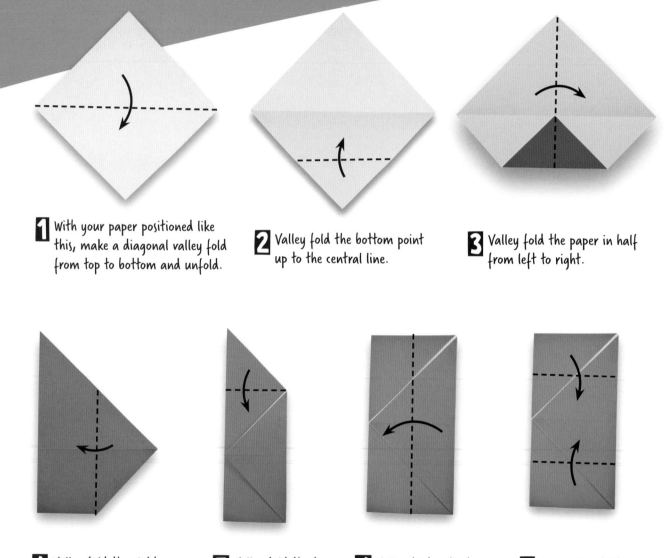

1 With your paper positioned like this, make a diagonal valley fold from top to bottom and unfold.

2 Valley fold the bottom point up to the central line.

3 Valley fold the paper in half from left to right.

4 Valley fold the right point to the left edge.

5 Valley fold the top point down to the central line.

6 Valley fold in half from right to left, then unfold.

7 Now valley fold the top edge and the bottom edge to the central line, then unfold.

8 Unfold the top left layer.

9 Valley fold the bottom edge up to the top triangle, as shown.

10 Valley fold the top point of the triangle forward and tuck it into the front pocket.

Push

11 Keep tucking until all of the triangle is inside the pocket.

Push   Push

12 Squeeze the sides and it will turn into a cup shape.

13 Your paper should look like this.

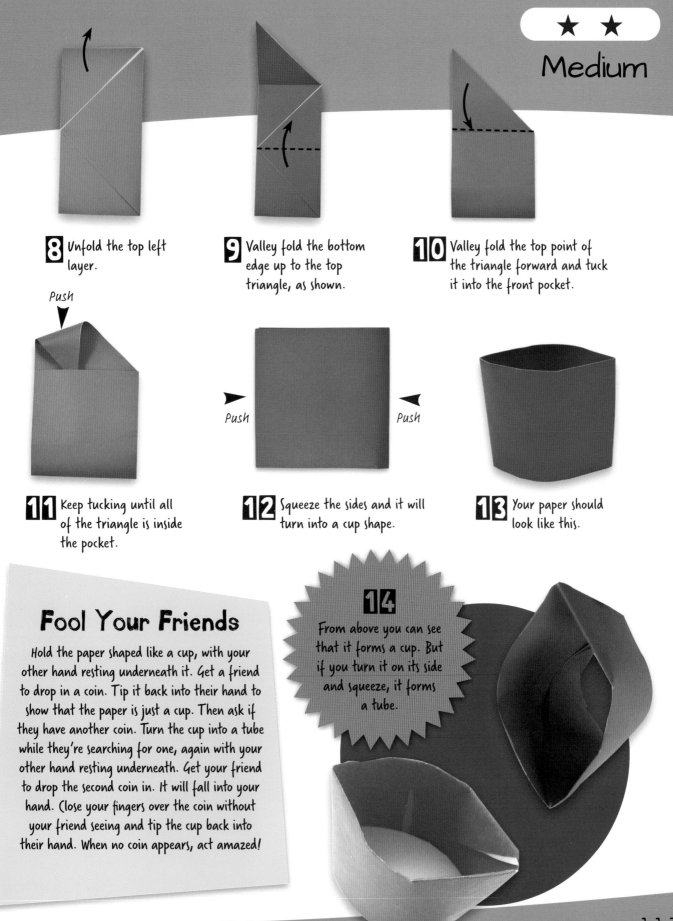

Fool Your Friends

Hold the paper shaped like a cup, with your other hand resting underneath it. Get a friend to drop in a coin. Tip it back into their hand to show that the paper is just a cup. Then ask if they have another coin. Turn the cup into a tube while they're searching for one, again with your other hand resting underneath. Get your friend to drop the second coin in. It will fall into your hand. Close your fingers over the coin without your friend seeing and tip the cup back into their hand. When no coin appears, act amazed!

14 From above you can see that it forms a cup. But if you turn it on its side and squeeze, it forms a tube.

117

FLAPPING BIRD

This classic origami crane has a hidden twist ... it can flap its wings! Follow these instructions to fold your own flapping bird.

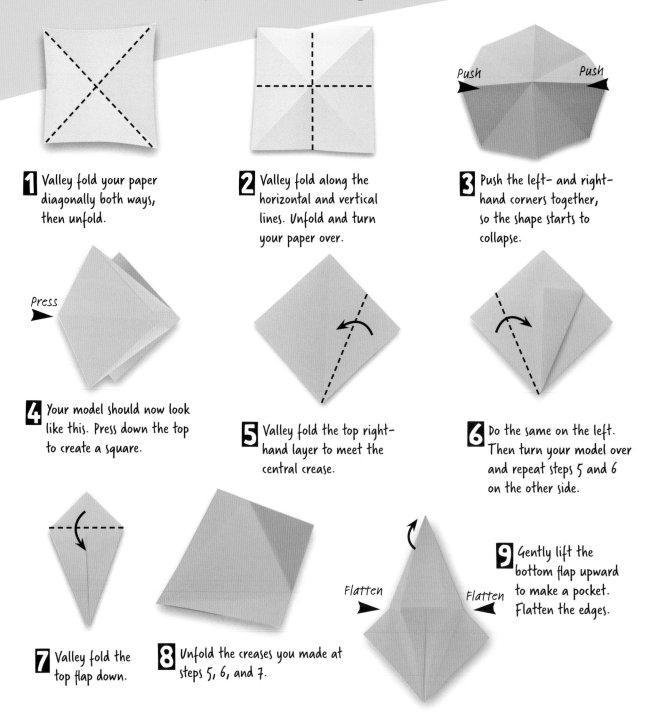

1 Valley fold your paper diagonally both ways, then unfold.

2 Valley fold along the horizontal and vertical lines. Unfold and turn your paper over.

3 Push the left- and right-hand corners together, so the shape starts to collapse.

Push *Push*

Press

4 Your model should now look like this. Press down the top to create a square.

5 Valley fold the top right-hand layer to meet the central crease.

6 Do the same on the left. Then turn your model over and repeat steps 5 and 6 on the other side.

7 Valley fold the top flap down.

8 Unfold the creases you made at steps 5, 6, and 7.

Flatten *Flatten*

9 Gently lift the bottom flap upward to make a pocket. Flatten the edges.

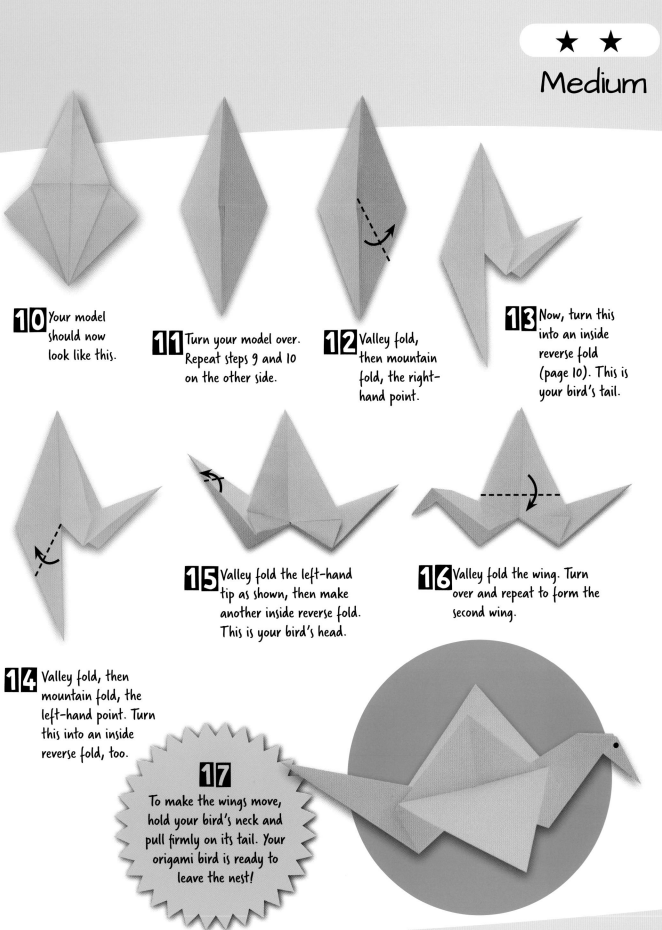

10 Your model should now look like this.

11 Turn your model over. Repeat steps 9 and 10 on the other side.

12 Valley fold, then mountain fold, the right-hand point.

13 Now, turn this into an inside reverse fold (page 10). This is your bird's tail.

14 Valley fold, then mountain fold, the left-hand point. Turn this into an inside reverse fold, too.

15 Valley fold the left-hand tip as shown, then make another inside reverse fold. This is your bird's head.

16 Valley fold the wing. Turn over and repeat to form the second wing.

17 To make the wings move, hold your bird's neck and pull firmly on its tail. Your origami bird is ready to leave the nest!

DOMINOES

It's great fun to send a row of dominoes toppling over. Follow these instructions to make a few, carefully line them up, and watch them fall!

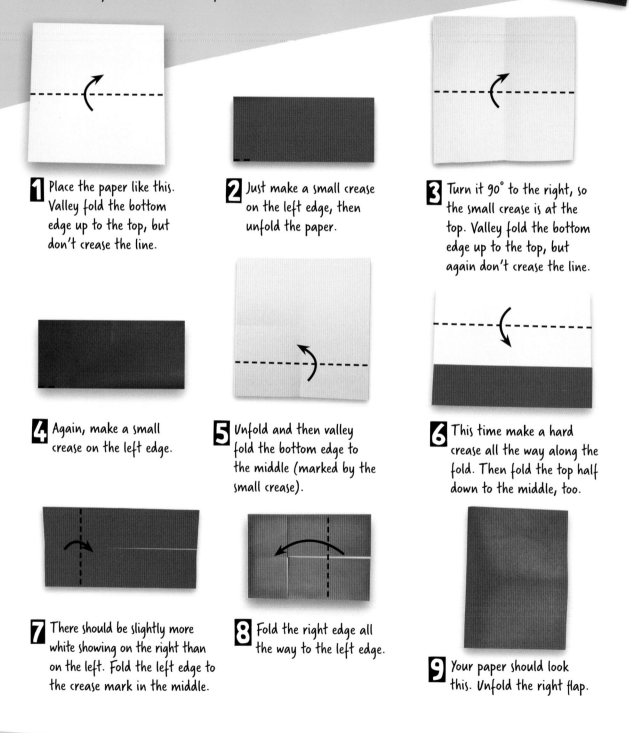

1 Place the paper like this. Valley fold the bottom edge up to the top, but don't crease the line.

2 Just make a small crease on the left edge, then unfold the paper.

3 Turn it 90° to the right, so the small crease is at the top. Valley fold the bottom edge up to the top, but again don't crease the line.

4 Again, make a small crease on the left edge.

5 Unfold and then valley fold the bottom edge to the middle (marked by the small crease).

6 This time make a hard crease all the way along the fold. Then fold the top half down to the middle, too.

7 There should be slightly more white showing on the right than on the left. Fold the left edge to the crease mark in the middle.

8 Fold the right edge all the way to the left edge.

9 Your paper should look this. Unfold the right flap.

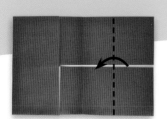

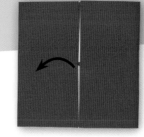

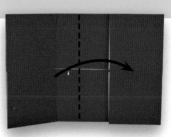

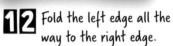

10 Fold the right edge over so it meets the edge of the left flap.

11 Your paper should now look like this. Unfold the left flap.

12 Fold the left edge all the way to the right edge.

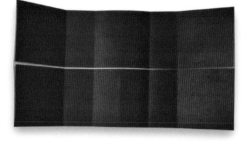

13 Your paper should look like this, with a vertical crease about a quarter of the way from the left edge, and a small horizontal crease on the right edge.

14 Completely unfold the two flaps, so your paper looks like this.

15 Curl the paper over and insert the left flap (the one with the crease mark) inside the right-hand flap (the one without a crease mark).

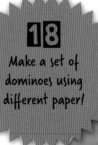

18 Make a set of dominoes using different paper!

16 Keep pushing the left flap inside the other flap.

17 Once it's all the way inside, your domino is ready.

LOTUS FLOWER

The lotus flower grows in water, floating on the surface. This project requires some strong finger power, as you'll need to fold the paper over several times.

1 Place the paper white side up, with one corner facing you. Make two valley folds as shown, then unfold.

2 Valley fold the left corner to the central line.

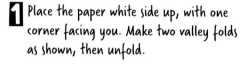

3 Repeat step 2 with the other three corners.

4 Fold the top left corner to the central line.

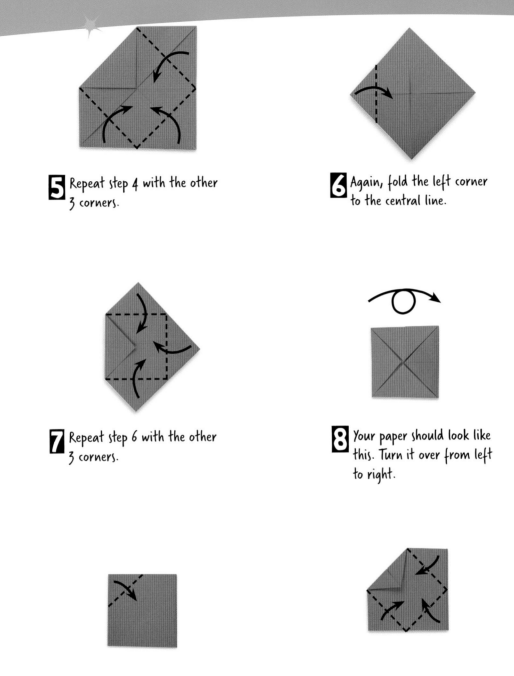

5 Repeat step 4 with the other 3 corners.

6 Again, fold the left corner to the central line.

7 Repeat step 6 with the other 3 corners.

8 Your paper should look like this. Turn it over from left to right.

9 For the final time, fold the top left corner to the central point.

10 Repeat step 9 with the other 3 sides.

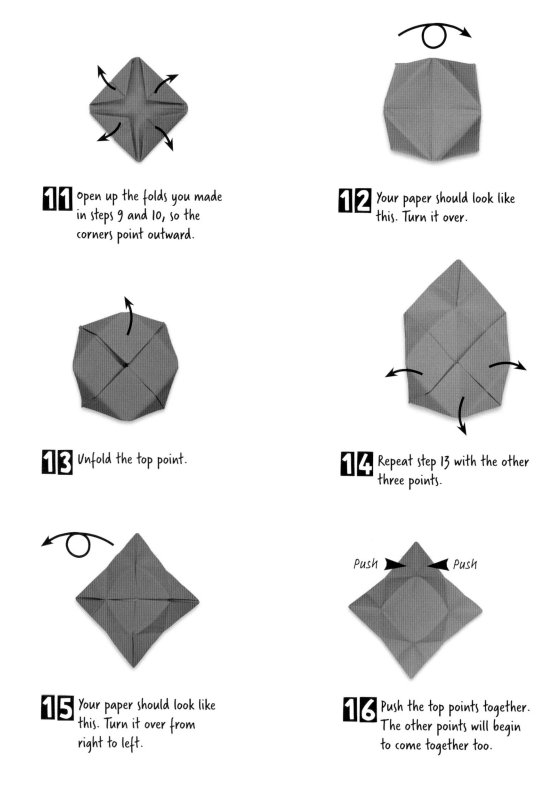

11 Open up the folds you made in steps 9 and 10, so the corners point outward.

12 Your paper should look like this. Turn it over.

13 Unfold the top point.

14 Repeat step 13 with the other three points.

15 Your paper should look like this. Turn it over from right to left.

16 Push the top points together. The other points will begin to come together too.

Push ◄ ► *Push*

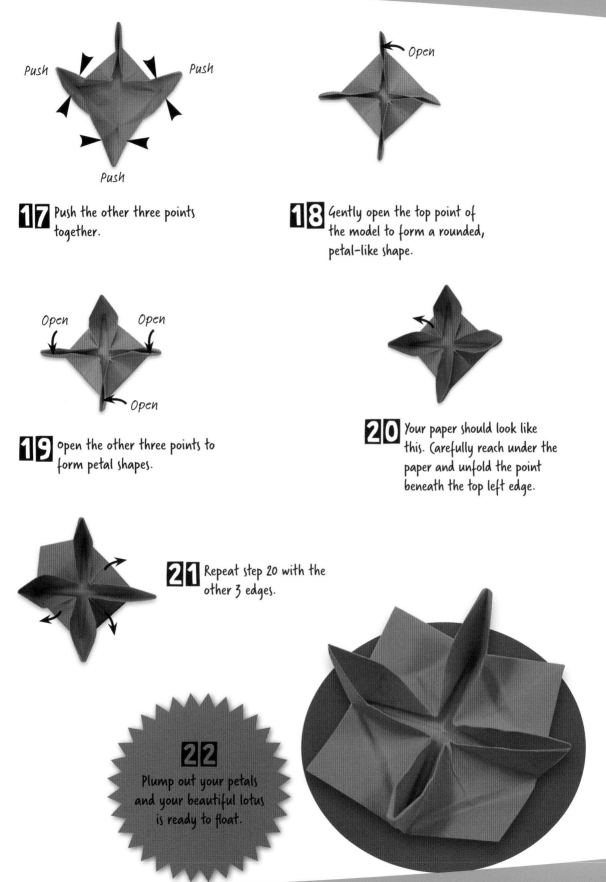

Push   Push

Push

Open

17 Push the other three points together.

18 Gently open the top point of the model to form a rounded, petal-like shape.

Open   Open

Open

19 Open the other three points to form petal shapes.

20 Your paper should look like this. Carefully reach under the paper and unfold the point beneath the top left edge.

21 Repeat step 20 with the other 3 edges.

22 Plump out your petals and your beautiful lotus is ready to float.

GULPING FISH

It only takes a few minutes of careful paper folding to create this hungry origami fish with its great, gulping mouth.

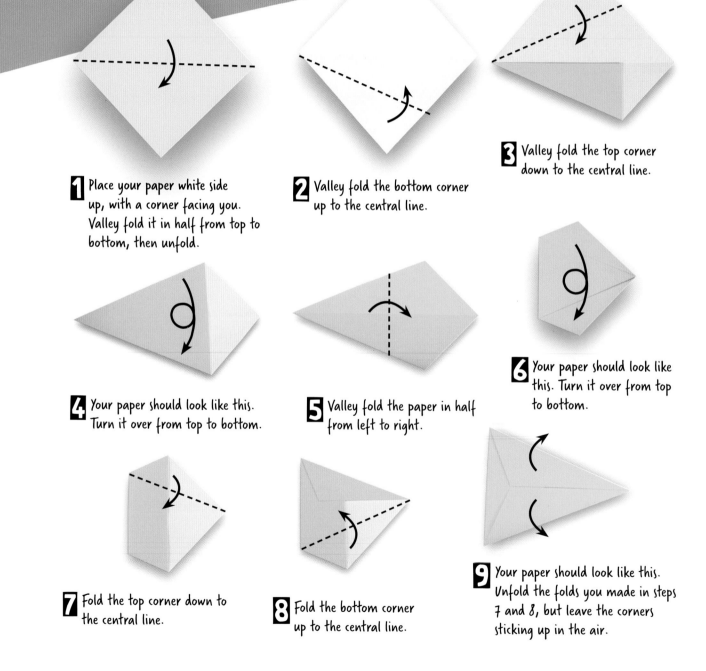

1 Place your paper white side up, with a corner facing you. Valley fold it in half from top to bottom, then unfold.

2 Valley fold the bottom corner up to the central line.

3 Valley fold the top corner down to the central line.

4 Your paper should look like this. Turn it over from top to bottom.

5 Valley fold the paper in half from left to right.

6 Your paper should look like this. Turn it over from top to bottom.

7 Fold the top corner down to the central line.

8 Fold the bottom corner up to the central line.

9 Your paper should look like this. Unfold the folds you made in steps 7 and 8, but leave the corners sticking up in the air.

10 Open up the horizontal flap in the middle and push it to the left.

11 As you push, the top and bottom flaps will start to fold inward, forming this shape. Flatten the paper down.

Push

12 On the top layer, fold up the right point, as shown. This will be the first tail fin.

14 Make another fold on the right-hand side, as shown, to form the second tail fin.

13 Your paper should look like this. Turn it over from top to bottom.

16 To make your fish gulp, simply take a tail fin in each hand. When you pull them apart, your fish will open its mouth. And when you push them together, it'll snap it shut again!

15 Your snapping origami fish is ready.

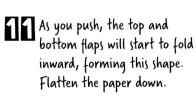

127

BARKING DOG

Woof, woof! This barking dog is very cute. Once you've mastered the folds, why not make him a few friends to play with?

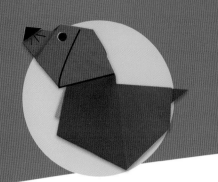

1 Place your paper as shown. Valley fold it in half from top to bottom.

2 Diagonally fold the bottom corner of the top layer up to meet the top edge.

3 Turn the paper over from left to right.

4 Again, diagonally fold the bottom corner of the top layer up to the top edge, so it matches the other side.

5 Valley fold the left corner of the top layer down to the bottom, as shown.

6 Turn the paper over from left to right and repeat step 5 on the other side.

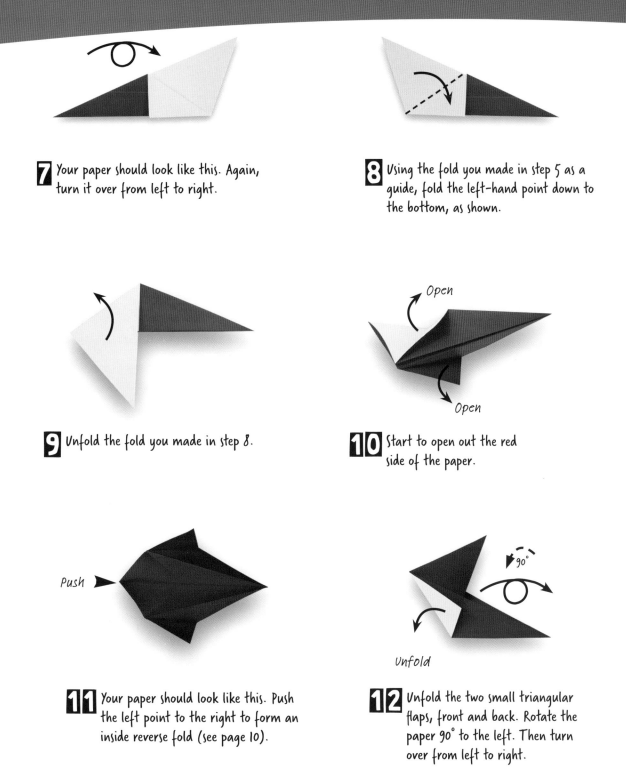

7 Your paper should look like this. Again, turn it over from left to right.

8 Using the fold you made in step 5 as a guide, fold the left-hand point down to the bottom, as shown.

9 Unfold the fold you made in step 8.

10 Start to open out the red side of the paper.

Open

Open

11 Your paper should look like this. Push the left point to the right to form an inside reverse fold (see page 10).

Push

12 Unfold the two small triangular flaps, front and back. Rotate the paper 90° to the left. Then turn over from left to right.

Unfold

90°

13 Make a valley fold in the left point, as shown.

14 Fold it back the other way so it's also a mountain fold.

15 Open up the left-hand point and start folding it the other way, as a mountain fold. Bring the sides down to create an outside reverse fold (see page 10).

16 Your paper should look like this. Flatten it down.

17 Start making the head by valley folding the left point back to the right, as shown. Fold it the other way so it's also a mountain fold.

18 Make another valley fold going back to the left. Again, fold it the other way, so it's also a mountain fold.

19 Now turn the folds you made in steps 17 and 18 into two inside reverse folds (see page 10), one inside the other.

20 Your paper should look like this. Make another small fold near the left-hand point and turn it into an outside reverse fold. This is the nose.

21 Make the tail by valley folding the right point back to the left, as shown. Fold it the other way so it's also a mountain fold.

22 Make another valley fold, slightly farther to the right, as shown. Again, fold it the other way so it's also a mountain fold.

24 Your dog is ready! To make him bark, simply hold his front feet and pull his tail. His head will nod up and down (you'll have to add the sound effects).

23 Now turn the folds you made in steps 21 and 22 into two inside reverse folds, one inside the other.

Pull

Hold here

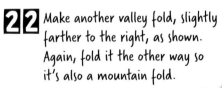

HELICOPTER

You may get dizzy watching this amazing spinning helicopter whirling around. The higher you drop it, the more it will spin!

1 Place the paper like this.

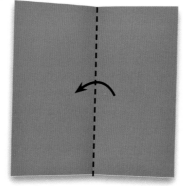

2 Valley fold it in half from right to left, then unfold.

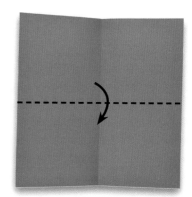

3 Now valley fold the paper in half from top to bottom, then unfold.

4 Turn the paper over. Then valley fold it in half diagonally from right to left.

5 Your paper should look like this.

6 Unfold the paper and turn it so the diagonal fold made in step 4 is now horizontal.

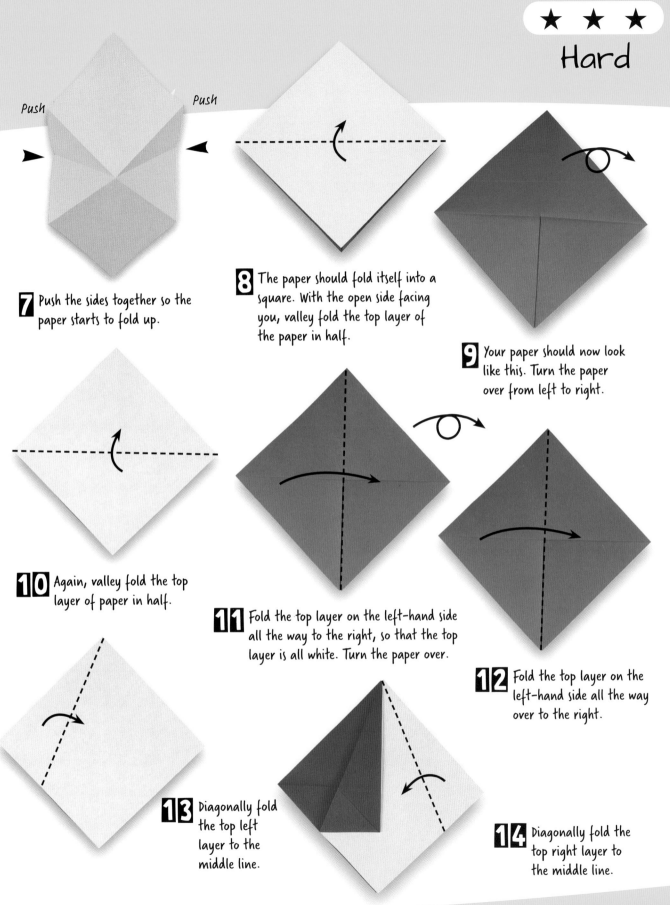

Push   Push

7 Push the sides together so the paper starts to fold up.

8 The paper should fold itself into a square. With the open side facing you, valley fold the top layer of the paper in half.

9 Your paper should now look like this. Turn the paper over from left to right.

10 Again, valley fold the top layer of paper in half.

11 Fold the top layer on the left-hand side all the way to the right, so that the top layer is all white. Turn the paper over.

12 Fold the top layer on the left-hand side all the way over to the right.

13 Diagonally fold the top left layer to the middle line.

14 Diagonally fold the top right layer to the middle line.

133

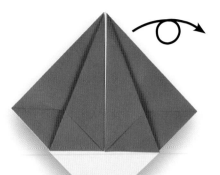

15 Your paper should look like this. Turn it over.

16 Fold the left-hand side to the middle line, like this. Then fold the right-hand side to the middle line, too.

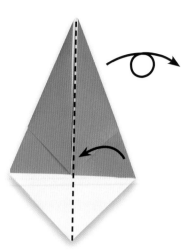

17 Fold the top right-hand layer over to the left so there's no more white showing. Turn the paper over.

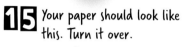

18 Again, fold the top right-hand layer over to the left so there's no more white showing.

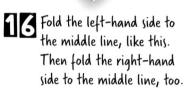

19 There should now be a clear gap in the bottom half of the paper. Valley fold the right flap up to the top.

20 Mountain fold the left-hand flap the other way.

21 Pull the flaps out so they're pointing in opposite directions, like this.

22 Hold the helicopter with the two flaps at the top, gently release it, and watch it spin.

MOTORBOAT

The motorboat zips across the water at great speeds. Here's how to make a sleek and streamlined origami version.

1 Place the paper white side up, with one corner facing you. Make two valley folds as shown, then unfold.

2 Valley fold the left corner to the central line.

3 Repeat step 2 with the other three corners.

4 Take the central left-hand point and valley fold it back to the left.

5 Repeat step 4 with the other three central points, as shown.

6 Your paper should now look like this. Unfold the top side.

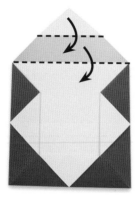

7 Fold forward the top point, then fold it over again so the point is hidden.

8 Your paper now looks like this. Repeat steps 6 and 7 on the bottom side.

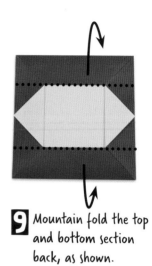

9 Mountain fold the top and bottom section back, as shown.

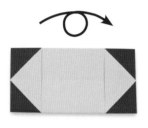

10 Your paper should look like this. Turn it over from left to right.

11 Fold the top left corner down to the central line.

12 Repeat step 11 with the other 3 corners.

13 Fold the top right corner down to meet the central line. Do the same with the other three corners.

14 Fold the top point down to the middle.

15 Fold the bottom point up to the middle.

16 Unfold the folds made in steps 13 to 15 and start to open up the central horizontal folds.

17 Your paper should look like this. Keep opening up the central folds.

18 When the folds are wide apart, like this, push the model up from below to turn the boat inside out, so the red side bulges outward.

19 Your paper should look like this. Turn it over.

20 Lift up the white fold of paper on the left side.

21 Now lift up the white fold of paper on the right side.

22 Your motorboat is ready to race!

DUCKLING

Quack, quack! Here comes an origami duckling paddling along the water. Why not make a whole family of ducks and take them all for a swim together?

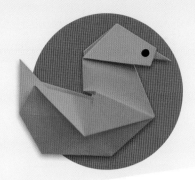

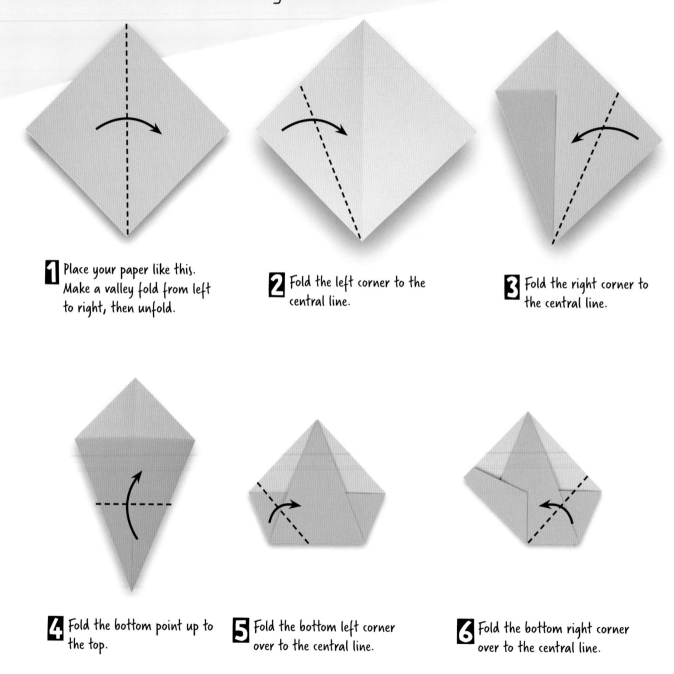

1 Place your paper like this. Make a valley fold from left to right, then unfold.

2 Fold the left corner to the central line.

3 Fold the right corner to the central line.

4 Fold the bottom point up to the top.

5 Fold the bottom left corner over to the central line.

6 Fold the bottom right corner over to the central line.

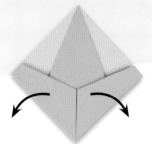

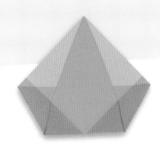

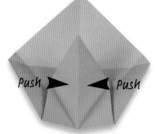

7 Open out the folds you made in steps 5 and 6.

8 Bring down the fold you made in step 4 so that the yellow side is pointing toward you.

9 Your paper should look like this. As you bring the point forward, press its sides together.

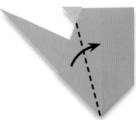

10 When the point is sticking straight at you, valley fold the whole paper in half from right to left.

11 Then make a diagonal valley fold as shown.

12 Now turn the fold you made in step 11 into a mountain fold, to crease the paper really well.

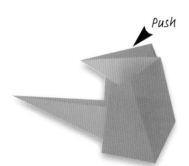

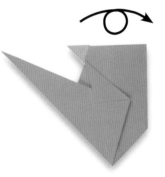

13 Open out the paper and turn the folds you made in steps 11 and 12 into an inside reverse fold (see page 10).

14 Flatten your paper down, so it looks like this. Valley fold the bottom central point, as shown.

15 Your paper should look like this. Turn it over from left to right, and repeat step 14 on the other side.

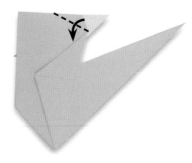

16 Your paper should look like this. Make a small valley fold on the top layer of paper.

17 Now fold the corner you just made the other way, as a mountain fold, and tuck it behind so it's out of sight. Then turn the paper over from left to right, and repeat steps 16 and 17 on the other side.

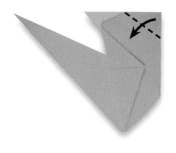

18 Your paper should look like this. Make another small valley fold, as shown.

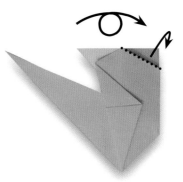

19 Fold the corner you just made the other way, as a mountain fold, and tuck it behind so it's out of sight. Turn the paper over and repeat steps 18 and 19 on the other side.

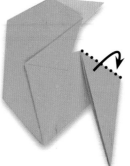

20 Your paper should look like this. Fold down the right point, as shown.

21 Fold the point the other way to make a mountain fold. Then flip it over to make an outside reverse fold (see page 10).

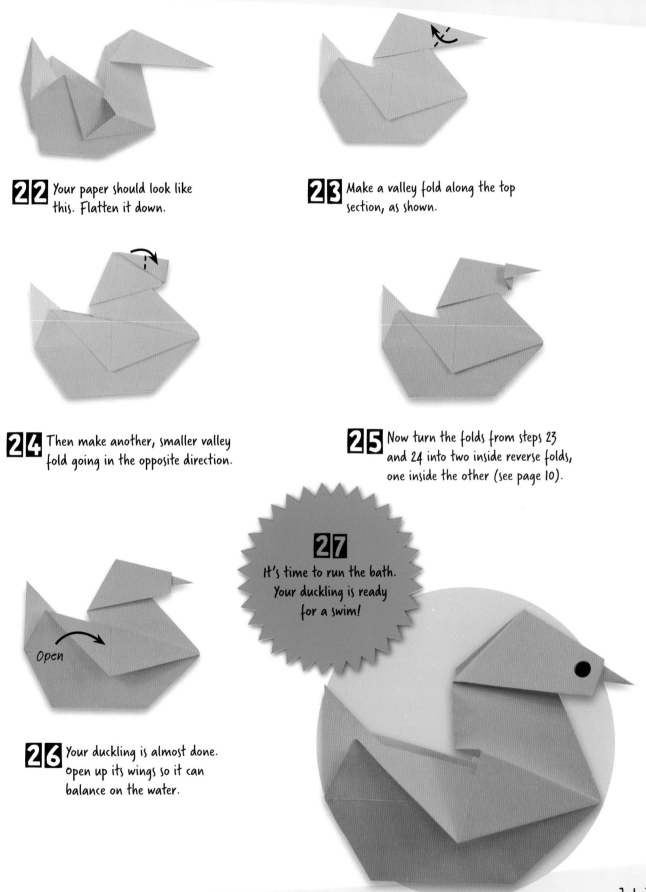

22 Your paper should look like this. Flatten it down.

23 Make a valley fold along the top section, as shown.

24 Then make another, smaller valley fold going in the opposite direction.

25 Now turn the folds from steps 23 and 24 into two inside reverse folds, one inside the other (see page 10).

27 It's time to run the bath. Your duckling is ready for a swim!

Open

26 Your duckling is almost done. Open up its wings so it can balance on the water.

Jumping Horse

This origami horse will perform forward somersaults right before your very eyes. You'll need scissors to complete your model, so ask an adult to help you.

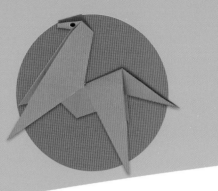

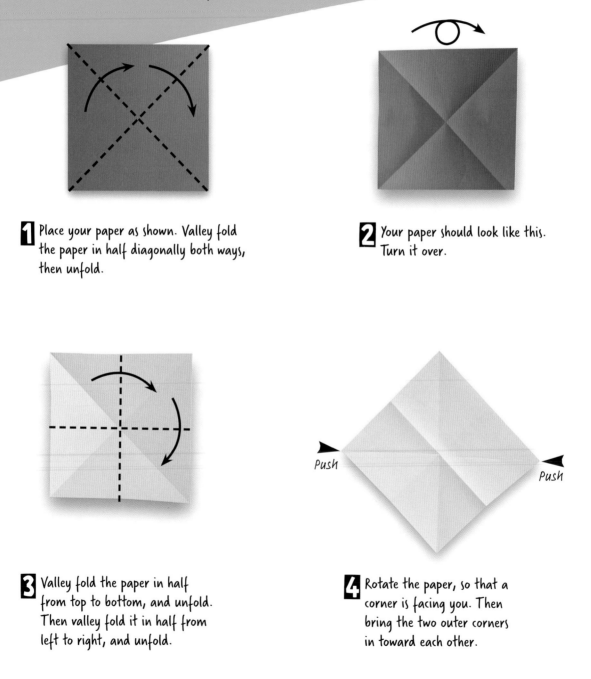

1 Place your paper as shown. Valley fold the paper in half diagonally both ways, then unfold.

2 Your paper should look like this. Turn it over.

3 Valley fold the paper in half from top to bottom, and unfold. Then valley fold it in half from left to right, and unfold.

4 Rotate the paper, so that a corner is facing you. Then bring the two outer corners in toward each other.

Push

Push

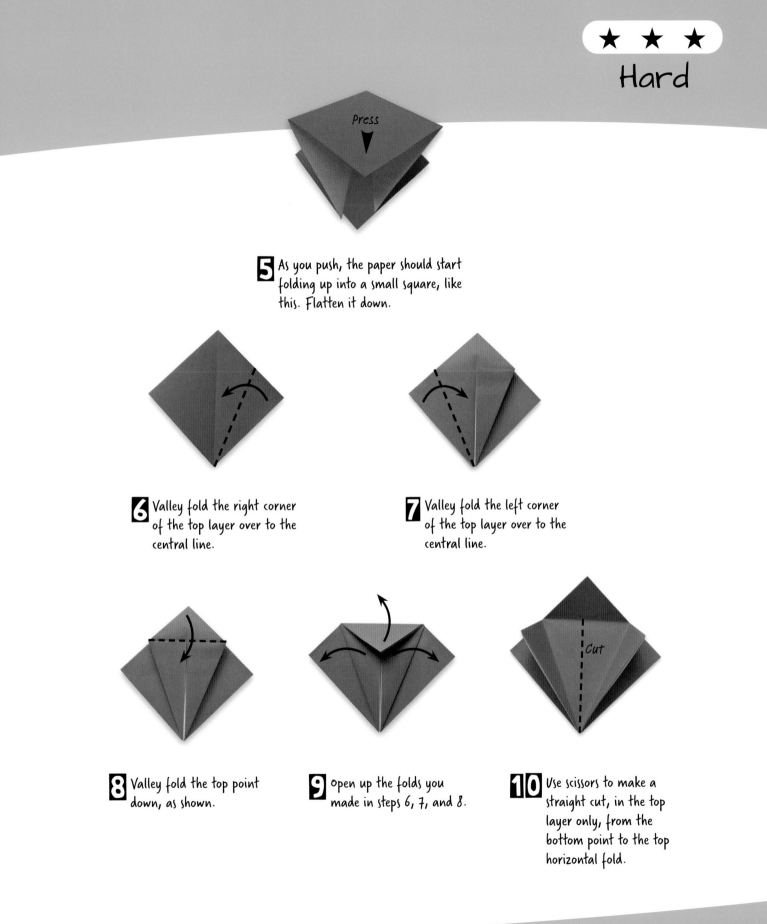

Press

5 As you push, the paper should start folding up into a small square, like this. Flatten it down.

6 Valley fold the right corner of the top layer over to the central line.

7 Valley fold the left corner of the top layer over to the central line.

8 Valley fold the top point down, as shown.

9 Open up the folds you made in steps 6, 7, and 8.

10 Use scissors to make a straight cut, in the top layer only, from the bottom point to the top horizontal fold.

Cut

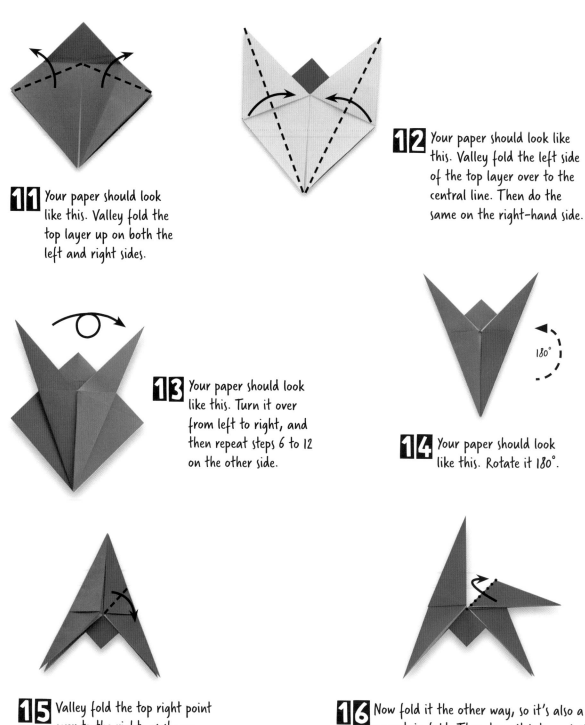

11 Your paper should look like this. Valley fold the top layer up on both the left and right sides.

12 Your paper should look like this. Valley fold the left side of the top layer over to the central line. Then do the same on the right-hand side.

13 Your paper should look like this. Turn it over from left to right, and then repeat steps 6 to 12 on the other side.

14 Your paper should look like this. Rotate it 180°.

15 Valley fold the top right point over to the right, as shown.

16 Now fold it the other way, so it's also a mountain fold. Then turn it into an inside reverse fold (see page 10). This is your horse's tail.

17 Make a valley fold near the tip of the top left point.

18 Now fold it the other way, so it's also a mountain fold. Then turn it into an inside reverse fold. This is your horse's head.

19 Start forming a nose by making a small valley fold at the end of the head.

20 Fold it the other way, so it's also a mountain fold. Then turn it into another inside reverse fold. Your horse is ready to perform!

21
To make your horse jump, flick its tail hard up in the air and it should perform a forward somersault ... and land on its feet!

Jet Plane

This sleek, streamlined plane is built for speed. Follow the instructions carefully to make sure it flies as fast as possible!

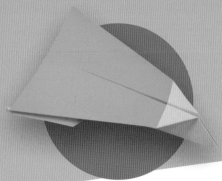

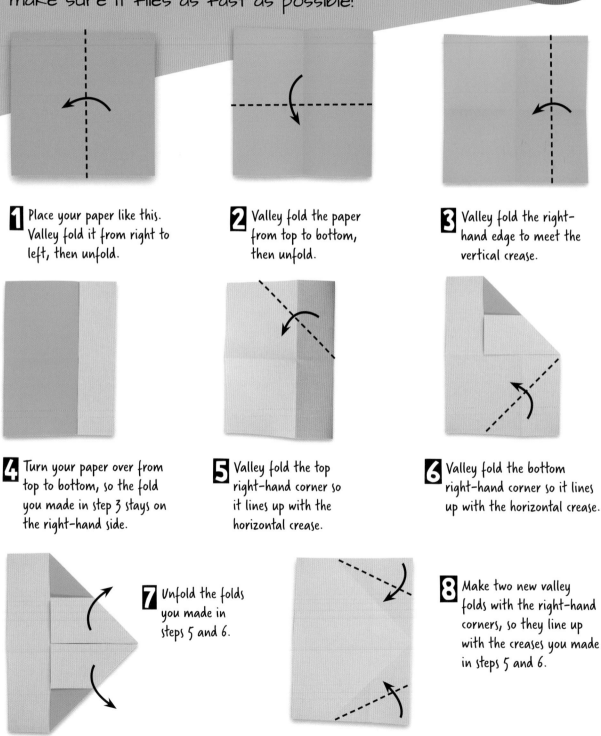

1 Place your paper like this. Valley fold it from right to left, then unfold.

2 Valley fold the paper from top to bottom, then unfold.

3 Valley fold the right-hand edge to meet the vertical crease.

4 Turn your paper over from top to bottom, so the fold you made in step 3 stays on the right-hand side.

5 Valley fold the top right-hand corner so it lines up with the horizontal crease.

6 Valley fold the bottom right-hand corner so it lines up with the horizontal crease.

7 Unfold the folds you made in steps 5 and 6.

8 Make two new valley folds with the right-hand corners, so they line up with the creases you made in steps 5 and 6.

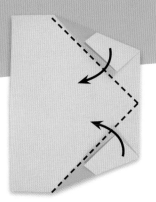

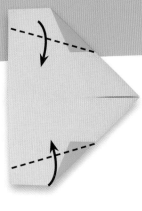

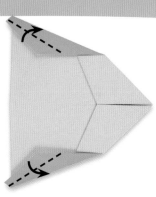

9 Fold the right-hand corners over again so that they line up with the crease in the middle. This is the nose of the jet.

10 Valley fold the outside of the wings so they line up with the edges of the nose section.

11 Valley fold the rear of the wings so they line up with the outside edges.

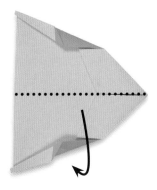

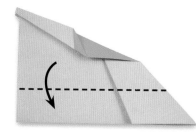

13 Valley fold the top wing down, as shown.

14 Turn the paper over.

12 Mountain fold the paper in half along the central crease.

16 Unfold the wings, even them up, and your plane is ready to take to the skies.

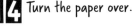

15 Repeat step 13 on the other side and your model is nearly complete.

Egg-Laying Hen

With just a single piece of paper you can make both a hen and a little egg. You'll need some scissors for the final stage, so ask an adult to help you.

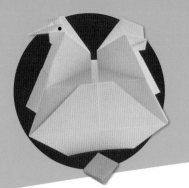

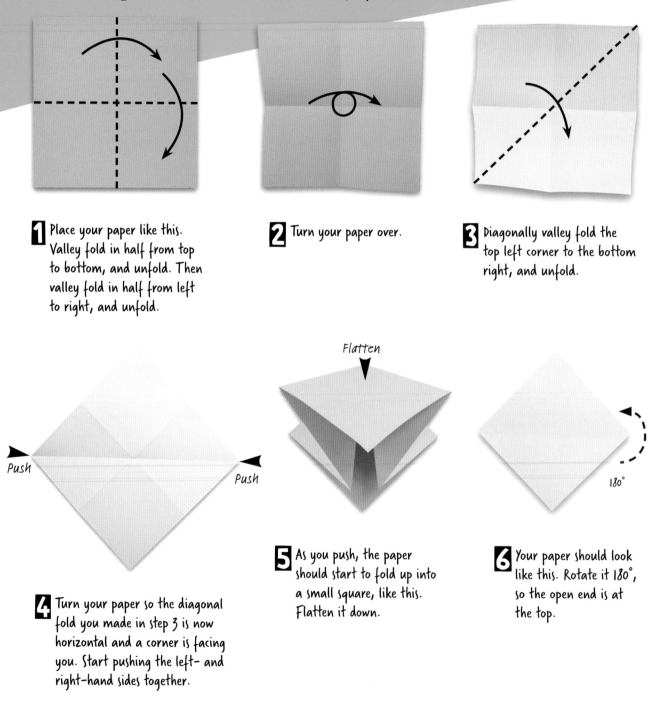

1 Place your paper like this. Valley fold in half from top to bottom, and unfold. Then valley fold in half from left to right, and unfold.

2 Turn your paper over.

3 Diagonally valley fold the top left corner to the bottom right, and unfold.

Push

Push

Flatten

180°

4 Turn your paper so the diagonal fold you made in step 3 is now horizontal and a corner is facing you. Start pushing the left- and right-hand sides together.

5 As you push, the paper should start to fold up into a small square, like this. Flatten it down.

6 Your paper should look like this. Rotate it 180°, so the open end is at the top.

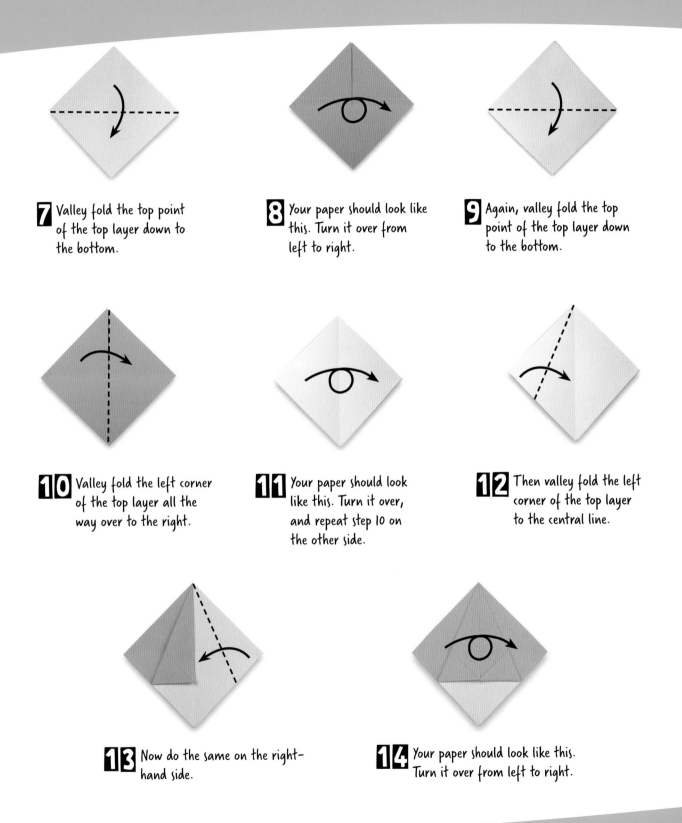

7 Valley fold the top point of the top layer down to the bottom.

8 Your paper should look like this. Turn it over from left to right.

9 Again, valley fold the top point of the top layer down to the bottom.

10 Valley fold the left corner of the top layer all the way over to the right.

11 Your paper should look like this. Turn it over, and repeat step 10 on the other side.

12 Then valley fold the left corner of the top layer to the central line.

13 Now do the same on the right-hand side.

14 Your paper should look like this. Turn it over from left to right.

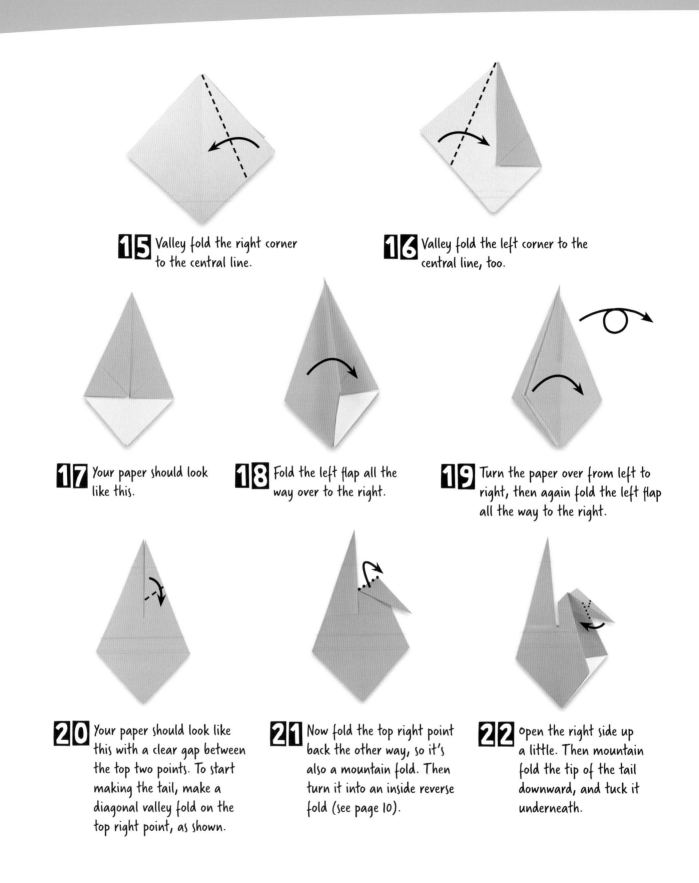

15 Valley fold the right corner to the central line.

16 Valley fold the left corner to the central line, too.

17 Your paper should look like this.

18 Fold the left flap all the way over to the right.

19 Turn the paper over from left to right, then again fold the left flap all the way to the right.

20 Your paper should look like this with a clear gap between the top two points. To start making the tail, make a diagonal valley fold on the top right point, as shown.

21 Now fold the top right point back the other way, so it's also a mountain fold. Then turn it into an inside reverse fold (see page 10).

22 Open the right side up a little. Then mountain fold the tip of the tail downward, and tuck it underneath.

23 Your paper should look like this. Flatten it down.

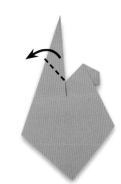

24 Start to make the head by valley folding the left point over to the left, as shown.

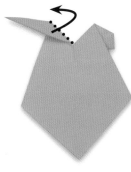

25 Now fold the point the other way, so it's also a mountain fold, then turn it into an inside reverse fold.

26 Your paper should look like this. Make a second, smaller inside reverse fold going the other way, to finish the head.

27 Make a third inside reverse fold going back the other way to form the beak.

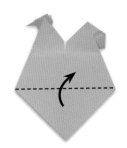

28 Your paper should look like this. Valley fold the bottom point of the top layer up, as shown.

Tuck

29 Tuck the point behind the middle flap.

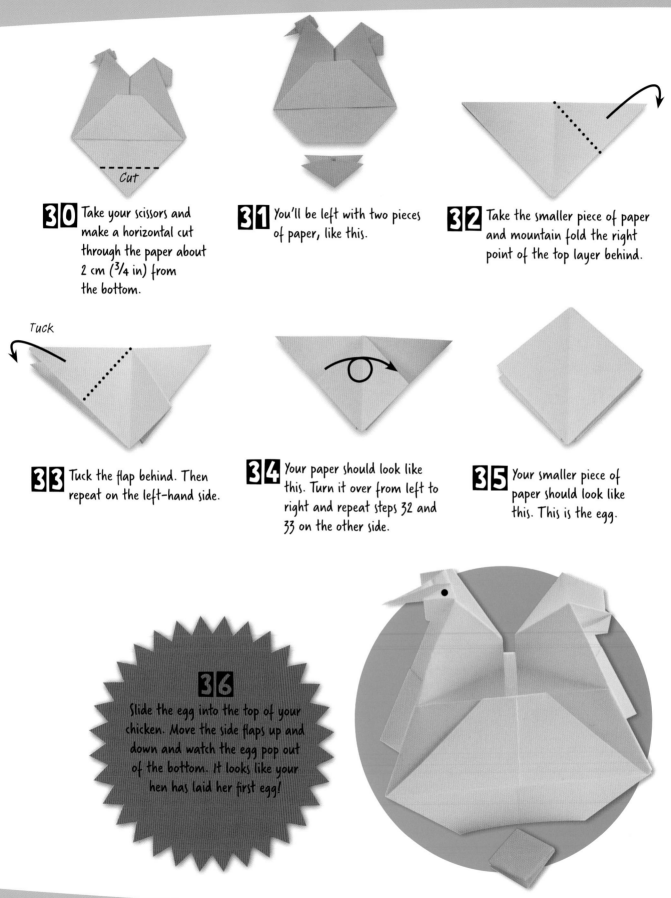

30 Take your scissors and make a horizontal cut through the paper about 2 cm (¾ in) from the bottom.

Cut

31 You'll be left with two pieces of paper, like this.

32 Take the smaller piece of paper and mountain fold the right point of the top layer behind.

Tuck

33 Tuck the flap behind. Then repeat on the left-hand side.

34 Your paper should look like this. Turn it over from left to right and repeat steps 32 and 33 on the other side.

35 Your smaller piece of paper should look like this. This is the egg.

36 Slide the egg into the top of your chicken. Move the side flaps up and down and watch the egg pop out of the bottom. It looks like your hen has laid her first egg!

CHAPTER 4

CHRISTMAS

It's Christmas! What better way to celebrate than to create your own festive models, from an elf to a snowflake. You'll even find a stocking to make.

SANTA

Christmas wouldn't be Christmas without Santa Claus! Follow these steps to fold your own St. Nick.

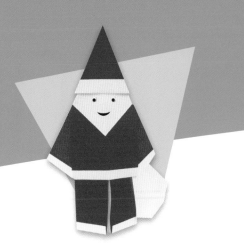

TO MAKE THE BODY

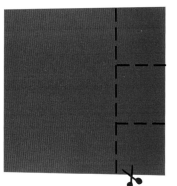

1 Valley fold the paper a third of the way from the right-hand edge. Cut along the fold. Fold the strip into thirds and cut along these folds, too.

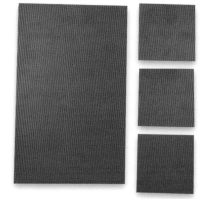

2 Your paper should look like this. Put the three small pieces of paper to one side.

3 Take the large piece of paper. Fold down the top edge and fold up the bottom edge, as shown.

4 Your paper will look like this. Turn it over.

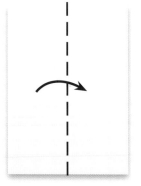

5 Fold the paper in half from left to right.

6 Your paper will look like this. Unfold it.

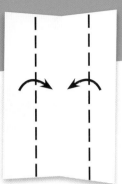 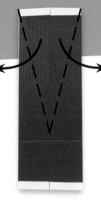 

7 Valley fold both edges in to the middle crease.

8 Valley fold both sides out from the middle, ending each fold a third of the way from the bottom edge.

9 Now fold the top down, like this.

To make the hat

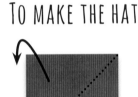 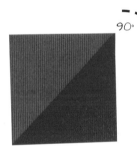

10 The body is finished. Put it to one side.

11 Take one of the small squares from step 2. Mountain fold it in half and unfold.

12 Rotate the paper 90°, so the crease in the middle is horizontal.

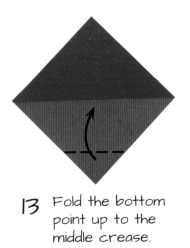 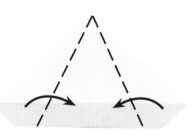

13 Fold the bottom point up to the middle crease.

14 Fold up again to meet the middle crease. Turn the paper over.

15 Valley fold both sides in, so they meet in the middle.

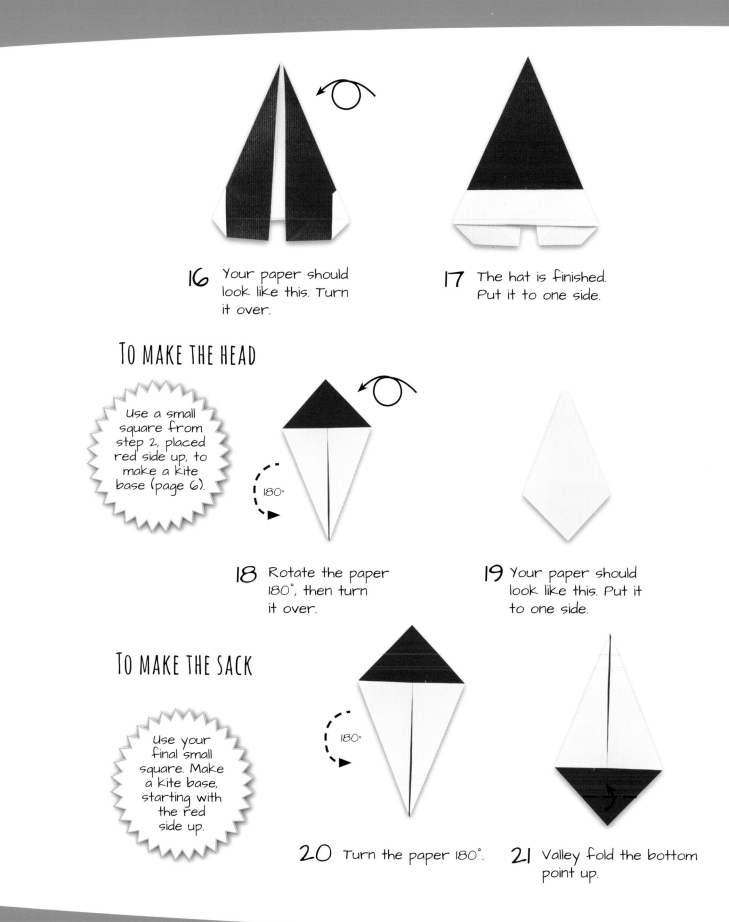

16 Your paper should look like this. Turn it over.

17 The hat is finished. Put it to one side.

TO MAKE THE HEAD

Use a small square from step 2, placed red side up, to make a kite base (page 6).

180°

18 Rotate the paper 180°, then turn it over.

19 Your paper should look like this. Put it to one side.

TO MAKE THE SACK

Use your final small square. Make a kite base, starting with the red side up.

180°

20 Turn the paper 180°.

21 Valley fold the bottom point up.

22 Your paper should look like this. Turn it over.

23 The sack is finished. Put it to one side.

To make Santa

24 Slide the hat on to the head.

25 Take the head and the body. Use sticky tape to attach the back of the head to the top of the body.

26 Tape the top of the sack to the back of Santa's sleeve.

27 Santa is ready to load his sleigh and deliver all those exciting presents!

Holly Leaves

Holly trees keep their leaves all year around and have red berries in the winter, making them perfect Christmas decorations.

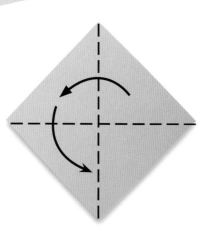

1 Valley fold your paper in half from top to bottom, and unfold. Then valley fold from right to left, and unfold.

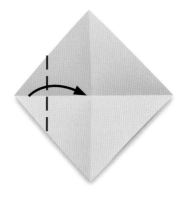

2 Valley fold the left point over to meet the middle crease.

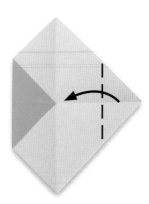

3 Valley fold the right point over to meet the middle crease, too.

4 Now, valley fold the left edge over to meet the middle crease.

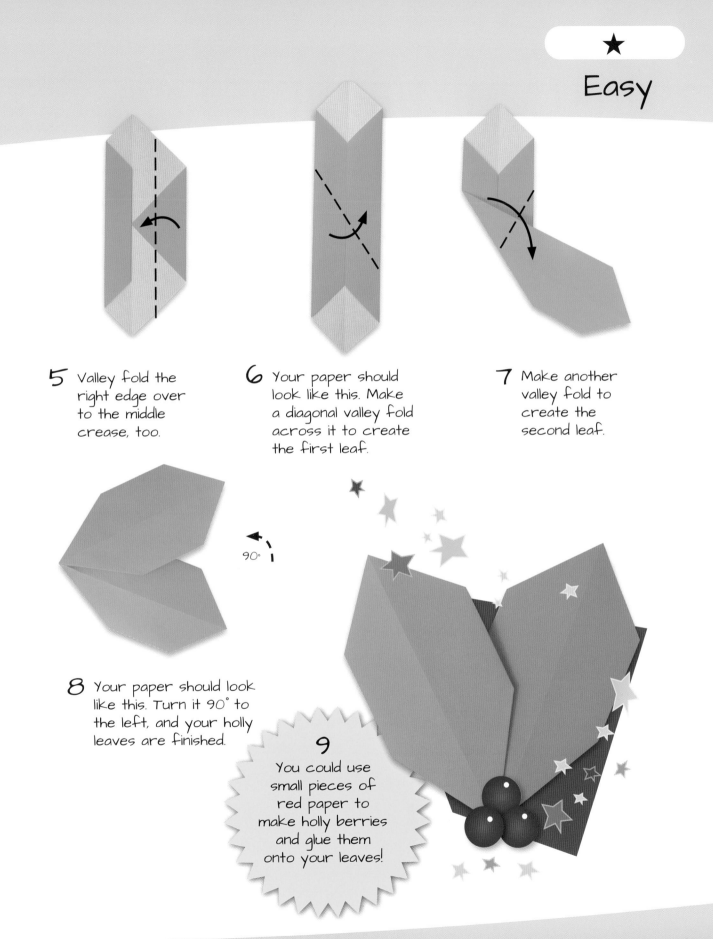

5 Valley fold the right edge over to the middle crease, too.

6 Your paper should look like this. Make a diagonal valley fold across it to create the first leaf.

7 Make another valley fold to create the second leaf.

90°

8 Your paper should look like this. Turn it 90° to the left, and your holly leaves are finished.

9 You could use small pieces of red paper to make holly berries and glue them onto your leaves!

Letter to Santa

Send Santa your wish list in this neat envelope. Then make sure you are good between now and Christmas!

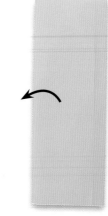

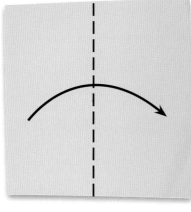

1 With the paper like this, valley fold the paper in half. Unfold.

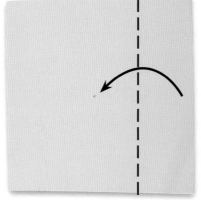

2 Fold the right-hand side to the middle crease. Unfold.

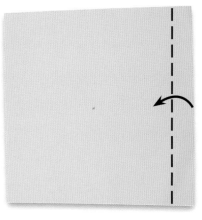

3 Fold the right edge back in, to meet the crease you made in step 2.

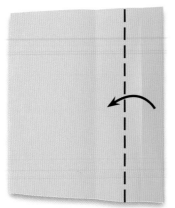

4 Now, fold the right-hand edge to meet the middle crease.

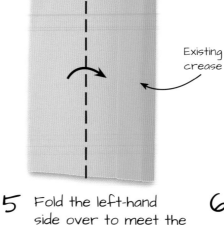

Existing crease

5 Fold the left-hand side over to meet the crease in the middle of the yellow side.

6 Your paper should look like this. Open out the fold on the left.

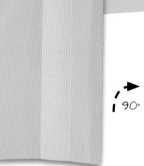

7 Turn the paper 90° to the right.

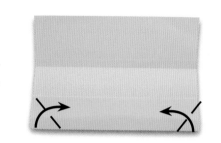

8 Valley fold the bottom corners up to meet the yellow edge.

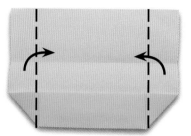

9 Make a vertical valley fold on each side.

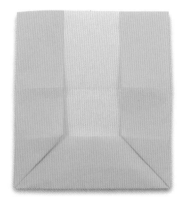

10 Fold the top left corner down to meet the crease line.

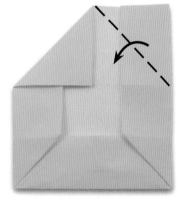

11 Repeat with the top right corner.

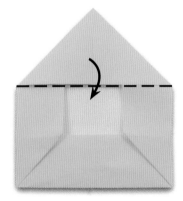

12 Fold the top point down along the crease.

13 Put your Christmas wish list inside the envelope and tuck in the flap.

14 Your letter is ready to be sent off to Santa. Now you just need to add his address...

REINDEER

Where would Santa be without his reindeer? They pull his sleigh to deliver presents on Christmas Eve.

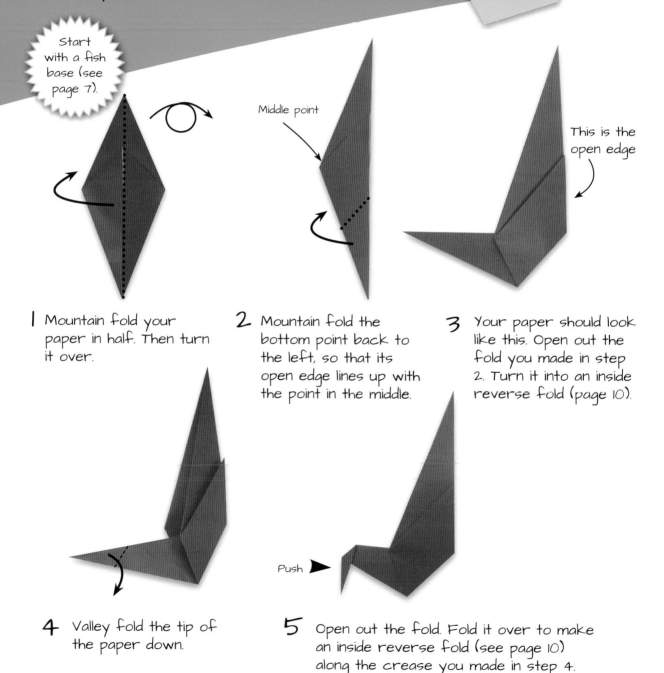

Start with a fish base (see page 7).

Middle point

This is the open edge

1 Mountain fold your paper in half. Then turn it over.

2 Mountain fold the bottom point back to the left, so that its open edge lines up with the point in the middle.

3 Your paper should look like this. Open out the fold you made in step 2. Turn it into an inside reverse fold (page 10).

4 Valley fold the tip of the paper down.

Push ▶

5 Open out the fold. Fold it over to make an inside reverse fold (see page 10) along the crease you made in step 4.

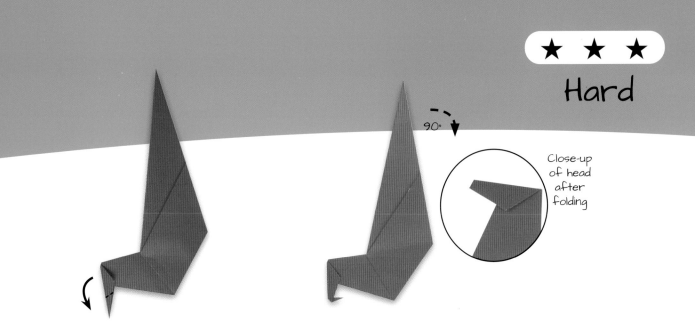

90°

Close-up
of head
after
folding

6   Make a diagonal valley fold in the bottom tip, like this. Fold it back the other way so it's also a mountain fold.

7   Open out the fold and turn it into an inside reverse fold. This is your reindeer's head. Now rotate your paper 90°.

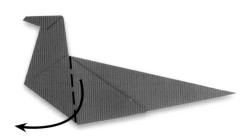

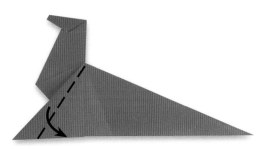

8   Valley fold the front flap to the left. Then valley fold the back flap in the same way.

9   Valley fold the front flap down, like this, to create a front leg. Repeat on the back flap, too.

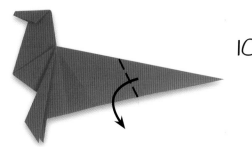

10   Valley fold the right-hand point down. Fold it the other way so it's also a mountain fold. Crease well.

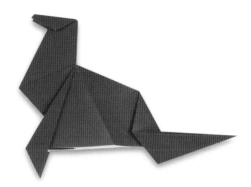

11 Make a valley fold pointing up. Turn it into a mountain fold too.

12 Open out the folds you made in steps 10 and 11.

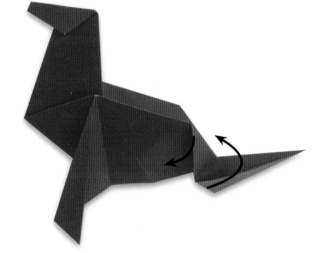

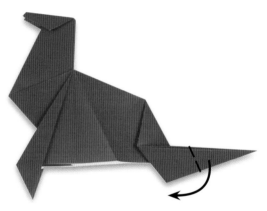

13 Turn these folds into two outside reverse folds (see page 10), one inside the other.

14 Your paper should look like this. Valley fold the point down, as shown. Fold it the other way, so it's also a mountain fold.

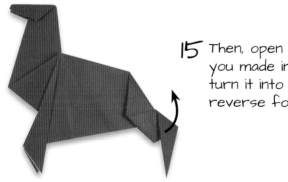

15 Then, open out the fold you made in step 14 and turn it into an outside reverse fold .

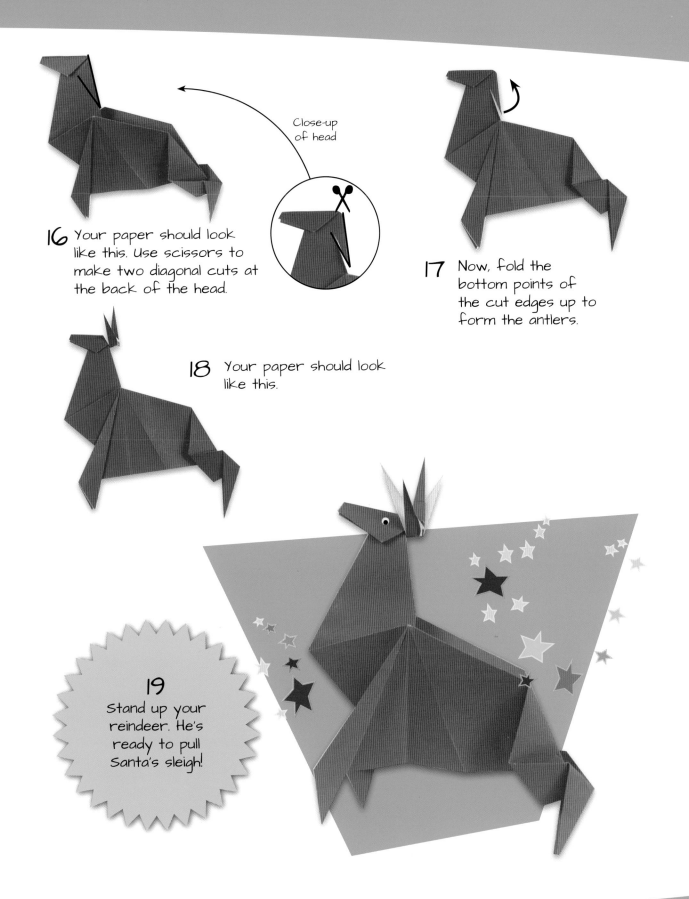

Close-up of head

16 Your paper should look like this. Use scissors to make two diagonal cuts at the back of the head.

17 Now, fold the bottom points of the cut edges up to form the antlers.

18 Your paper should look like this.

19 Stand up your reindeer. He's ready to pull Santa's sleigh!

CHRISTMAS TREE

Follow these simple steps to fold your own paper Christmas tree!

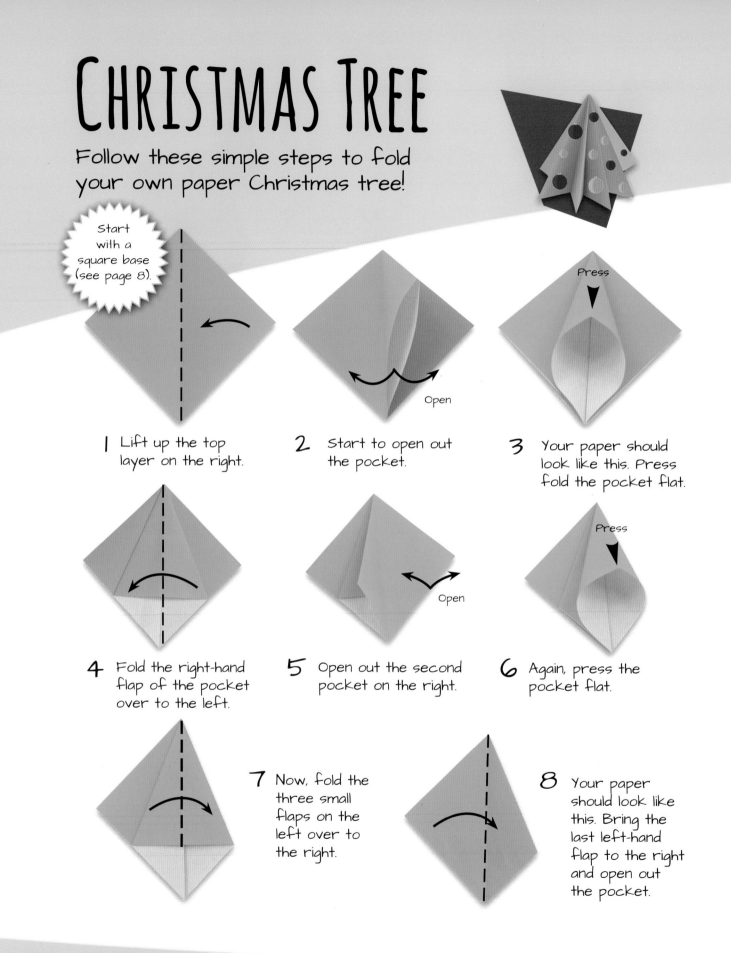

Start with a square base (see page 8).

1 Lift up the top layer on the right.

2 Start to open out the pocket.

Open

3 Your paper should look like this. Press fold the pocket flat.

Press

4 Fold the right-hand flap of the pocket over to the left.

5 Open out the second pocket on the right.

Open

6 Again, press the pocket flat.

Press

7 Now, fold the three small flaps on the left over to the right.

8 Your paper should look like this. Bring the last left-hand flap to the right and open out the pocket.

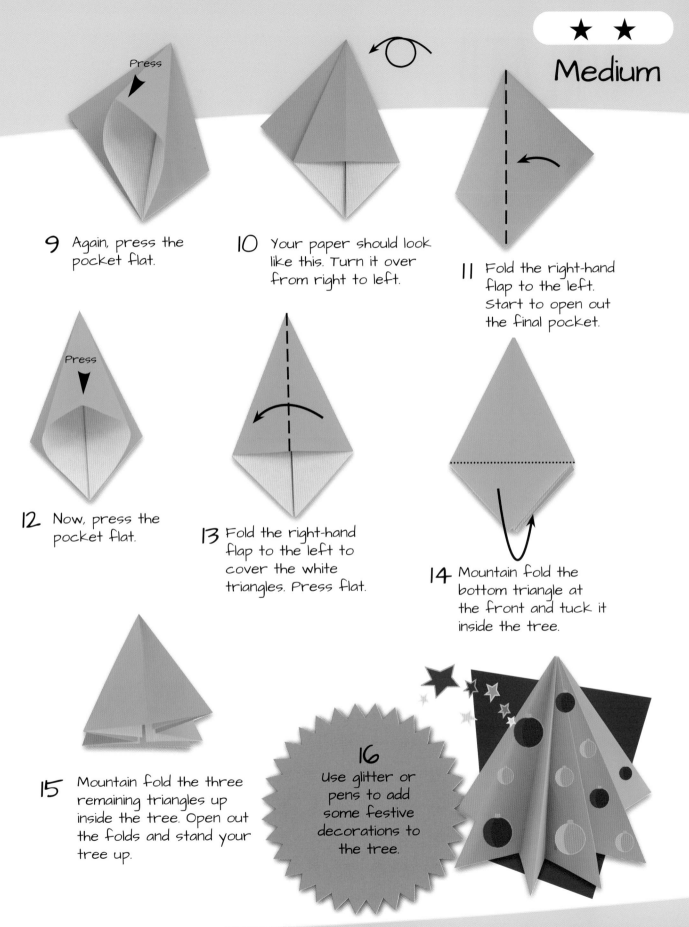

Press

9 Again, press the pocket flat.

10 Your paper should look like this. Turn it over from right to left.

11 Fold the right-hand flap to the left. Start to open out the final pocket.

Press

12 Now, press the pocket flat.

13 Fold the right-hand flap to the left to cover the white triangles. Press flat.

14 Mountain fold the bottom triangle at the front and tuck it inside the tree.

15 Mountain fold the three remaining triangles up inside the tree. Open out the folds and stand your tree up.

16 Use glitter or pens to add some festive decorations to the tree.

Wreath

Hanging a wreath on your door at Christmas time is a lovely way to welcome visitors.

You will need four sheets of paper for this project.

1 Place your first piece of paper like this. Valley fold it in half from right to left and open it out again.

2 Now, valley fold it in half from top to bottom.

3 Make a valley fold, like this, bringing the bottom tip up.

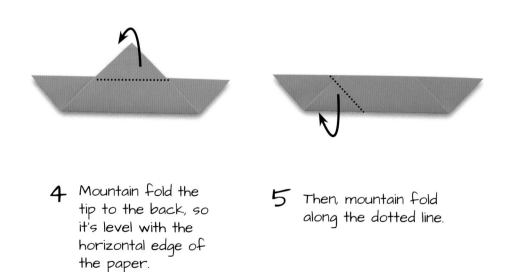

4 Mountain fold the tip to the back, so it's level with the horizontal edge of the paper.

5 Then, mountain fold along the dotted line.

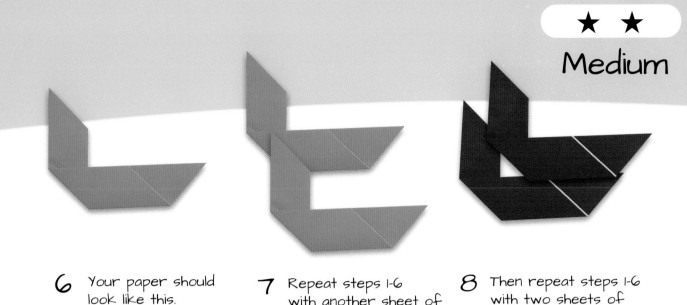

6 Your paper should look like this.

7 Repeat steps 1-6 with another sheet of green paper.

8 Then repeat steps 1-6 with two sheets of red paper. You should now have four pieces.

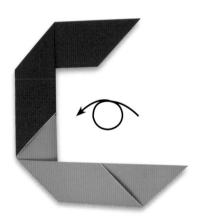

9 Take one red and one green piece and place them like this. Start to slide the top of the green shape inside the pocket of the red shape.

10 Turn the paper over.

11 Slide the end of the red shape inside the pocket of the green shape. Turn the paper over again.

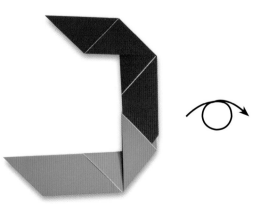

169

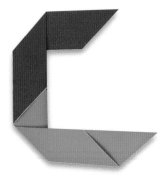

12 Your paper should look like this. Make sure it is secure. Then, repeat steps 9-11 with the other two pieces.

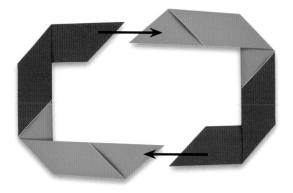

13 Place the two halves so they are facing each other, like this. Slide them together, using the same method you used in steps 9-11.

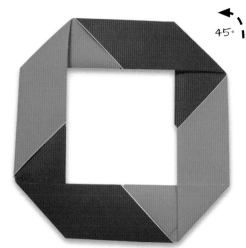

45°

14 Turn the shape 45° to the left so one of the smaller flat edges is facing you.

15
Decorate your wreath in any way you like and hang it on your bedroom door.

REINDEER FACE

★ ★ ★

Hard

Santa's reindeers have beautiful antlers, just like this paper version.

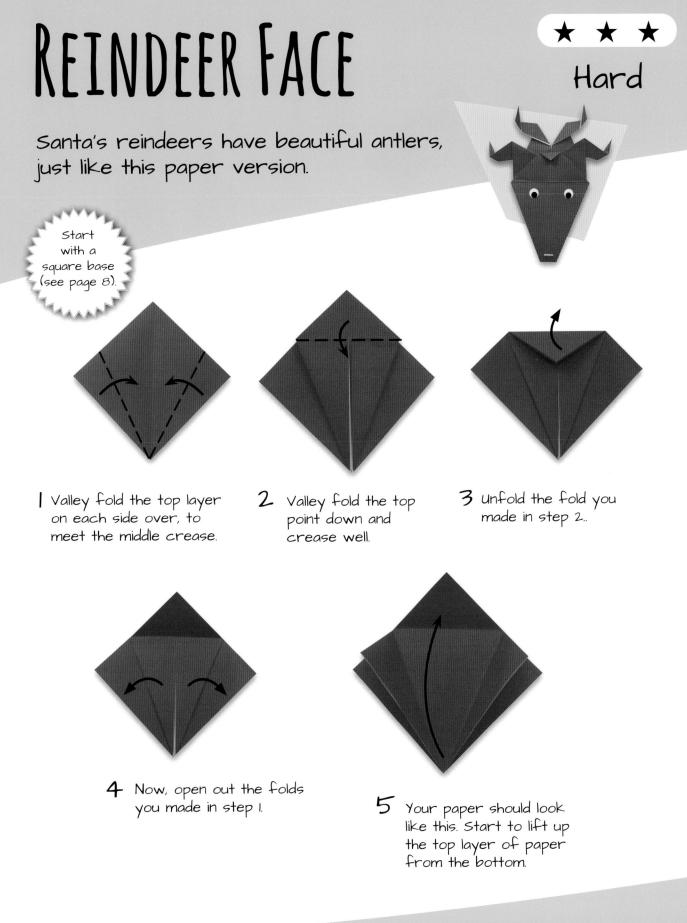

Start with a square base (see page 8).

1 Valley fold the top layer on each side over, to meet the middle crease.

2 Valley fold the top point down and crease well.

3 Unfold the fold you made in step 2..

4 Now, open out the folds you made in step 1.

5 Your paper should look like this. Start to lift up the top layer of paper from the bottom.

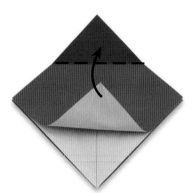

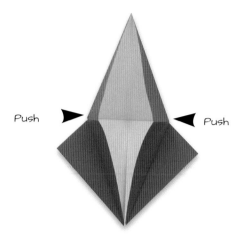

6 Keep lifting up the top layer to open out the pocket. Use your finger to help it fold along the horizontal crease you made in step 2.

7 Gently push in the sides to create a kite shape. Press the paper flat.

8 Your paper should look like this. Turn it over.

9 Repeat steps 1-7 on the other side.

10 Your paper should look like this. Make a valley fold on the bottom left-hand point, as shown. Fold it the other way, so it's also a mountain fold. Then turn it into an inside reverse fold (see page 10).

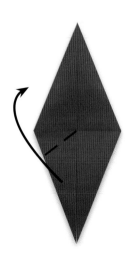

11 Your paper should look like this. Press the fold on the left flat.

12 Repeat steps 10-11 on the right-hand side.

13 Your paper should look like this now. Mountain fold the top flap down.

14 Make a small valley fold in the bottom tip.

Close-up

15 Now, valley fold the bottom of the paper over again.

Close-up

16 Valley fold the point of the triangle at the front of your paper down.

17 Then valley fold the left point down and across.

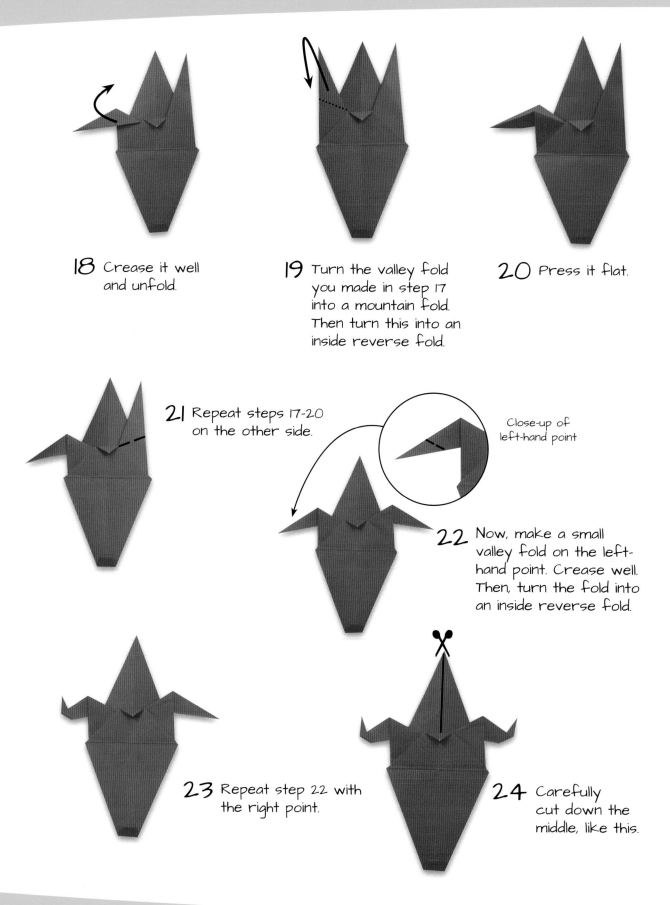

18 Crease it well and unfold.

19 Turn the valley fold you made in step 17 into a mountain fold. Then turn this into an inside reverse fold.

20 Press it flat.

21 Repeat steps 17-20 on the other side.

Close-up of left-hand point

22 Now, make a small valley fold on the left-hand point. Crease well. Then, turn the fold into an inside reverse fold.

23 Repeat step 22 with the right point.

24 Carefully cut down the middle, like this.

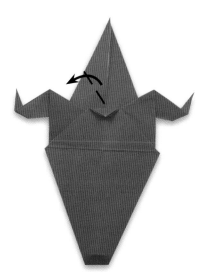

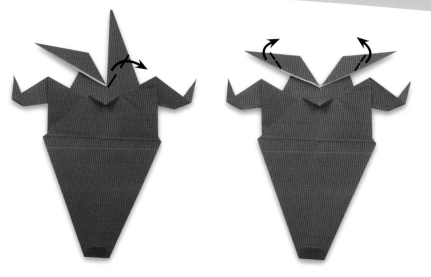

25 Make a valley fold in the left-hand point, so it sticks out sideways.

26 Do the same on the right-hand side.

27 Valley fold the tip of each point up, like this, to complete your reindeer's antlers.

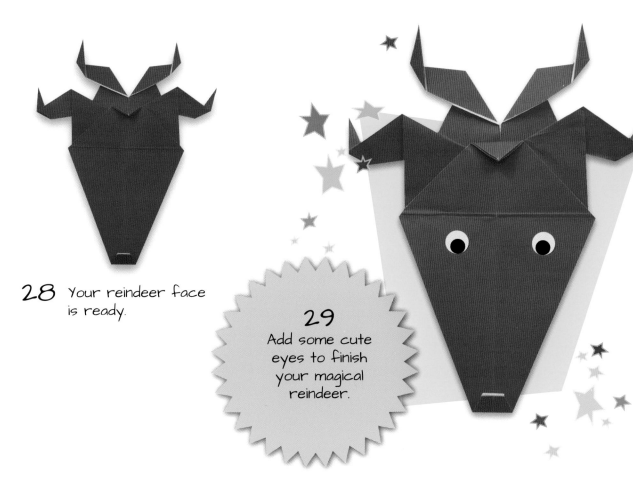

28 Your reindeer face is ready.

29 Add some cute eyes to finish your magical reindeer.

ELF

Santa's elves make the Christmas toys. You'll need two sheets of paper to make this cute little helper!

TO MAKE THE BODY

1 With the paper like this, make valley folds on the left and right sides.

2 Turn the paper 90°.

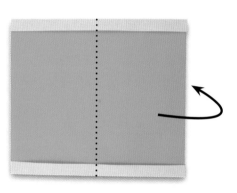

3 Mountain fold the paper down the middle.

4 Your paper should look like this. Unfold all folds and turn it over.

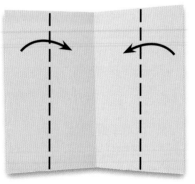

5 Fold both sides to the middle crease.

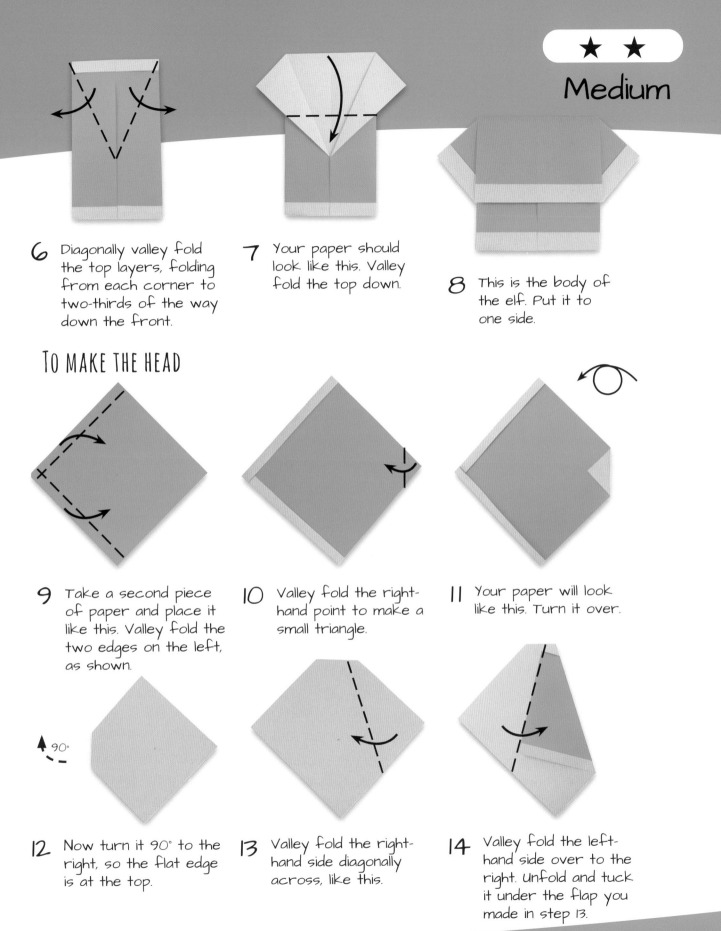

6 Diagonally valley fold the top layers, folding from each corner to two-thirds of the way down the front.

7 Your paper should look like this. Valley fold the top down.

8 This is the body of the elf. Put it to one side.

TO MAKE THE HEAD

9 Take a second piece of paper and place it like this. Valley fold the two edges on the left, as shown.

10 Valley fold the right-hand point to make a small triangle.

11 Your paper will look like this. Turn it over.

90°

12 Now turn it 90° to the right, so the flat edge is at the top.

13 Valley fold the right-hand side diagonally across, like this.

14 Valley fold the left-hand side over to the right. Unfold and tuck it under the flap you made in step 13.

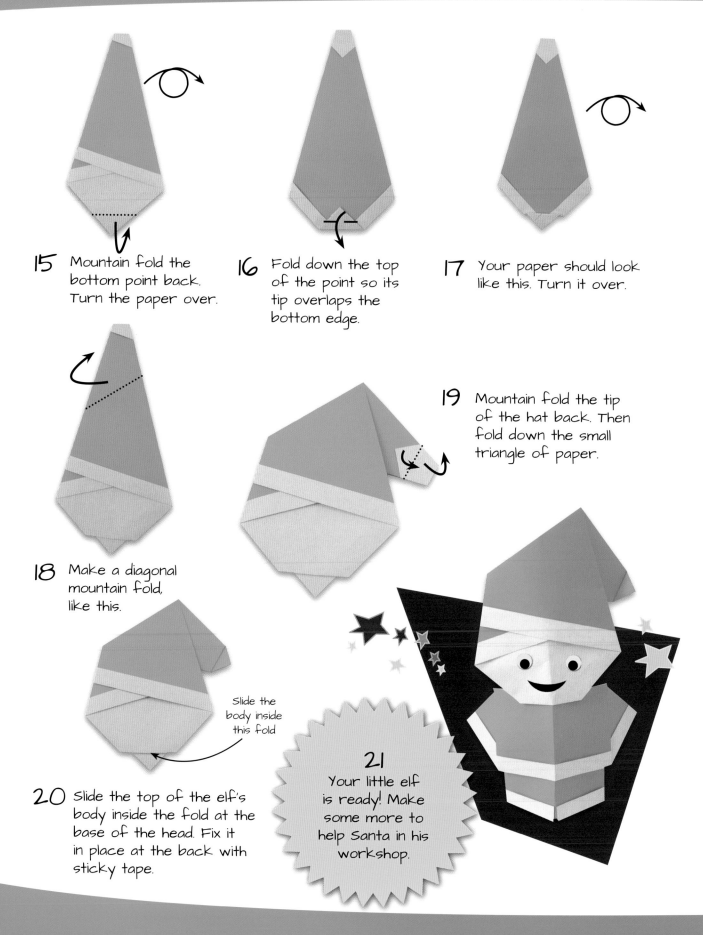

15 Mountain fold the bottom point back. Turn the paper over.

16 Fold down the top of the point so its tip overlaps the bottom edge.

17 Your paper should look like this. Turn it over.

18 Make a diagonal mountain fold, like this.

19 Mountain fold the tip of the hat back. Then fold down the small triangle of paper.

Slide the body inside this fold

20 Slide the top of the elf's body inside the fold at the base of the head. Fix it in place at the back with sticky tape.

21 Your little elf is ready! Make some more to help Santa in his workshop.

STOCKING

This cheerful Christmas stocking makes a great decoration. You could stuff it with little candies, too!

Start with a kite base (see page 6).

1 Turn the paper over.

2 Valley fold the top triangle down.

3 Open out the fold.

4 Valley fold the top point down to where the creases cross.

5 Valley fold the top of the paper down to the horizontal crease.

6 Now fold the top of the paper down again along the crease line.

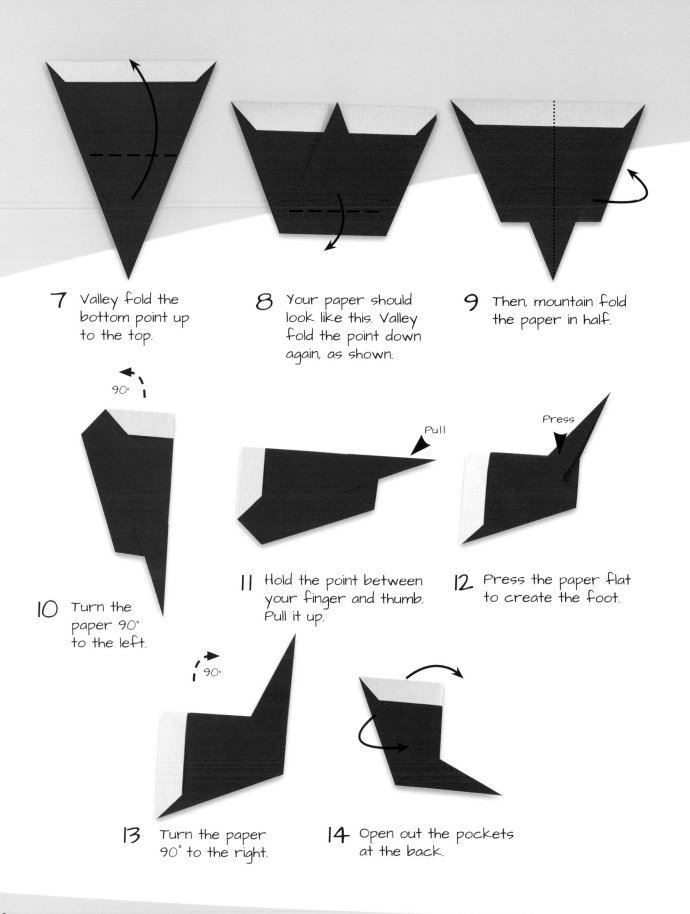

7 Valley fold the bottom point up to the top.

8 Your paper should look like this. Valley fold the point down again, as shown.

9 Then, mountain fold the paper in half.

90°

10 Turn the paper 90° to the left.

Pull

11 Hold the point between your finger and thumb. Pull it up.

Press

12 Press the paper flat to create the foot.

90°

13 Turn the paper 90° to the right.

14 Open out the pockets at the back.

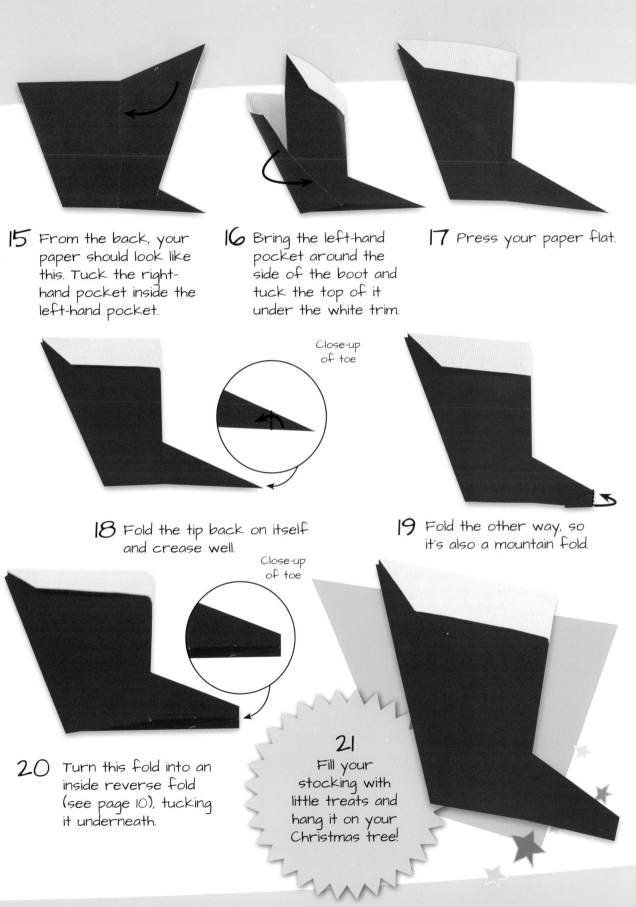

15 From the back, your paper should look like this. Tuck the right-hand pocket inside the left-hand pocket.

16 Bring the left-hand pocket around the side of the boot and tuck the top of it under the white trim.

17 Press your paper flat.

Close-up of toe

18 Fold the tip back on itself and crease well.

19 Fold the other way, so it's also a mountain fold.

Close-up of toe

20 Turn this fold into an inside reverse fold (see page 10), tucking it underneath.

21 Fill your stocking with little treats and hang it on your Christmas tree!

SNOWFLAKE

Paper cut snowflakes are a classic Christmas decoration.

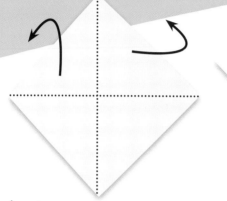

1 With your paper like this, make a mountain fold from right to left, and unfold. Then, make a mountain fold from top to bottom.

2 Your paper should look like this. Turn it over, so the point is facing upward.

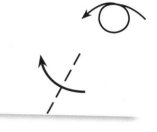

3 Valley fold the right-hand corner up and to the left, so the tip sticks out on the other side. Turn your paper over.

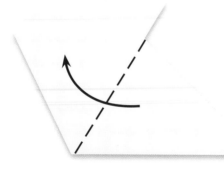

4 Now, valley fold the second bottom corner up and to the left.

5 Your paper should look like this. Turn it over.

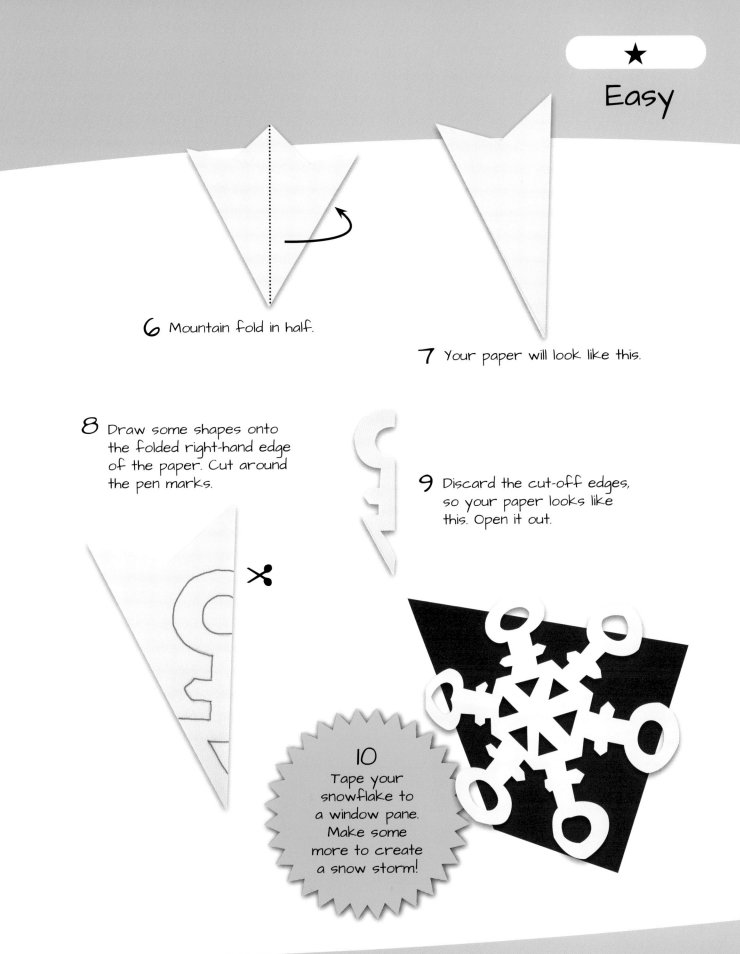

6 Mountain fold in half.

7 Your paper will look like this.

8 Draw some shapes onto the folded right-hand edge of the paper. Cut around the pen marks.

9 Discard the cut-off edges, so your paper looks like this. Open it out.

10
Tape your snowflake to a window pane. Make some more to create a snow storm!

Candy Cane

These cute paper candy canes are a great way to brighten up your Christmas tree.

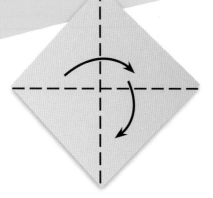

1 Place your paper like this. Valley fold your paper in half from top to bottom, and unfold. Then valley fold from left to right, and unfold.

2 Fold the right-hand side to the left, making the fold about 6 mm (¼ in) to the right of the middle crease.

3 Your paper should look like this. Turn it over from top to bottom.

4 Valley fold the right-hand edge along the crease line.

5 Keep folding the flap over and over, creasing well each time, until there is no more paper left to fold.

6 Now, make a diagonal valley fold a third of the way down, as shown.

7 Your paper should look like this. Turn it over.

8 Valley fold the tip of the paper down, as shown.

9 Turn the paper over.

10 Make some more canes to hang from the branches of your Christmas tree!

CANDLE

You'll need two pieces of yellow or orange paper to fold your own Christmas candle.

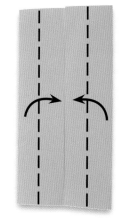

TO MAKE THE CANDLE

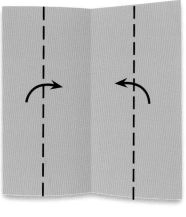

1 Place the first piece of paper like this. Valley fold it in half and unfold.

2 Fold in both sides to meet the middle crease.

3 Valley fold the sides in again to meet the middle crease.

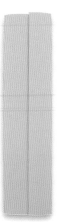

4 Your paper should look like this. Open out all the folds.

5 Valley fold the top, 2.5cm (1 in) from the top edge.

6 Your paper will look like this. Open the fold you made in step 5.

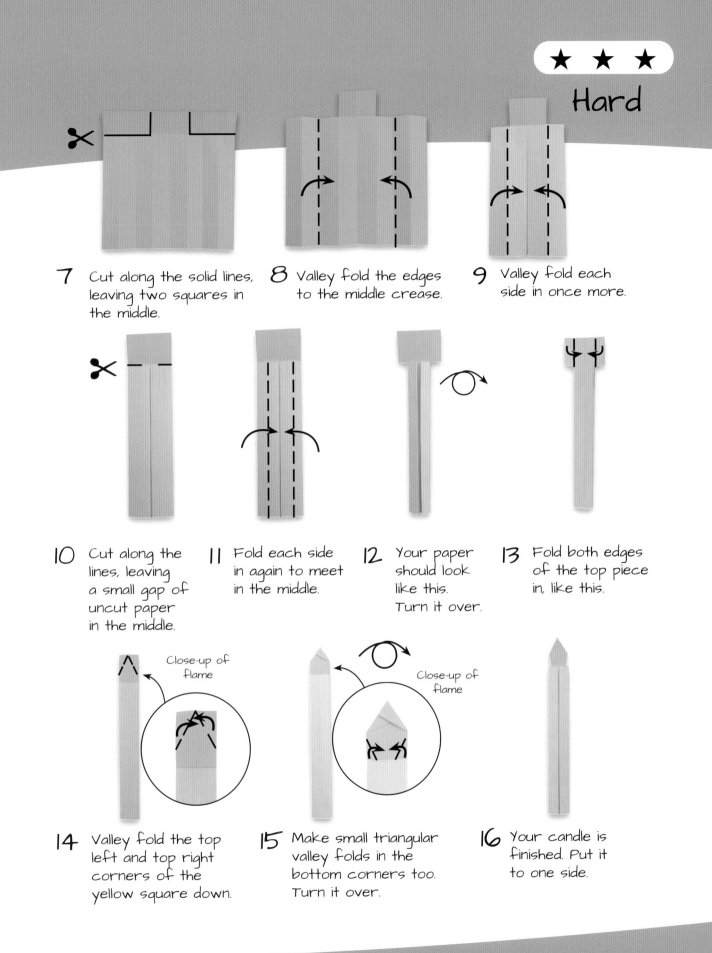

7 Cut along the solid lines, leaving two squares in the middle.

8 Valley fold the edges to the middle crease.

9 Valley fold each side in once more.

10 Cut along the lines, leaving a small gap of uncut paper in the middle.

11 Fold each side in again to meet in the middle.

12 Your paper should look like this. Turn it over.

13 Fold both edges of the top piece in, like this.

Close-up of flame

14 Valley fold the top left and top right corners of the yellow square down.

Close-up of flame

15 Make small triangular valley folds in the bottom corners too. Turn it over.

16 Your candle is finished. Put it to one side.

To make the candle's base

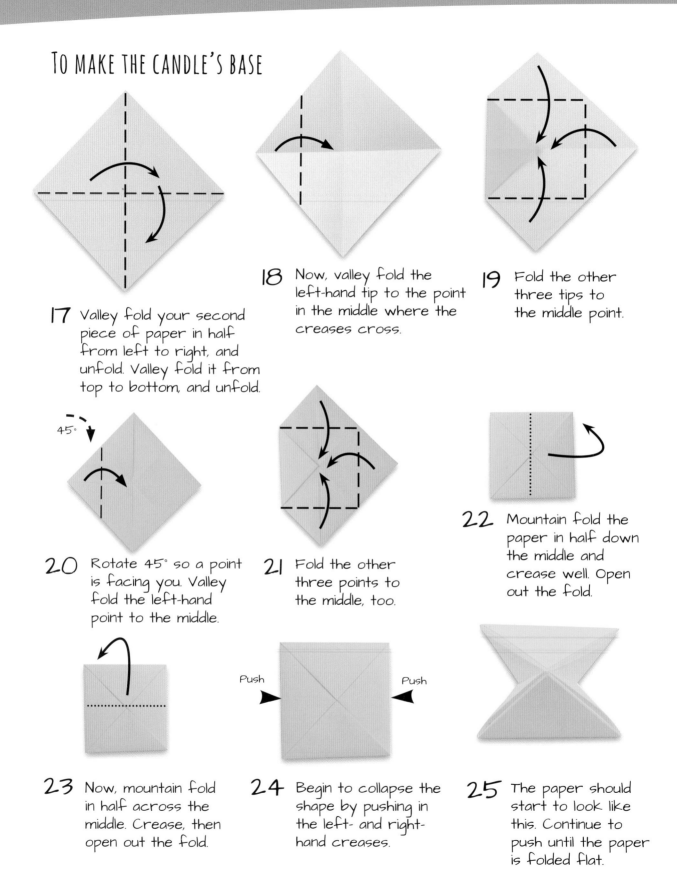

17 Valley fold your second piece of paper in half from left to right, and unfold. Valley fold it from top to bottom, and unfold.

18 Now, valley fold the left-hand tip to the point in the middle where the creases cross.

19 Fold the other three tips to the middle point.

45°

20 Rotate 45° so a point is facing you. Valley fold the left-hand point to the middle.

21 Fold the other three points to the middle, too.

22 Mountain fold the paper in half down the middle and crease well. Open out the fold.

23 Now, mountain fold in half across the middle. Crease, then open out the fold.

Push   Push

24 Begin to collapse the shape by pushing in the left- and right-hand creases.

25 The paper should start to look like this. Continue to push until the paper is folded flat.

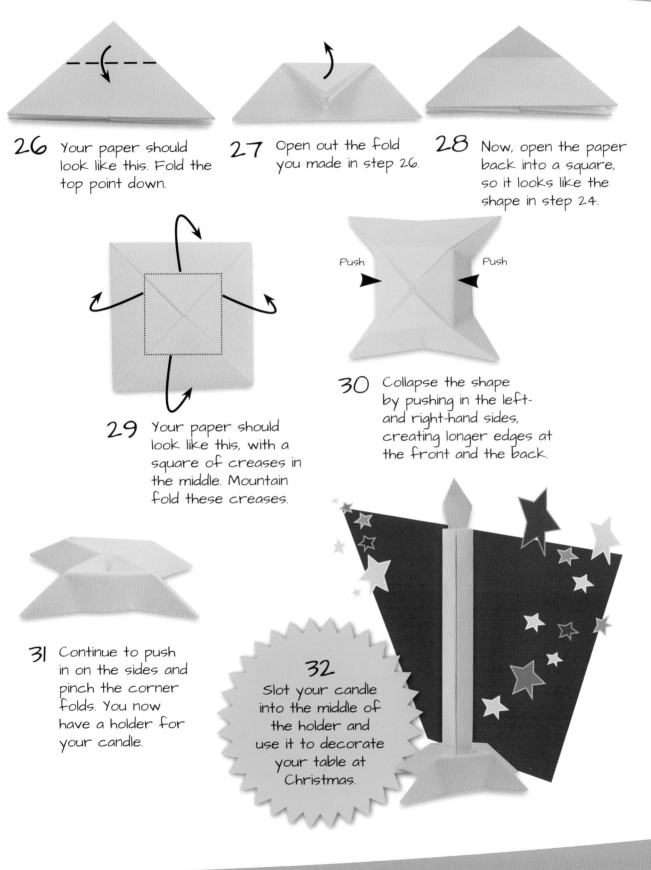

26 Your paper should look like this. Fold the top point down.

27 Open out the fold you made in step 26.

28 Now, open the paper back into a square, so it looks like the shape in step 24.

29 Your paper should look like this, with a square of creases in the middle. Mountain fold these creases.

30 Collapse the shape by pushing in the left- and right-hand sides, creating longer edges at the front and the back.

Push

Push

31 Continue to push in on the sides and pinch the corner folds. You now have a holder for your candle.

32 Slot your candle into the middle of the holder and use it to decorate your table at Christmas.

SLEIGH

Fold your own paper sleigh for Santa to pack with presents!

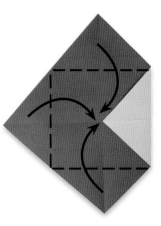

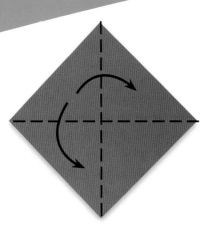

1 With the paper like this, make a horizontal valley fold, and unfold. Then make a vertical valley fold, and unfold.

2 Fold the right-hand point to the middle point.

3 Fold the other three points to the middle point.

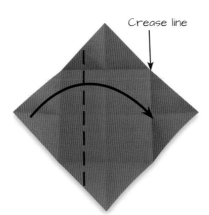

Crease line

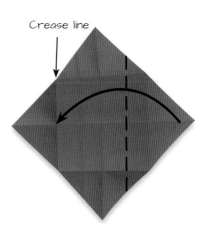

Crease line

4 Your paper should look like this. Open out the folds.

5 Fold the left point over to the right to meet the crease you made in step 2. Unfold.

6 Fold the right point over to meet the crease you made on the left in step 3. Unfold.

7 Fold the top point down to meet the crease you made in the bottom at step 3.

8 Your paper should look like this. Unfold.

9 Fold the bottom point up to meet the crease you made in the top at step 3.

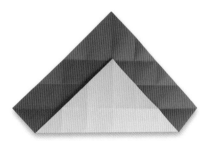

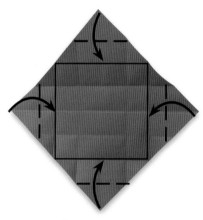

10 Your paper should look like this. Open out the fold.

11 Fold in each point so they meet the creases indicated by the square above.

12 Your paper should look like this. Open out the folds.

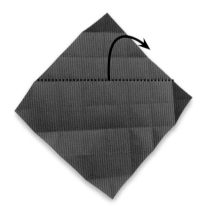

13 Mountain fold along the dotted line. This is the crease you made in step 7.

14 Mountain fold along the dotted line. Then rotate the paper 180°.

15 Your paper should look like this. Make diagonal valley folds in the squares shown.

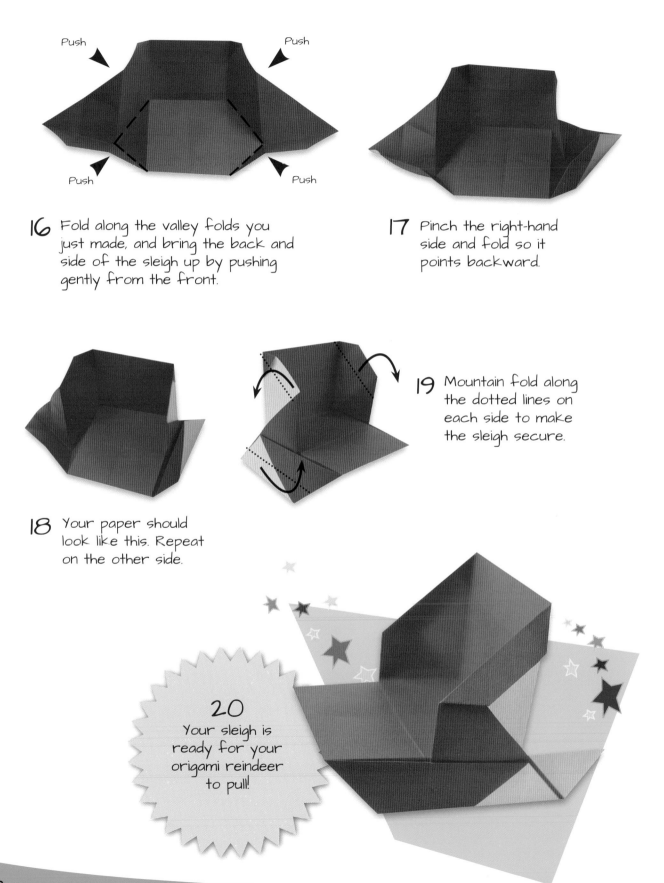

Push   Push

Push   Push

16 Fold along the valley folds you just made, and bring the back and side of the sleigh up by pushing gently from the front.

17 Pinch the right-hand side and fold so it points backward.

19 Mountain fold along the dotted lines on each side to make the sleigh secure.

18 Your paper should look like this. Repeat on the other side.

20
Your sleigh is ready for your origami reindeer to pull!

PRESENT

★ ★

Medium

Make a pretty present for your workshop scene. You'll need two pieces of paper for this model.

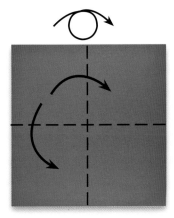

1 With the paper like this, make two valley folds, as shown. Unfold and turn the paper over.

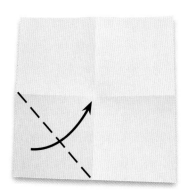

2 Fold the bottom left corner to the middle point.

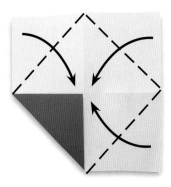

3 Fold the other three points to the middle.

4 Fold the left-hand edge to the middle point.

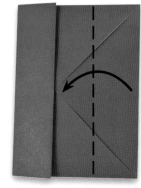

5 Fold the right-hand edge to the middle point.

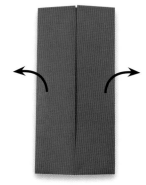

6 Open out the folds.

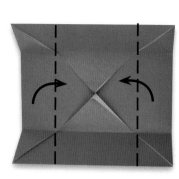

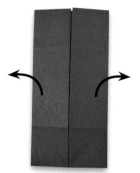

7 Your paper should look like this. Turn it 90°.

8 Repeat the folds you made at steps 4 and 5.

9 Open out the folds.

Push

10 Open out the top and bottom flaps.

11 Fold the left and right sides up, to form two sides of the box.

12 Holding the sides, push in along the top left diagonal fold.

Push

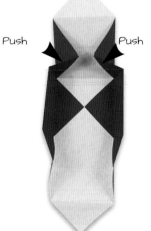

Push   Push

Push

13 Your paper should look like this. Repeat step 12 on the other side, pushing in along the top right fold.

14 Continue to push along the diagonal folds until the two points meet. Press the folds flat.

15 Fold the top point down, like this.

Push

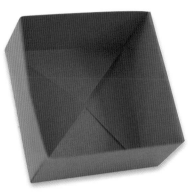

16 Press the tip of the flap in and down to meet the other two points, forming another side of the box.

17 Your paper should look like this. Now repeat steps 12-16 on the other side.

18 This is one half of your box.

19 Repeat steps 1-18 to make the other half of your box. Squeeze the sides slightly to slot it into the first half.

20 Your Christmas box is ready. Put a little present inside and give it to someone special!

Snowman

You'll need two pieces of paper to make this jolly snowman. He's dressed for the weather in his warm hat and scarf.

To make the body

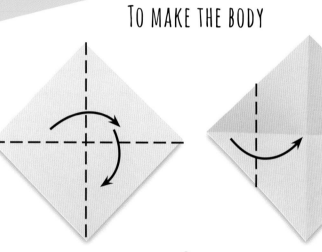

1 Place your paper like this. Make one valley fold from top to bottom, and unfold. Make another one from left to right, and unfold.

2 Your paper should look like this. Fold the left-hand point to meet the middle crease.

3 Fold the tip back to meet the left-hand edge.

4 Your paper should look like this. Unfold the fold you made in step 3.

5 Now, fold the tip back to meet the crease you made in step 3.

6 Valley fold the white triangle in half, so the edge meets the crease made in step 3, too.

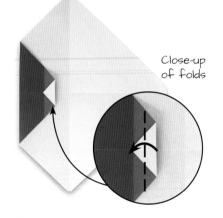

Close-up of folds

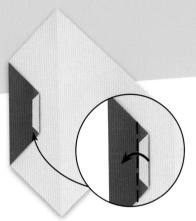

Horizontal crease

7 Fold the paper over once more, along the crease you made in step 3.

8 Your paper should look like this. Turn it over from top to bottom.

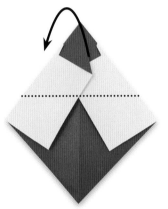

9 Place your finger on the horizontal crease. Valley fold the top point down. The tip on the left should meet the vertical crease.

90°

10 Your paper should look like this. Rotate it 90° to the right.

11 Make another diagonal valley fold, as shown.

12 Your paper should look like this. Mountain fold the top down then unfold.

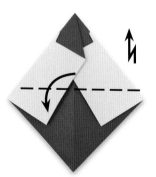

13 Now make a valley fold just below your mountain fold. Turn them into a step fold (page 6).

14 Valley fold the left-hand side. The tip should touch the middle crease.

15 Now valley fold the right-hand side in the same way.

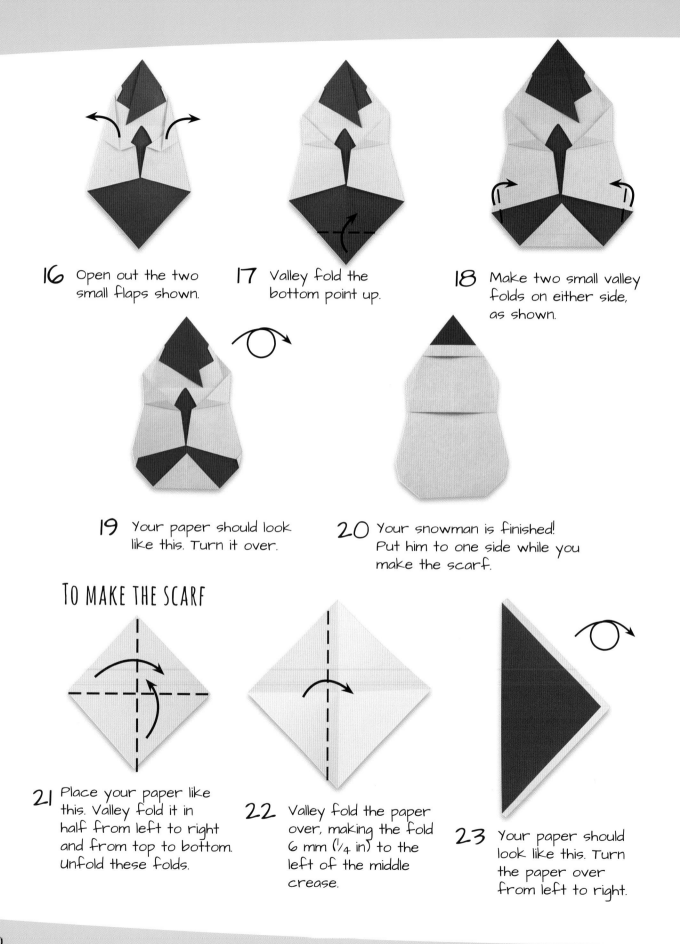

16 Open out the two small flaps shown.

17 Valley fold the bottom point up.

18 Make two small valley folds on either side, as shown.

19 Your paper should look like this. Turn it over.

20 Your snowman is finished! Put him to one side while you make the scarf.

To make the scarf

21 Place your paper like this. Valley fold it in half from left to right and from top to bottom. Unfold these folds.

22 Valley fold the paper over, making the fold 6 mm (¼ in) to the left of the middle crease.

23 Your paper should look like this. Turn the paper over from left to right.

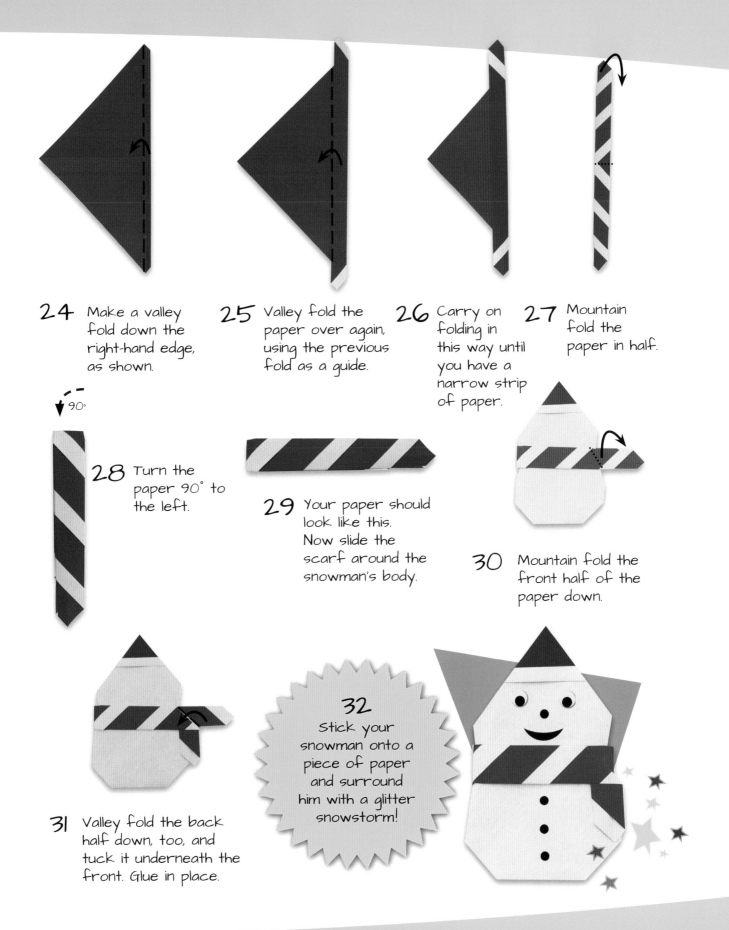

24 Make a valley fold down the right-hand edge, as shown.

25 Valley fold the paper over again, using the previous fold as a guide.

26 Carry on folding in this way until you have a narrow strip of paper.

27 Mountain fold the paper in half.

90°

28 Turn the paper 90° to the left.

29 Your paper should look like this. Now slide the scarf around the snowman's body.

30 Mountain fold the front half of the paper down.

31 Valley fold the back half down, too, and tuck it underneath the front. Glue in place.

32 Stick your snowman onto a piece of paper and surround him with a glitter snowstorm!

Star Chain

Hang this pretty star decoration around your home for a festive feel.

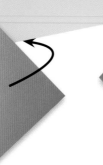

Start with a square base (see page 8).

1 Mountain fold your paper in half.

2 Your paper will look like this.

3 Use tracing paper to transfer the shape of half a star down the folded edge of the paper Cut out the star.

4 Open out the four folded stars and fan out the folds of the original piece of paper.

5 Overlap the stars, one above the other, and glue them together where they touch. Glue the top of the top star to the bottom point of the folded paper.

6 Add a loop of thin string or cotton to hang up your stars as a decoration.

CHAPTER 5

MONSTERS

From snakes and spiders to werewolves and dragons, these projects are monsterously fun! Or try making a witch or a wizard from a single piece of paper—that really is magic!

DRACULA

Let's start with the most famous undead character of them all–the dastardly count, Dracula. Watch your necks!

1

Place your paper like this with a corner facing you. Valley fold it in half from left to right, and unfold. Then valley fold it from top to bottom, and unfold.

2

Fold the top point down to the middle crease.

3

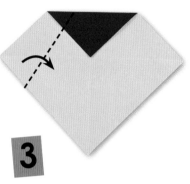

Fold the top left edge over at an angle, as shown.

4

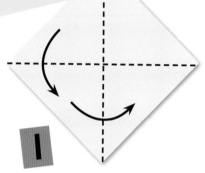

Repeat Step 3 with the top right edge.

5

TURN OVER

Your paper should look like this. Turn it over from left to right.

6

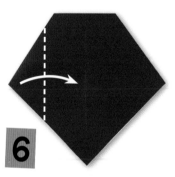

Fold the left-hand corner over to the middle crease.

7

Repeat Step 6 with the right-hand corner.

8

Fold up the bottom point to meet the other two central points.

9 Fold the left and right central points to the sides, as shown.

UNFOLD

10 Unfold the left flap you made in Step 9, as shown.

LIFT

11 Lift the lower point and move it up and to the left so the flap forms a triangle shape.

FLATTEN

12 Flatten the paper down.

13 Repeat Steps 10 and 11 on the right-hand side.

14 Fold up the bottom left corner so it lines up with the flap you made in Steps 10 and 11.

15 Repeat Step 14 on the right-hand side.

TURN OVER

16 Your paper should look like this. Turn it over from left to right.

AAARGH!

17 Add a sinister face and fangs. It looks like Dracula is hungry—let's get him a bite to eat.

VAMPIRE FANGS

Here's how to make a pair of super-sharp vampire teeth. Make sure you crease all your folds well.

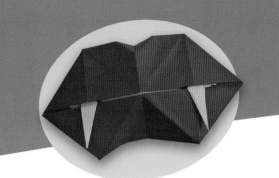

1 Place your paper like this. Valley fold it in half from left to right, and unfold. Then valley fold it from top to bottom, and unfold.

2 Fold the left corner over to the middle crease.

3 Repeat Step 2 with the other three corners.

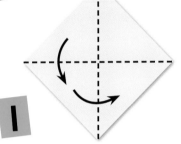

4 Fold the bottom left corner up to the middle point.

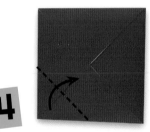

5 Repeat Step 4 with the other three corners.

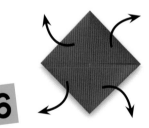

6 Open out the folds you made in Steps 4 and 5.

7 Fold the left edge over to the middle.

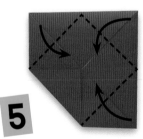

8 Fold the right edge over to the middle.

UNFOLD **UNFOLD**

9 Unfold the folds you made in Steps 7 and 8.

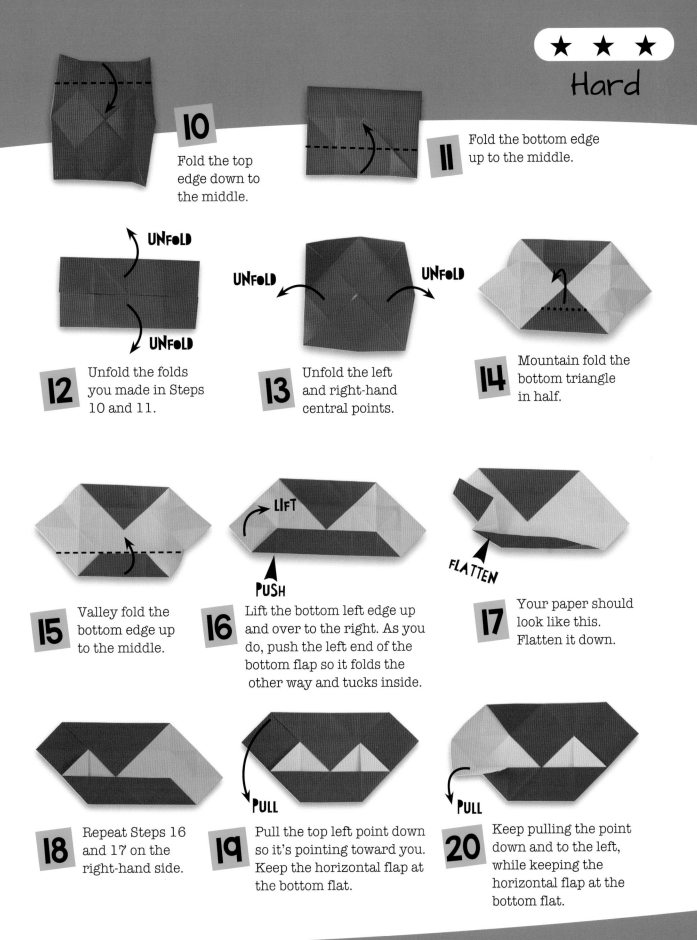

10 Fold the top edge down to the middle.

11 Fold the bottom edge up to the middle.

12 Unfold the folds you made in Steps 10 and 11.

13 Unfold the left and right-hand central points.

14 Mountain fold the bottom triangle in half.

15 Valley fold the bottom edge up to the middle.

16 Lift the bottom left edge up and over to the right. As you do, push the left end of the bottom flap so it folds the other way and tucks inside.

17 Your paper should look like this. Flatten it down.

18 Repeat Steps 16 and 17 on the right-hand side.

19 Pull the top left point down so it's pointing toward you. Keep the horizontal flap at the bottom flat.

20 Keep pulling the point down and to the left, while keeping the horizontal flap at the bottom flat.

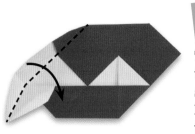

21 The top-left edge of the paper should start to flip over. Fold it down along the line shown.

22 Repeat Steps 19 to 21 on the right-hand side.

23 Your paper should look like this. Open up the two middle flaps where they meet at the top. Keep the bottom points in position so your paper looks like the image in Step 24.

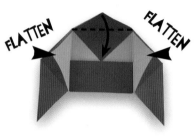

24 Fold the top edge down and over while flattening down the white triangles at the side.

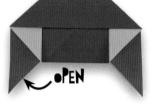

25 Open up the bottom left point so it forms a cone shape.

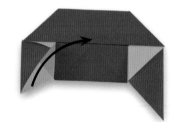

26 Bring the point up and to the right. Flatten it down so it matches the image in Step 27.

27 Repeat Steps 25 and 26 on the right-hand side.

28 Fold the bottom left point of the upper layer up to the middle.

29 Fold the top-left point of the upper layer down to the middle.

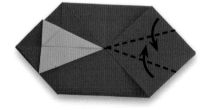

30 Repeat Steps 28 and 29 on the right-hand side.

31 Pinch the left white triangle so it forms a beak-like shape.

32 Bring the beak shape down. Flatten it so it's pointing down. This is your first fang.

33 Repeat Steps 31 and 32 on the right-hand side. This is your other fang.

OPEN

TUCK INSIDE

TUCK INSIDE

OPEN

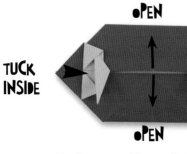

34 Open up the red pieces of paper in the middle and tuck inside everything apart from the tips of the fangs, which should be left hanging down over the lower lip.

35 Make a Cupid's bow by pinching the top of the paper to form a small V-shaped mountain fold around a vertical valley fold.

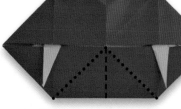

36 Go over some folds you've already made to form a V-shaped mountain fold around a vertical valley fold at the bottom of the lips.

37 **And there are your vampire fangs—all sharp and ready to bite. Time to find some necks.**

207

ALIEN

Do you believe in aliens? Making this project may just convince you. It's out of this world!

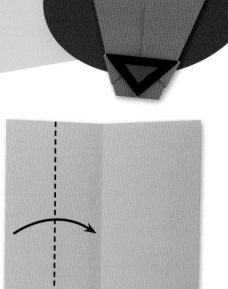

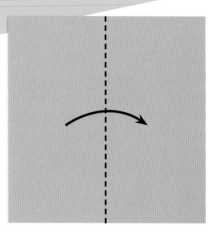

 Place your paper like this, white side up, with a straight facing you. Fold it in half from left to right, then unfold.

 Fold the left-hand edge over to the middle crease.

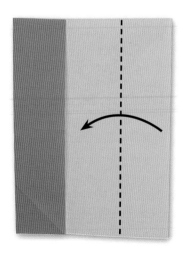

 Fold the right-hand edge over to the middle crease.

 Fold the top point of the upper layer across to the left edge.

208

5

Repeat Step 4 with the other three corners.

6

Fold the top left point over to the middle crease.

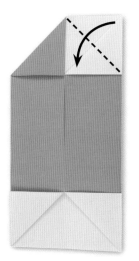

7

Fold the top right point over to the middle crease.

UNFOLD   UNFOLD

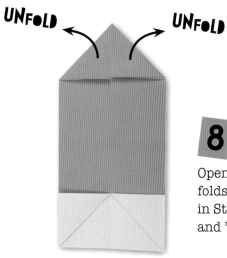

8

Open out the folds you made in Steps 6 and 7.

PUSH

q

Bring the top left point over to the middle crease again. As you do, push up the fold that's been highlighted from below so that it becomes a mountain fold.

FLATTEN

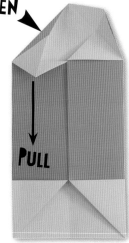

PULL

10

Pull the point of the mountain fold down, as shown. Flatten it down. This is your alien's first eye.

11

Your paper should look like this. Repeat Steps 9 and 10 on the right-hand side.

12

Mountain fold the top point over and behind.

13

Fold up the bottom edge, as shown, to create a new flap.

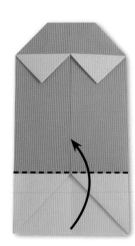

14

Fold the top left point of the new flap down to the bottom edge.

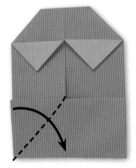

15

Repeat Step 14 on the right-hand side.

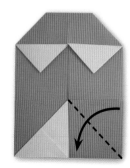

16

Fold up the left point of the upper layer, as shown.

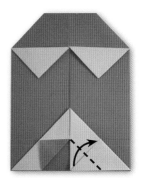

17

Repeat Step 16 on the right-hand side.

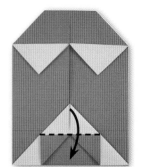

18

Fold the middle point over and down so it touches the bottom edge.

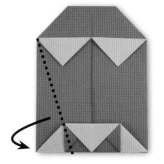

19

Mountain fold the left-hand side of the paper at an angle.

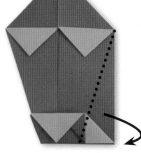

20

Repeat Step 19 on the right-hand side.

21

Add some spooky-looking eyes and your alien is ready to board its spaceship.

TAKE ME TO YOUR LEADER!

GIANT SNAKE

This snake may be a giant but it moves so quietly that it can easily sneak up on you—make sure you stay out of biting range!

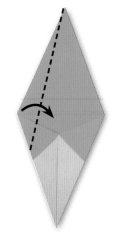

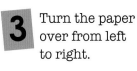

1 Place your paper white side up with a corner facing you. Valley fold it in half from right to left, and unfold.

2 Fold the left and right top edges to the middle crease, as shown.

3 Turn the paper over from left to right.

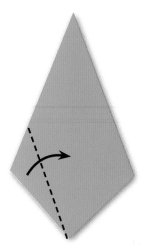

4 Fold the bottom left edge over to the middle crease.

5 Repeat step 4 on the right-hand side.

6 Fold the top left edge over to the middle crease.

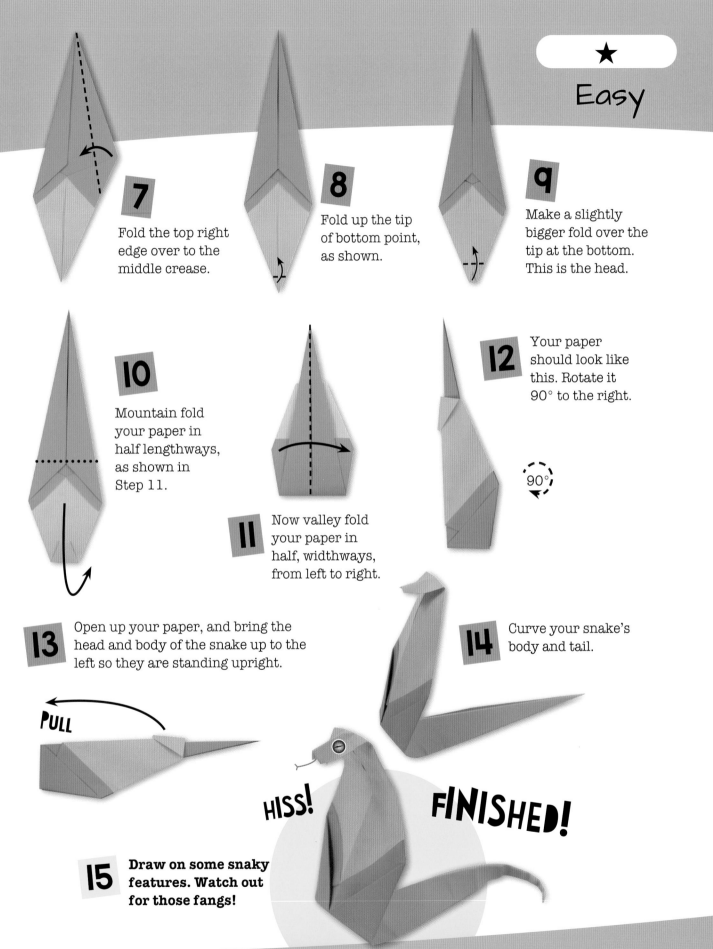

7 Fold the top right edge over to the middle crease.

8 Fold up the tip of bottom point, as shown.

9 Make a slightly bigger fold over the tip at the bottom. This is the head.

10 Mountain fold your paper in half lengthways, as shown in Step 11.

11 Now valley fold your paper in half, widthways, from left to right.

12 Your paper should look like this. Rotate it 90° to the right.

90°

13 Open up your paper, and bring the head and body of the snake up to the left so they are standing upright.

14 Curve your snake's body and tail.

PULL

HISS!

FINISHED!

15 Draw on some snaky features. Watch out for those fangs!

Snapping Nessie

There's no need for you to search for the Loch Ness Monster, the world's most mysterious lake creature. You can just make your own!

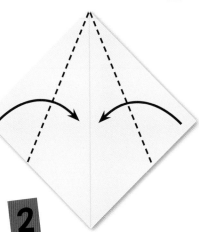

1

Place your paper white side up with a corner facing you. Valley fold it in half from left to right, and unfold.

2

Fold the left and right top edges to the middle crease, as shown.

3

Fold the bottom left and bottom right edges over to the middle crease.

4

Fold the paper in half from bottom to top.

5

Fold the top point of the upper layer down to the bottom edge.

6

Fold the top point of the bottom layer down and to the left, as shown.

7

Fold the bottom point up and to the left.

UNFOLD

8 Unfold the fold you made in Step 6.

9 Now valley fold the point over and down to the right.

UNFOLD

10 Open up the fold again.

PUSH ◀ **PUSH**

11 Push the paper together along the fold lines you made in Steps 6 and 9 until it makes a pointed shape sticking straight up at you.

PUSH ▶

12 Your paper should look like this. Push the shape you made in Step 11 over to the right and flatten it down.

13 Now unfold the fold you made in Step 7 and repeat Steps 8 to 12 on this side too.

14 Mountain fold the lower half of the paper in half to create the neck.

15 Add some eyes and Nessie is ready to peer out of the water. If you open and close the neck, Nessie will snap its jaws.

OPEN AND CLOSE

SNAP!

OPEN AND CLOSE

WITCH AND BROOMSTICK

Hubble, bubble, toil and ... hopefully not too much folding trouble. You'll need two pieces of paper and some scissors for this one.

THE WITCH

1

Let's start with the witch. Place your paper like this, white side up, with a corner facing you. Fold it in half from left to right, and unfold.

2

Fold the left and right top edges to the middle crease, as shown.

3

Fold the bottom point up to meet the flaps you made in Step 2.

4

Make a fold in the left-hand upper layer as shown.

5

Repeat Step 4 on the right-hand side.

6

Your paper should look like this. Fold it in half from right to left.

7 Fold the top point down and to the left, as shown, to create a new flap.

8 Unfold the fold you made in step 7.

OPEN

9 Open up the flap you made in step 7. Be sure to open all four layers.

FLATTEN

FLATTEN

10 Make sure the white layers inside the flap are separated and form a triangle shape. Flatten the paper down.

11 Fold the left-hand point back to make the witch's hat—and to reveal the witch's face.

12 Your paper should look like this. Rotate it to the left so it matches the image in Step 13.

13 Make a small fold, as shown, to give the witch's hat a brim.

14 **Add a face and your witch is ready to cast her first spell. She's not quite ready to travel, however. So put her to one side and go grab the other piece of paper.**

WITCH AND BROOMSTICK

THE BROOMSTICK

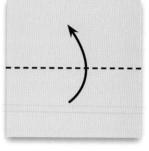

1 Fold the paper in half from bottom to top, then unfold.

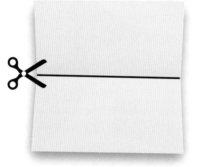

2 Use the scissors to cut your paper in half along the crease you made in Step 1.

3 Take one of the halves and fold it in half from bottom to top, then unfold.

4 Fold the top edge down to the middle crease.

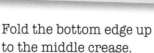

5 Fold the bottom edge up to the middle crease.

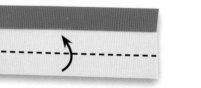

6 Fold the right edge back to the left. Make the crease just under half the distance from the right edge to the middle.

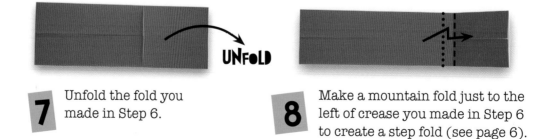

UNFOLD

7 Unfold the fold you made in Step 6.

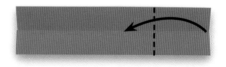

8 Make a mountain fold just to the left of crease you made in Step 6 to create a step fold (see page 6).

FLATTEN ▶

9 Flatten the step fold down.

10 Fold the top edge that's to the left of the step fold straight down to just over the middle crease. But fold the top edge that's to the right of the step fold down at an angle, as shown.

FLATTEN   **FLATTEN**

11 Flatten the paper down.

12 Fold the bottom edge that's to the left of the step fold up to just below the top edge.

13 Fold the bottom edge that's to the right of the step fold up at an angle, as shown.

TURN OVER

14 Your paper should look like this. Turn it over from top to bottom.

15 Time to give your witch her transport—get the first piece of paper.

16 Place your witch carefully on her broomstick—you don't want her to fall off.

I'VE PUT A SPELL ON YOU!

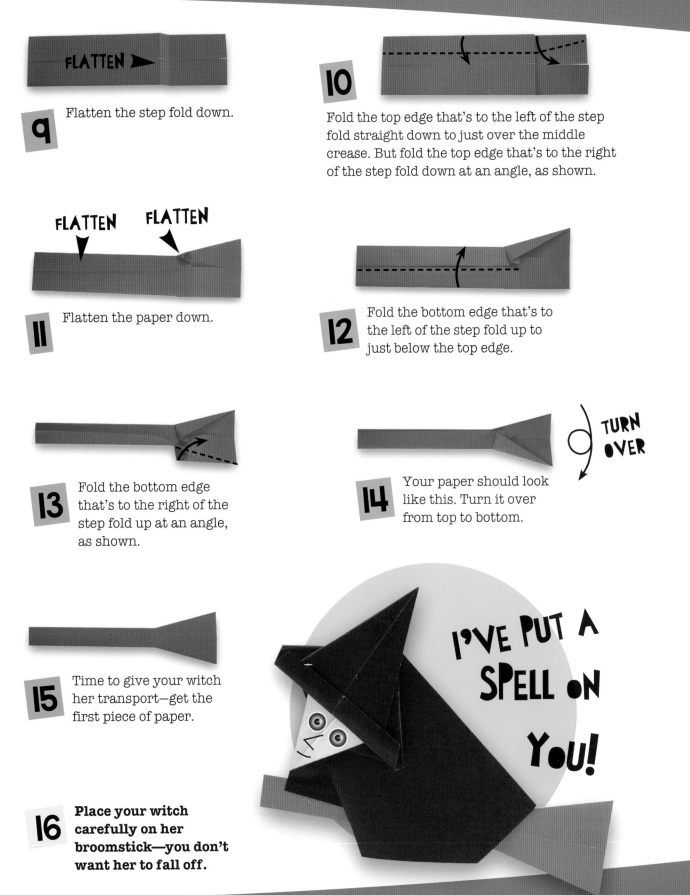

219

WITCH'S CAT

A witch's best friend is her magical cat. Once you've mastered the folds, try it again with a piece of paper a quarter of the size—to get a cat that can sit on the broomstick, too.

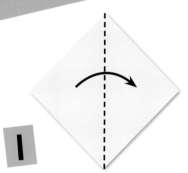

1 Fold the paper in half from left to right, then unfold.

2 Fold the left and right bottom edges to the middle crease.

3 Fold the left and right points over to the middle crease, as shown, to create two new flaps.

4 Fold up the bottom point so it goes just above where the middle left and right points meet.

5 Fold the point back down again to create a step fold (see page 6), as shown.

6 Fold the paper in half from right to left.

7 Make a diagonal fold on the upper layer as shown, so the paper opens into a point at the top.

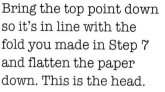

8 Bring the top point down so it's in line with the fold you made in Step 7 and flatten the paper down. This is the head.

9 Rotate the paper slightly to the left.

10 Fold the bottom point up.

11 Fold it the other way so it's also a mountain fold, then turn it into an outside reverse fold (see page 10).

12 Mountain fold up the bottom point and tuck it inside.

13 Repeat Step 12 on the opposite side.

14 Fold up the bottom point of the face.

15 Fold the point down again to form the cat's nose.

MEOW!

16 Make two step folds on either side of the face to form the ears.

17

Add some eyes and whiskers. Try to make your cat look as magical as possible.

WEREWOLF

Just a normal person by day, but a fiendish wolf by night—you don't want to meet this monster when the moon is full!

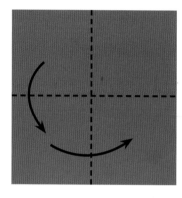

1 Place your paper like this, white side down. Valley fold it in half from top to bottom, and unfold. Then valley fold it in half from left to right, and unfold.

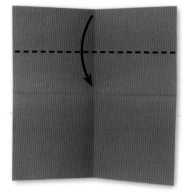

2 Valley fold the top edge down to the middle crease.

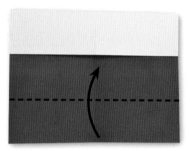

3 Fold the bottom edge up to the middle crease.

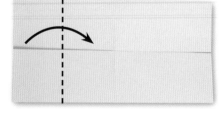

4 Valley fold the left edge to the middle crease.

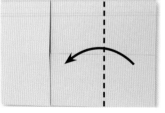

5 Valley fold the right edge to the middle crease.

UNFOLD | UNFOLD

6 Unfold the folds you made in Steps 4 and 5.

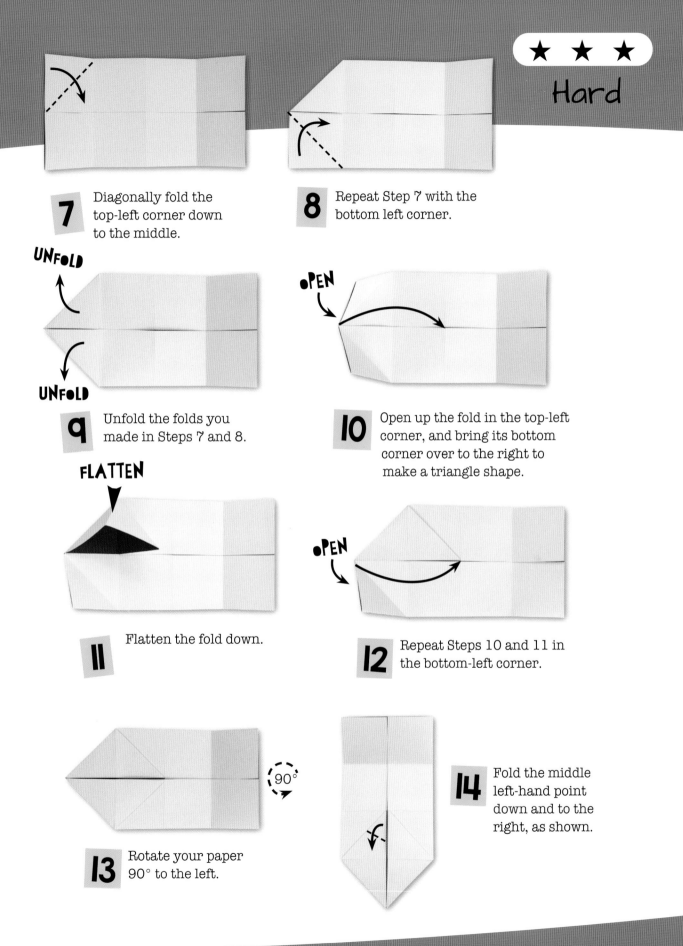

7 Diagonally fold the top-left corner down to the middle.

8 Repeat Step 7 with the bottom left corner.

UNFOLD

UNFOLD

9 Unfold the folds you made in Steps 7 and 8.

OPEN

10 Open up the fold in the top-left corner, and bring its bottom corner over to the right to make a triangle shape.

FLATTEN

11 Flatten the fold down.

OPEN

12 Repeat Steps 10 and 11 in the bottom-left corner.

90°

13 Rotate your paper 90° to the left.

14 Fold the middle left-hand point down and to the right, as shown.

15

Repeat Step 14 with the middle right-hand point.

16

Make a small fold to the top two layers on the middle left side, as shown, so that the paper matches the image for Step 17.

17

Repeat step 16 on the right-hand side.

 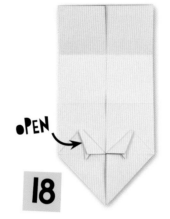

18

Open out the fold you made in Step 16.

19

Now fold both layers of the fold you made in Step 16 the other way, so it's now a mountain fold. Tuck it behind and flatten it down.

20

Repeat steps 18 and 19 on the right-hand side.

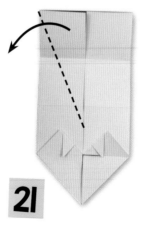

21

Fold the top-left middle point over to the left and down.

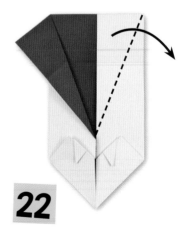

22

Repeat Step 21 on the right-hand side.

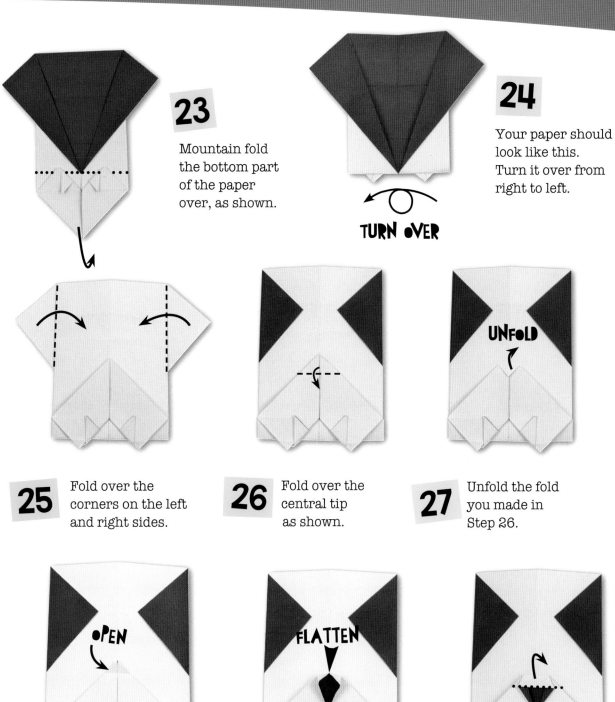

23 Mountain fold the bottom part of the paper over, as shown.

24 Your paper should look like this. Turn it over from right to left.

TURN OVER

25 Fold over the corners on the left and right sides.

26 Fold over the central tip as shown.

27 Unfold the fold you made in Step 26.

UNFOLD

OPEN

FLATTEN

28 Open out the tip and start to pull it apart so it looks like the image for Step 29.

29 Flatten the paper down along the fold you made in Step 26 so it makes a triangle shape.

30 Mountain fold the paper above the triangle, as shown, and tuck it behind.

31

Fold the top-left and top-right corners over.

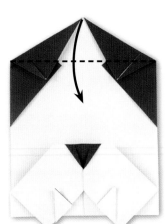

32

Fold over the top point

33

Make a step fold in the top left corner (see page 6) to form the first ear.

34

Repeat step 33 on the right-hand side.

35

Add scary eyes and your werewolf is ready to go on the prowl.

WIZARD

Unfortunately, there isn't a spell to create a magical origami wizard—so you'll just have to follow these instructions instead.

1 Place your paper white side up with a corner facing you. Valley fold it in half from left to right, then unfold.

2 Fold the left and right top edges down to the middle crease, as shown.

3 Fold the top point down to the right-hand point.

UNFOLD

4 Unfold the fold you made in Step 3.

5 Fold the top point down to the left-hand point.

UNFOLD

6 Unfold the fold you made in Step 5.

PUSH **PUSH**

7 The creases you made in Steps 3 and 5 should have made a cross shape. Push the paper together either side of the cross, so that it starts folding in on itself.

FLATTEN **FLATTEN**

8 Your paper should form a pointed beak-like shape, like this. Flatten the sides down.

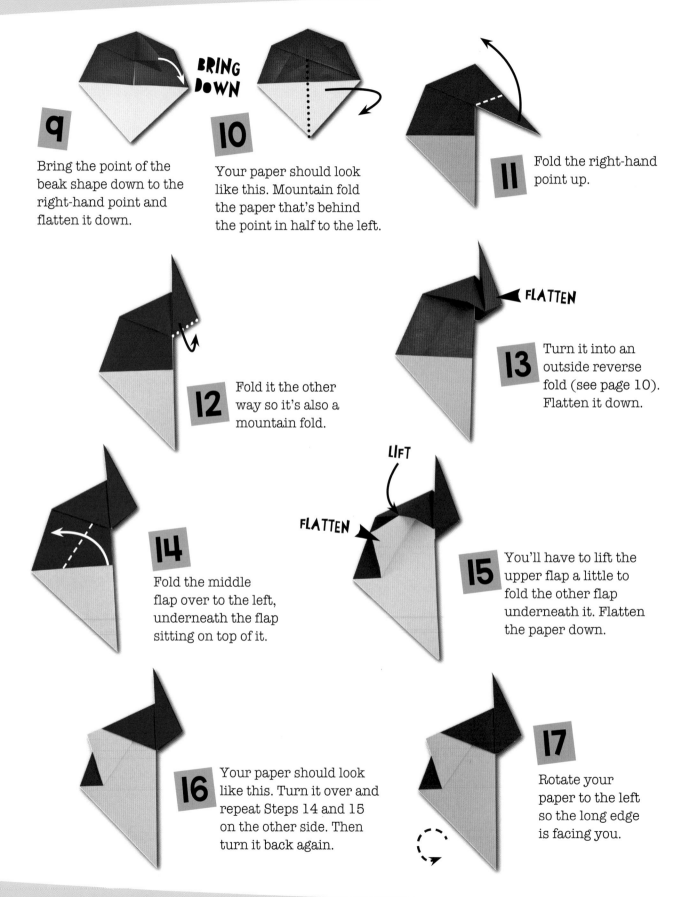

9 Bring the point of the beak shape down to the right-hand point and flatten it down.

BRING DOWN

10 Your paper should look like this. Mountain fold the paper that's behind the point in half to the left.

11 Fold the right-hand point up.

12 Fold it the other way so it's also a mountain fold.

FLATTEN

13 Turn it into an outside reverse fold (see page 10). Flatten it down.

14 Fold the middle flap over to the left, underneath the flap sitting on top of it.

LIFT

FLATTEN

15 You'll have to lift the upper flap a little to fold the other flap underneath it. Flatten the paper down.

16 Your paper should look like this. Turn it over and repeat Steps 14 and 15 on the other side. Then turn it back again.

17 Rotate your paper to the left so the long edge is facing you.

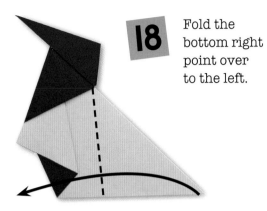

18 Fold the bottom right point over to the left.

19 Unfold the fold you made in step 18.

UNFOLD

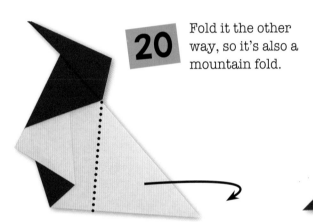

20 Fold it the other way, so it's also a mountain fold.

21 Turn it into an inside reverse fold (see page 10), tucking it through the middle of the paper, then flatten it down.

FLATTEN

22 Rotate your paper slightly to the right, so it matches the image in Step 23.

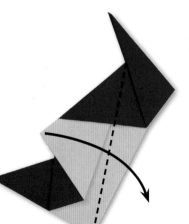

23 Fold the middle left point down and over to the right, as shown.

24

Turn your paper over. Repeat step 23 on the opposite side, then turn your paper back.

25

Fold the left-hand point over to the right.

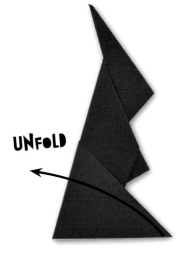

UNFOLD

26

Unfold the fold you made in Step 25.

27

Fold it the other way so it's also a mountain fold.

FLATTEN

28

Turn it into an inside reverse fold, tucking it through the other flaps of paper. Flatten the paper down.

29

Fold the bottom right point back over to the left, as shown.

30 Make another fold going the other way to create a step fold (see page 6).

31

Unfold the folds you made in Steps 29 and 30.

UNFOLD

32 Fold the folds you made in Steps 29 and 30 the other way, then tuck them inside one another so you've got an inside reverse fold inside another inside reverse fold.

◄ TUCK

33 Open up your wizard's cloak a little and he should be able to stand up. Why not decorate his hat and cloak with stars and magical symbols?

SPIDER

Cobwebs are one of the main ingredients of magic potions and this scary spider must produce lots of them. You'll need your scissors for this project.

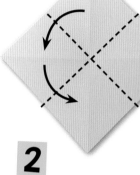

1

Place your paper white side down with a corner facing you. Valley fold it in half from top to bottom, and unfold. Then valley fold it in half from left to right, and unfold.

2

Turn the paper over. Fold the top right edge down to the bottom, and unfold. Then fold the top left edge down to the bottom, and unfold.

3

Start pushing the left and right corners in toward each other.

FLATTEN

4

As you push, the paper should start folding up into a small square like this. Flatten it down.

5

Your paper should look like this. With the open end facing you, fold the left point of the upper layer to the middle line.

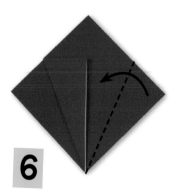

6

Valley fold the right bottom edge of the upper layer over to the middle line.

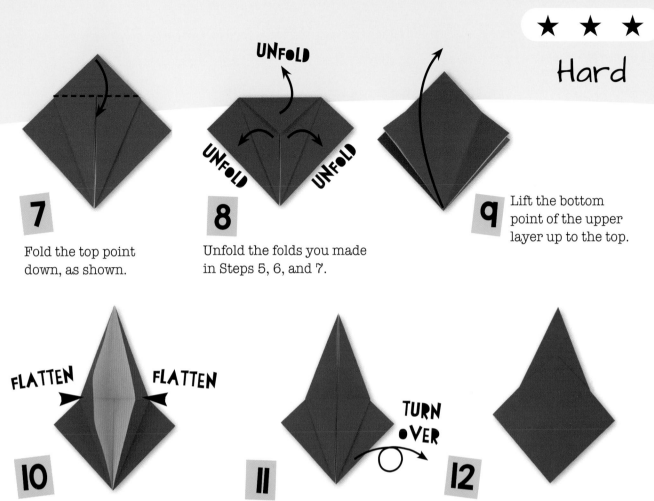

7
Fold the top point down, as shown.

8
Unfold the folds you made in Steps 5, 6, and 7.

9
Lift the bottom point of the upper layer up to the top.

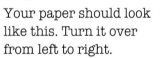

10
Your paper should form a shape a bit like a bird's mouth. Flatten the sides down.

11
Your paper should look like this. Turn it over from left to right.

12
Now repeat Steps 5 to 10 on this side.

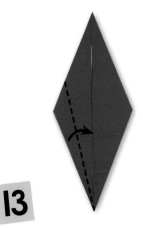

13
With the open end facing you, fold the left bottom edge of the upper layer over to the middle line.

14
Repeat Step 13 on the right-hand side.

15
Turn the paper over from left to right.

16 Repeat Steps 13 and 14 on this side.

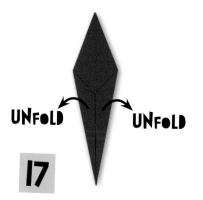

UNFOLD   UNFOLD

17 Open out the folds you made in Steps 13 to 16, front and back.

18 Take your scissors and carefully make a cut through the fold lines you made on the lower left-hand side up to the halfway crease. Cut through all the layers.

19 Repeat Step 18 on the right-hand side.

TURN OVER

20 Turn the paper over to the left a half turn so you can see the gap between the points at the top.

21 Make a cut, only in the upper layer, from the bottom tip to the halfway crease. Be careful not to accidentally cut any other layers.

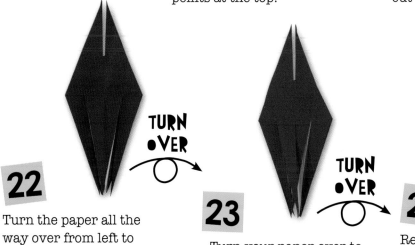

TURN OVER

22 Turn the paper all the way over from left to right and repeat Step 21 on the other side.

TURN OVER

23 Turn your paper over to the right a half turn.

TURN OVER

24 Refold the folds you made in Steps 13 to 16, on both sides.

25

Your paper should look like this. Fold the top point of the upper layer down, as shown.

26

Turn the paper over from left to right.

TURN OVER

27

Repeat Step 25 on this side.

28

Mountain fold the bottom right point formed by the upper two layers to the right.

29

Repeat Step 28 on the left-hand side.

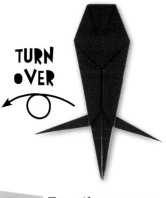

TURN OVER

30

Turn the paper over from right to left.

31

Valley fold the bottom right point formed by the upper two layers up to the right.

32

Repeat Step 31 on the left-hand side.

33

Valley fold the bottom right point formed by the upper two (unattached) layers to the right.

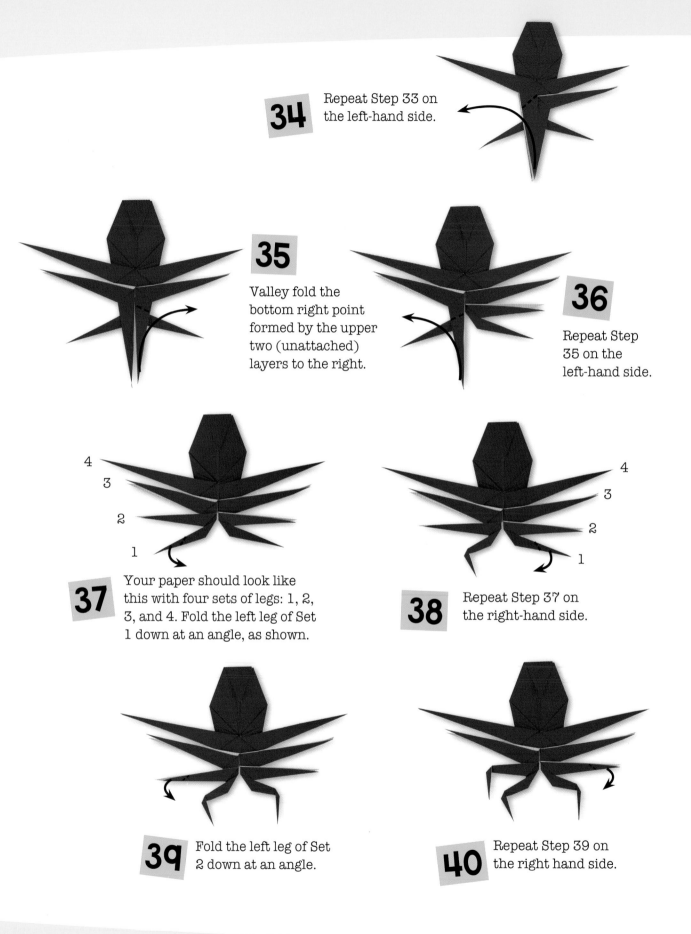

34 Repeat Step 33 on the left-hand side.

35 Valley fold the bottom right point formed by the upper two (unattached) layers to the right.

36 Repeat Step 35 on the left-hand side.

37 Your paper should look like this with four sets of legs: 1, 2, 3, and 4. Fold the left leg of Set 1 down at an angle, as shown.

38 Repeat Step 37 on the right-hand side.

39 Fold the left leg of Set 2 down at an angle.

40 Repeat Step 39 on the right hand side.

41

Fold both legs of Set 3 up at an angle.

42

Fold both legs of Set 4 up at an angle.

TURN OVER

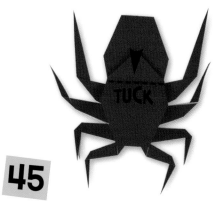

43

Your paper should look like this. Turn it over from left to right.

44

Fold the top edge of the upper layer down to the bottom.

TUCK

45

Valley fold the middle triangle and tuck it inside the lower flap.

46

Add some eyes before your spider goes scuttling off.

THE MUMMY

Beware the mummy's curse! This scary, bandaged figure is said to haunt anyone who displeases it, so make sure you fold yours carefully!

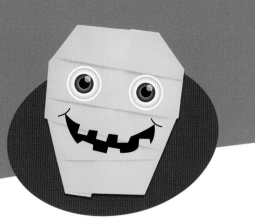

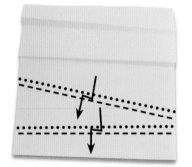

1 Place your paper like this, white side down, with a straight edge facing you. Make a step fold (see page 6) at the top, at a slight angle.

2 Make another step fold just below the first, again at a slight angle.

3 Make another two angled step folds so your paper matches the image in Step 4.

4 Flatten all your folds down.

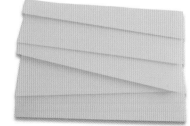

TURN OVER

5 Your paper should look like this. Turn it over from left to right.

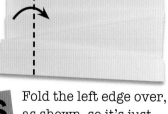

6 Fold the left edge over, as shown, so it's just short of the middle.

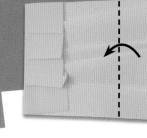

7

Repeat Step 6 on the right-hand side, so there's a small gap between the left and right edges.

8

Fold the bottom left point up and across, as shown.

9

Repeat Step 8 on the right-hand side.

10

Fold the top left point down and across, as shown to make a slightly smaller flap than in Steps 8 and 9.

TURN OVER

11

Repeat Step 10 on the right-hand side.

12

Your paper should look like this. Turn it over from right to left.

13

Add a mouth and some scary-looking eyes.

I WANT MY MUMMY!

DRAGON

This dragon may not be able to breathe flames, but it's still pretty scary!

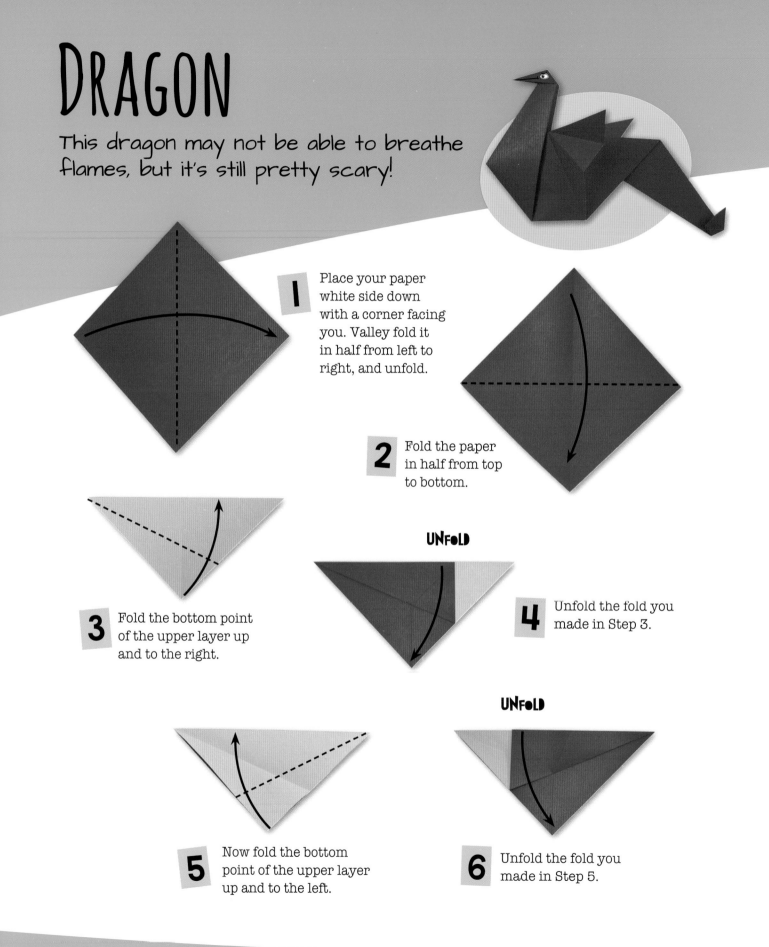

1 Place your paper white side down with a corner facing you. Valley fold it in half from left to right, and unfold.

2 Fold the paper in half from top to bottom.

3 Fold the bottom point of the upper layer up and to the right.

UNFOLD

4 Unfold the fold you made in Step 3.

5 Now fold the bottom point of the upper layer up and to the left.

UNFOLD

6 Unfold the fold you made in Step 5.

Hard

PUSH ▶ ◀ **PUSH**

7 Pinch the paper together either side of the bottom point and bring it up to the top along the crease lines made in Steps 3 and 5.

FLATTEN

8 As you move the paper up, it should form a corner pointing toward you, like this. Flatten it down to the left.

TURN OVER

9 Your paper should look like this. Turn it over from left to right.

10 Repeat Steps 3 to 8 on this side, but this time flatten the point in Step 8 down to the right.

TURN OVER

11 Your paper should look like this. Turn it back over from left to right.

12 Fold the right-hand point down, as shown.

13 Fold it the other way, so it's also a mountain fold, then turn it into an inside reverse fold (see page 10).

14 Fold the bottom right tip up and over to the left.

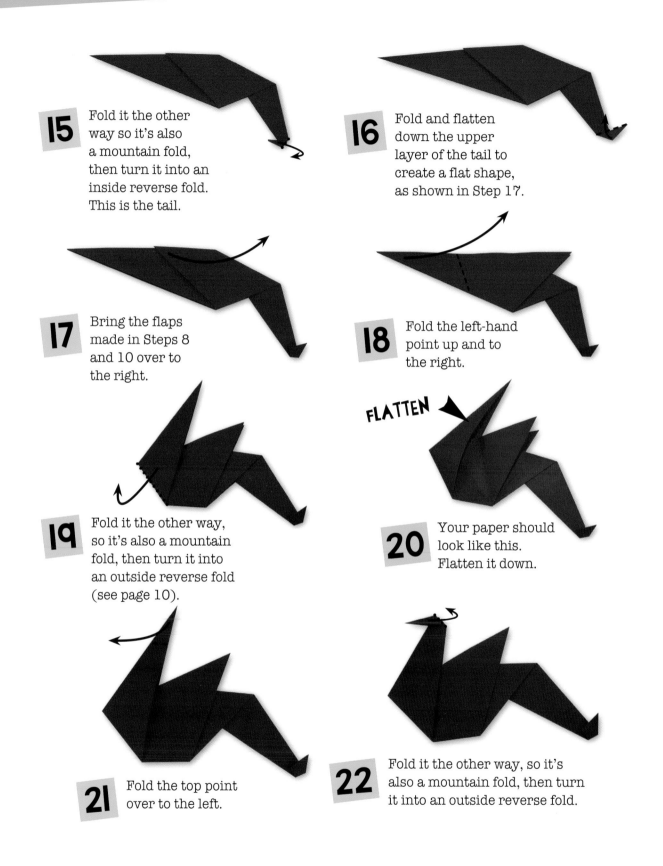

15 Fold it the other way so it's also a mountain fold, then turn it into an inside reverse fold. This is the tail.

16 Fold and flatten down the upper layer of the tail to create a flat shape, as shown in Step 17.

17 Bring the flaps made in Steps 8 and 10 over to the right.

18 Fold the left-hand point up and to the right.

FLATTEN

19 Fold it the other way, so it's also a mountain fold, then turn it into an outside reverse fold (see page 10).

20 Your paper should look like this. Flatten it down.

21 Fold the top point over to the left.

22 Fold it the other way, so it's also a mountain fold, then turn it into an outside reverse fold.

23 Bring the central flap back over to the left.

24 Fold the point of the flap back to the right and down, as shown.

25 Make another fold with the flap to the left and down. That's your first wing complete.

26 Repeat Steps 23 to 25 on the opposite side.

27 Pull the wings up and out and your dragon will be complete.

PULL

28 Your dragon is now ready to attack any knight who tries to steal its treasure.

FINISHED!

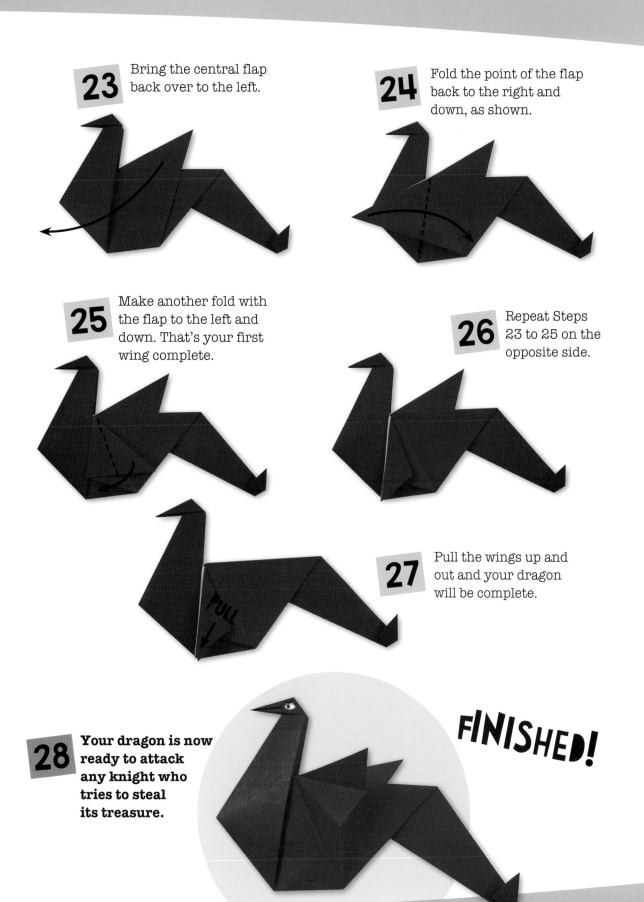

THE GRIM REAPER

According to legend, the Grim Reaper visits everyone just before their death, You'll need two pieces of paper to complete this eerie figure.

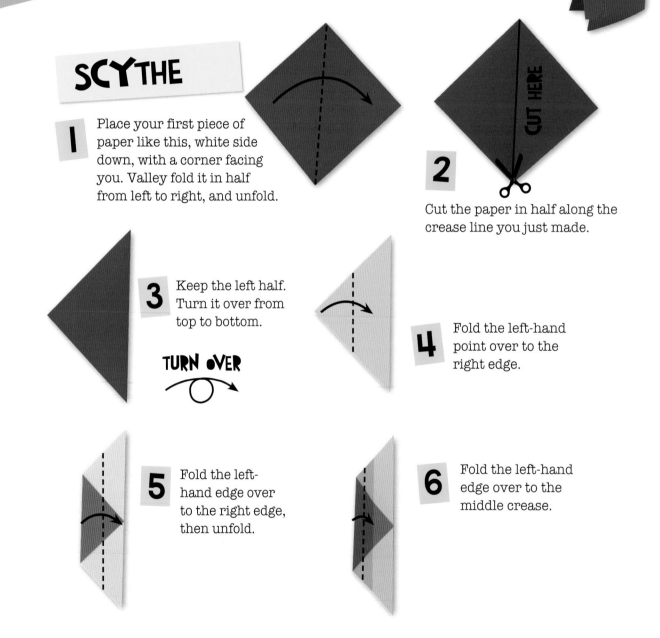

SCYTHE

1 Place your first piece of paper like this, white side down, with a corner facing you. Valley fold it in half from left to right, and unfold.

2 Cut the paper in half along the crease line you just made.

CUT HERE

3 Keep the left half. Turn it over from top to bottom.

TURN OVER

4 Fold the left-hand point over to the right edge.

5 Fold the left-hand edge over to the right edge, then unfold.

6 Fold the left-hand edge over to the middle crease.

7 Fold the left edge all the way over to the right edge.

8 Fold the paper in half again, so the left edge meets up with the right edge.

9 Fold the top of the scythe down and over to the right, as shown.

10 Mountain fold the top point of the scythe over so a small white triangle of paper is showing.

11 Fold the bottom point of the scythe up, as shown.

12 Fold it the other way, so it's also a mountain fold.

13 Now turn it into an inside reverse fold (see page 10) and tuck it inside the scythe.

◄ TUCK

14 Your scythe is ready to start collecting souls. Put it to one side while you make the Reaper himself.

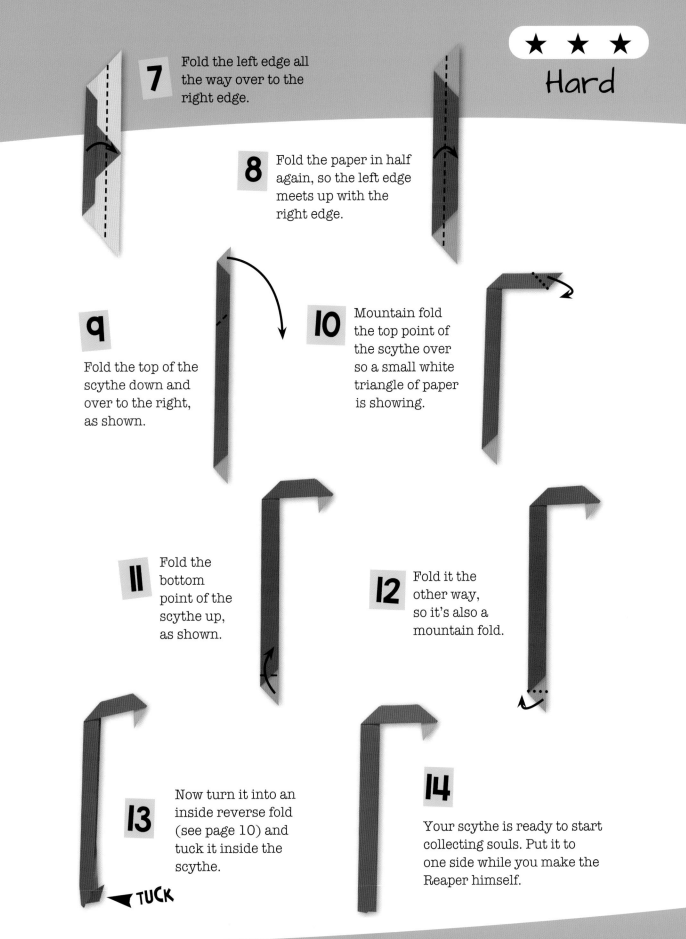

FIGURE

1 Place your second piece of paper white side up, with a straight edge facing you. Fold it in half from right to left, and unfold. Then fold it from top to bottom, and unfold.

2 Fold down the top edge so that it's just above the middle crease, as in the image for Step 3.

3 Your paper should look like this. Turn it over from left to right.

4 Fold the top left corner over to the middle crease.

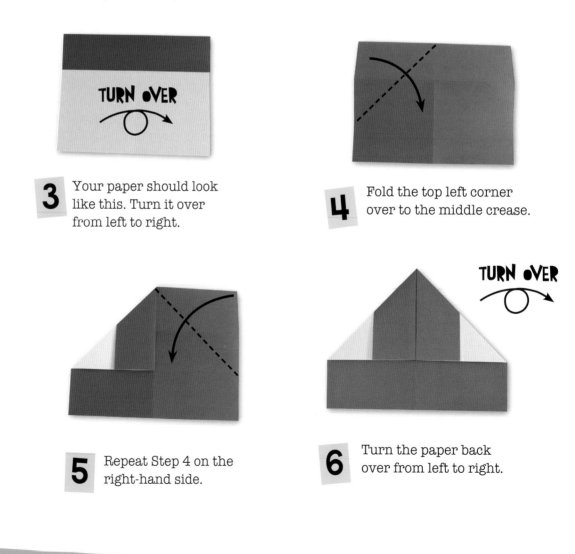

5 Repeat Step 4 on the right-hand side.

6 Turn the paper back over from left to right.

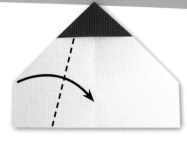

7 Fold the left-hand point over at an angle to the middle crease. The top triangle-shaped flap should stay where it is.

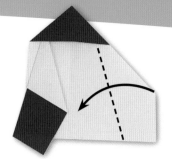

8 Repeat Step 7 on the right-hand side.

LIFT

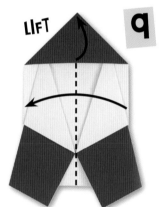

9 Fold the paper in half from right to left. As you do, lift up the middle of the triangle-shaped flap to form the Reaper's head.

OPEN

10 Open the middle flap and lift the left-hand point so that it forms a cone shape.

11 Your paper should look like this. Flatten it down so it forms a triangular shape with a horizontal top edge. This is the first arm.

FLATTEN

12 Turn the paper over from left to right.

TURN OVER

13 Repeat Steps 10 and 11 on this side.

14 Turn the paper back over from right to left.

TURN OVER

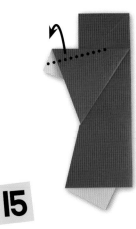

15

Mountain fold over the top edge of the arm, as shown.

16

Turn the paper over from left to right. Repeat Step 15 on the opposite side, then turn the paper back again.

TUCK INSIDE

17

Fold the white triangle at the bottom of the model up into the paper, on both sides.

18

Make a step fold (see page 6) at an angle, just above the arm to make the reaper's hood.

19

Repeat Step 18 on the opposite side.

20

Pull your paper apart slightly and your Reaper should stand up.

FINISHED!

21

Give him his scythe and your Grim Reaper is ready to start his dastardly work.

Octopod

Be careful if you visit the planet where this scary creature lives, as it might try to grab you with its long tentacles!

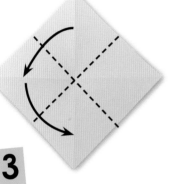

TURN OVER

1

Place your paper like this, white side down, with a corner facing you. Fold it in half from left to right, and unfold. Then fold it from top to bottom, and unfold.

2

Turn the paper over from left to right.

3

Fold the top right edge down to the bottom, and unfold. Then fold the top left edge down to the bottom, and unfold.

PUSH ▶   **PUSH** ◀

4

Start pushing the left and right corners in toward each other.

FLATTEN ⌄

5

As you push, the paper should start folding up into a small square like this. Flatten it down.

6

Bring the right point of the upper layer over to the middle.

249

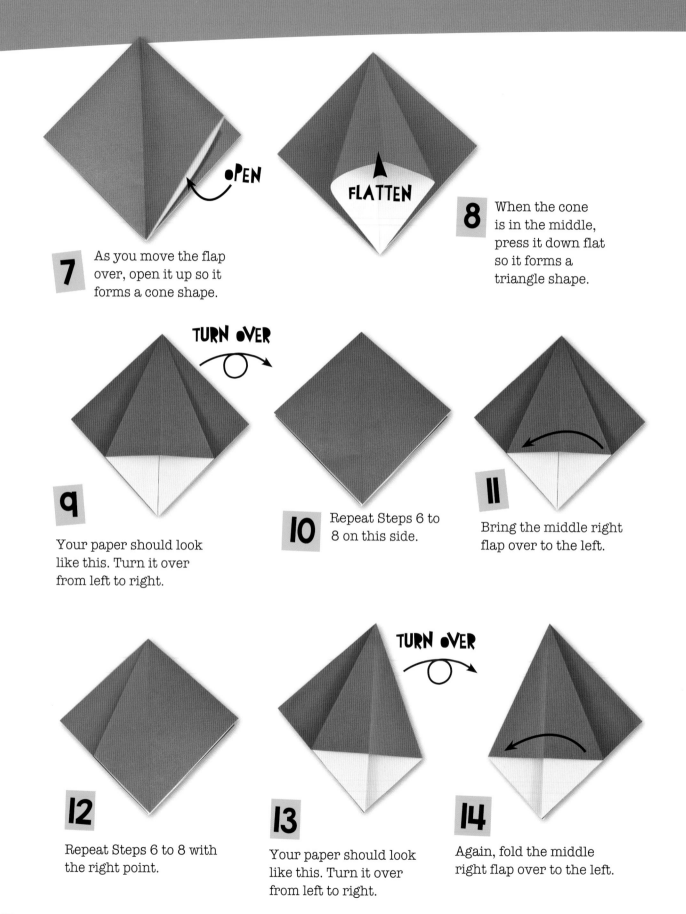

OPEN

7 As you move the flap over, open it up so it forms a cone shape.

FLATTEN

8 When the cone is in the middle, press it down flat so it forms a triangle shape.

TURN OVER

9 Your paper should look like this. Turn it over from left to right.

10 Repeat Steps 6 to 8 on this side.

11 Bring the middle right flap over to the left.

12 Repeat Steps 6 to 8 with the right point.

13 Your paper should look like this. Turn it over from left to right.

TURN OVER

14 Again, fold the middle right flap over to the left.

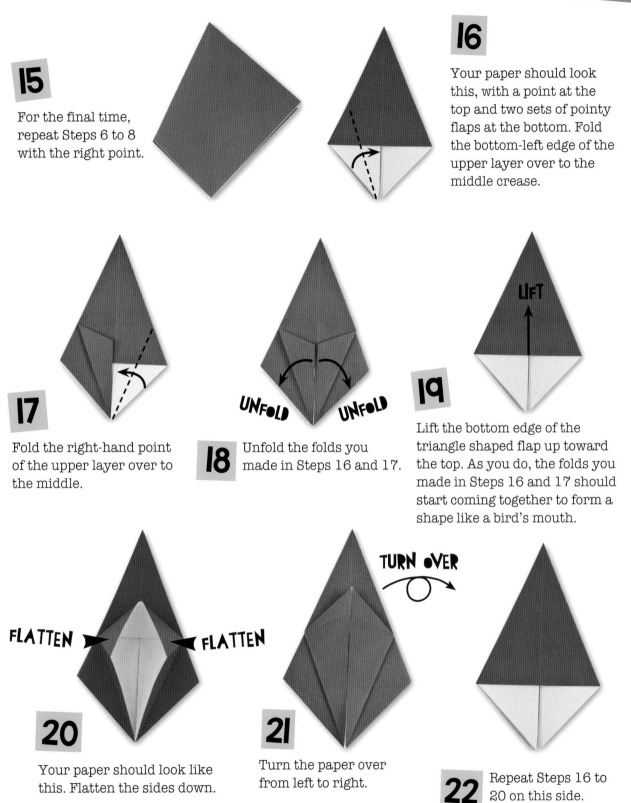

15

For the final time, repeat Steps 6 to 8 with the right point.

16

Your paper should look this, with a point at the top and two sets of pointy flaps at the bottom. Fold the bottom-left edge of the upper layer over to the middle crease.

17

Fold the right-hand point of the upper layer over to the middle.

18

Unfold the folds you made in Steps 16 and 17.

UNFOLD   UNFOLD

19

LIFT

Lift the bottom edge of the triangle shaped flap up toward the top. As you do, the folds you made in Steps 16 and 17 should start coming together to form a shape like a bird's mouth.

20

FLATTEN   FLATTEN

Your paper should look like this. Flatten the sides down.

21

Turn the paper over from left to right.

TURN OVER

22

Repeat Steps 16 to 20 on this side.

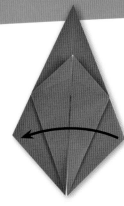

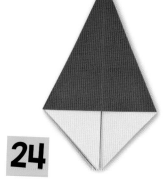

23

Bring the far right-hand point of the upper layer over to the left.

24

Repeat Steps 16 to 20 on this side too.

25

Turn your paper over from left to right.

TURN OVER

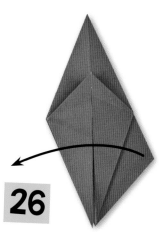

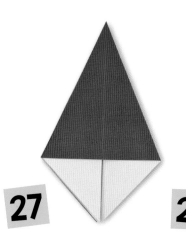

26

Again, fold the right-hand corner of the upper layer over to the left.

27

For the final time, repeat Steps 16 to 20.

28

Your paper should look like this. Bring the right-hand point of the upper layer over to the left.

TURN OVER

29

Turn the paper over from left to right.

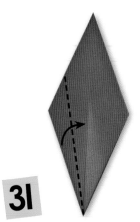

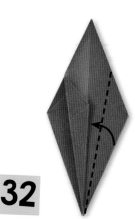

30

Again, bring the right-hand point of the upper layer over to the left.

31

Fold the bottom left edge of the upper layer over to the middle.

32

Fold the bottom right edge of the upper layer over to the middle.

33

Repeat Steps 31 and 32 on the other three sides.

34

Your paper should look like this. Fold the bottom point of the upper layer up to the top.

35

Repeat Step 34 on the other three sides. You'll have to open the paper up a little to do this.

36

Bring the flaps you made in Steps 34 and 35 down so they form the arms of a star shape, as in the image for Step 37.

37

Use your scissors to cut one of the arms in half. These are your first tentacles.

38

Repeat Step 37 with the other three arms to make eight tentacles in total.

40

Shape and curl the legs downward.

39

Inflate the octopus's head by blowing into it from below.

BLOW

41

Your eight-legged Octopod is ready to scuttle around its alien world. Use more paper to create a whole Octopod alien army.

FINISHED!

GHOST

We've made our ghost from a piece of white paper, for that classic sheet look. You might want to create a brighter, more friendly-looking ghost.

1 Place your paper like this with a corner facing you. Valley fold it in half from left to right, and unfold.

2 Fold the top left and right edges down to the middle crease, as shown.

3 Fold the bottom left edge over to the middle crease.

4 Repeat step 3 on the right-hand side.

5 Your paper should look like this. Unfold the fold you made in Step 3.

UNFOLD

PULL

6 Pull the middle point up along the central line, so that it forms a flap shaped like a triangle.

FLATTEN ▶

7 Flatten the paper down.

8 Repeat Steps 5 to 7 on the right-hand side.

INDEX

Alien 208-211
Angel 176-178
Apatosaurus 98-100
Argentinosaurus 94-97

Barking Dog 128-131
Bird, Flapping 118-119
Boat 135-137
Broomstick 216-219

Candle 186-189
Candy Cane 184-185
Christmas Tree 166-167
Cup, Magic 116-117

Dice 102-105
Dinosaur Egg 90-93
Dog, Barking 128-131
Dominoes 120-121
Dracula 202-203
Dragon 240-243
Duckling 138-141

Egg-laying Hen 148-152
Egg, Dinosaur 90-93
Elf 193-195

Fangs, Vampire 204-207
Fish, Gulping 126-127
Flapping Bird 118-119
Flower, Lotus 122-125
Fox 20-21
Frog, Kissing 111-115

Ghost 254-255
Giant Snake 212-213

Gorilla 12-15
Grim Reaper 244-248
Gulping Fish 126-127

Helicopter 132-134
Hen, Egg-laying 148-152
Holly Leaves 158-159
Horse, Jumping 142-145

Ichthyosaurus 66-67

Jet Plane 146-147
Jumping Horse 142-145

Kissing Frog 111-115

Letter to Santa 160-161
Lion 34-35
Lotus Flower 122-125

Magic Cup 116-117
Magician's Rabbit 106-110
Megalosaurus 54-57
Monkey 22-26
Motorboat 135-137
Mummy 238-239

Narwhal 45-47
Nessie, Snapping 214-215

Octopod 249-253

Parasaurolophus 76-81
Parrot 48-50
Plane, Jet 146-147
Present 193-195

Polar Bear 30-33
Pteranodon 73-75

Quetzalcoatlus 82-83

Rabbit, Magician's 106-110
Reindeer 162-165
Reindeer Face 171-175

Santa 154-157
Seahorse 16-19
Sleigh 190-192
Snake, Giant 212-213
Snapping Nessie 214-215
Snowflake 182-183
Snowman 196-199
Spider 232-237
Spinosaurus 84-89
Squid 27-29
Squirrel 36-39
Star Chain 200
Stocking 179-181

Triceratops 58-65

Utahraptor 68-72

Vampire Fangs 204-207
Velociraptor 52-53
Vulture 40-44

Werewolf 222-226
Witch and Broomstick 216-219
Witch's Cat 220-221
Wizard 227-231
Wreath 168-170

9

Your paper should look like this. Turn it over from left to right.

TURN OVER

10

Fold the left-hand point over to the middle.

11

Repeat Step 10 on the right-hand side.

12

Turn the paper over from right to left.

TURN OVER

13

Fold the middle left point down, as shown.

14

Repeat Step 13 on the right hand side.

15

Mountain fold over the top point.

16

Mountain fold over the bottom point at an angle to make the tail.

18

Add a spooky face and your ghost is ready to do its first haunting.

Boo!

17

Make another mountain fold in the tail, again at a slight angle. Your ghost should now be able to stand up.

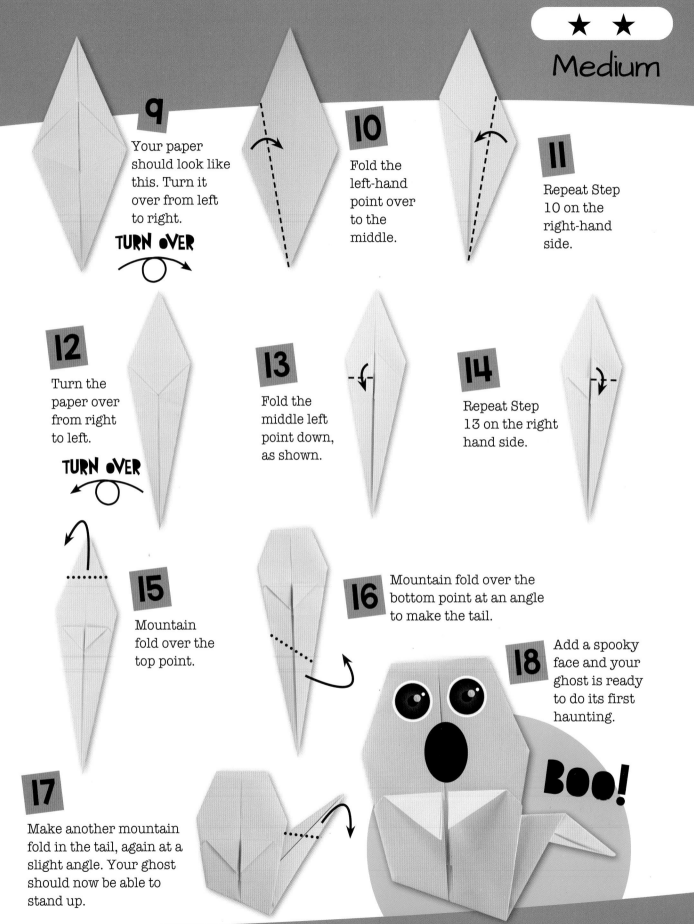